Reshaping the Boundaries

Reshaping the Boundaries

The Christian Intersection of China and the West in the Modern Era

Edited by Song Gang

HKU PRESS
香港大學出版社

Hong Kong University Press
The University of Hong Kong
Pokfulam Road
Hong Kong
www.hkupress.org

© 2016 Hong Kong University Press

ISBN 978-988-8390-55-7 (*Hardback*)

All rights reserved. No portion of this publication may be reproduced or transmitted in any form or by any means, electronic or mechanical, including photocopy, recording, or any information storage or retrieval system, without prior permission in writing from the publisher.

British Library Cataloguing-in-Publication Data
A catalogue record for this book is available from the British Library.

10 9 8 7 6 5 4 3 2 1

Printed and bound by Paramount Printing Co., Ltd. in Hong Kong, China

Contents

Boundary-Crossing Words, Beliefs, and Experiences: Late Imperial China's Encounter with the Modern West   1
Song Gang

1. "Sinarum gentes ... omnium sollertissimae": Encounters between the Middle Kingdom and the Low Countries, 1602–92   9
   Thijs Weststeijn

2. Russian-Chinese Cultural Exchanges in the Early Modern Period: Missionaries, Sinologists, and Artists   35
   Nikolay Samoylov

3. The Wind *Qin*: Hearing and Reading Chinese Reactions to the Pipe Organ   48
   David Francis Urrows

4. "Supreme Nation": The British Image in Karl Gützlaff's Novels *Shifei lüelun* and *Dayingguo tongzhi*   59
   John T. P. Lai

5. "Sacred Heart" and the Appropriation of Catholic Faith in Nineteenth-Century China   76
   Ji Li

6. Local Magistrates and Foreign Mendicants: Chinese Views of Shanxi's Franciscan Mission during the Late Qing   91
   Anthony E. Clark

7. A Religious Rhetoric of Competing Modernities: Christian Print Culture in Late Qing China   106
   Melissa Wei-Tsing Inouye

List of Contributors   123
Index   125

Boundary-Crossing Words, Beliefs, and Experiences
Late Imperial China's Encounter with the Modern West

Song Gang

The rise of China as a leading power in today's world has attracted increasing scholarly attention to the country's encounter with the West (primarily referring to Europe and North America in this volume) in the modern era, i.e., from the late sixteenth to the early twentieth centuries. While more recent research began to shift away from the model of a tradition–modernity polarity in explaining late imperial Chinese history, new approaches have been proposed to explore a broader range of subjects tied with the richly documented exchanges between China and the West since the sixteenth century. However, there is still a lack of collaborative effort to examine how Western culture, long shaped by the dominant Christian religion, was conceptualized and imagined by late imperial Chinese people, and vice versa, how Confucian-based Chinese culture was understood and interpreted in modern Europe and North America. Indeed, the multilayered two-way flows of words, beliefs, and experiences in such a significant cross-cultural encounter open up intriguing possibilities for further investigation. This volume, which consists of seven studies, presents cutting-edge research on the formation and transformation of different types of knowledge, perceptions, and representations exchanged between China and the West through the modern period. It aims to shed new light and provide refreshing perspectives for future exploration of related subjects in this field.

The findings in this volume suggest a process of boundary-crossing interactions between Chinese and Western cultures. On the one hand, some long-standing ideologies, religious beliefs, and cultural tastes have been modified or redefined due to Chinese people's more frequent contacts with Westerners. Whether they were emperors, officials, literati, or peasants, they often moved beyond conventional thinking to try to make sense of Western religion and culture. In this respect, David Francis Urrows, Ji Li, and Anthony Clark unfold an impressive list of new boundaries drawn by those Chinese who reinterpreted traditional thoughts, built regional, national as well as transnational networks, and promoted expedient means of interpersonal and intercultural adaptations. On the other hand, the stereotyped Sinocentric mentality (embedded in such terms as *Tianxia* 天下 and *Hua-Yi* 華夷) continued to carry a heavy load of cultural imperatives that frequently challenged the thoughts and behaviors of Western (including Russian) missionaries, Sinologists, and artists. They also felt the urgent need to mark new religious, ethical, and aesthetic boundaries of self-identity when meeting with Chinese people and their unyielding cultural pride. This aspect receives particular attention in the studies of Thijs Weststeijn, Nikolay Samoylov, John T. P. Lai, and Melissa Wei-Tsing Inouye, who carefully examine a number of missionary sources to measure the limits of transcultural understandings at spiritual, intellectual, and ideological levels.

A reader may keenly notice the interweaving of both Chinese and Western perspectives in this volume. The syncretic approach resists a simple alignment with the established theories, and it sets a framework in which the contributors can fully address the distinctive feature of "in-betweenness" embedded in a variety of boundary-crossing words, beliefs, and experiences. This key concept, frequently seen in literary criticisms, translation studies, and cross-cultural studies, also helps advance our understanding of the historical encounter between China and the West in three significant aspects. First, it entails more room for comprehensive research, thereby avoiding the limitations of some influential theories and methodological models, e.g., the "Eurocentric approach" (with its critique *Orientalism*), the "impact and response" thesis, the "China-centered approach," and the "transmission" and the "reaction" frameworks. For Catholic missions in late imperial China, for example, it was not always the case that missionaries played a role as the *transmitters* while the Chinese were the *receivers*. As Ji Li has convincingly argued, the roles could be reversed when Chinese Christians managed to have their voices heard in Europe. In addition, largely due to the reshaped boundaries, messages being transmitted between different locations and through different media could be altered at various degrees in the process and therefore not be complete or faithful to the original meanings and purposes. Second, the "in-between" feature highlights the interactiveness and interdependence that characterized the contacts between China and the West in early modern history. It would be a questionable claim that the encounter of China and the West between the sixteenth and the eighteenth centuries, often seen as a period of reciprocal influences, came to an end in 1800, while hostile confrontations incurred by Western arrogance and Chinese humiliation dominated Sino-Western relations through the nineteenth century. The observation overlooks the subtlety of some cases highlighted in this volume, e.g., a Protestant missionary may use the traditional Chinese concept of ideal society to promote his model image of the West, or there could be self-contradictory expressions of modernity in late Qing missionary publications. These cases suggest that the key actually lies in how the participants responded to an "in-between" situation when defining new ideological, religious, and cultural boundaries in reality. Third, the reshaping of boundaries not only embodied dynamic transcultural experiences, but they also marked new public and private spheres without fixed borders between traditional and modern, native and foreign, or central and marginal. By means of official records, personal letters, musical instruments, news reports, translated texts, rumors, and miracle stories, the new spheres enabled the participants to interact with each other in expansive networks and produce many "in-between" thoughts, images, and identities, neither Chinese nor Western by nature. Considering the above three aspects, we should focus on the "in-between" feature as the key in our investigation of the boundary-crossing cases, which in many ways affected late imperial Chinese history and modern Western history.

The contributors of this volume are experts in history, religious studies, music history, as well as cultural studies. They not only display pioneering research on subjects that have not been fully digested in previous research, but also make effective use of existing and newly found sources to reconstruct the "in-between" experiences of Chinese and Western peoples in the modern era. Their studies represent different areas of interests, but they share the same concern about how ideological, religious, and cultural boundaries may have been reshaped on both sides in the Sino-Western encounter.

The volume is organized into seven chapters. In Chapter 1, Thijs Weststeijn presents a penetrating survey of the multilayered cultural exchanges between China and the Low Countries during the seventeenth century. Traders and missionaries from the remote place of the "red-haired barbarians" became regular visitors to the Middle Kingdom and the South China Sea in this period. The intermediary role of the Low Countries travelers in transacting cultural products between the two ends of the world depended on a fortuitous combination of factors: the global "Jesuit information network" was complemented with and sometimes catalyzed by the interests of the Dutch trading company. Bearing in mind the recent studies on early modern Netherlandish Jesuitica, Weststeijn is keen enough to pay attention to the significant work of a group of Jesuit missionaries from the Low Countries, such as Nicolas Trigault, Philippe Couplet, and Ferdinand Verbiest. Their voyages and writings, involving publishers from the Dutch Republic, contributed to the vital exchange of knowledge. Weststeijn's research on European Sinology and humanistic scholarship also gives him a solid footing to analyze Sino-Dutch exchanges in linguistic and philological terms: the Jesuits' introduction of the Chinese writing system was consciously adopted and fantasized by European scholars in their search for a universal script. Meanwhile, the Jesuits' collaborative translation of Confucian classics in *Confucius Sinarum philosophus* disclosed a carefully reinterpreted version of Confucianism filtered through the Christian truth, and it aroused a series of later translations and commentaries bouncing between ancient Chinese wisdom and post-Renaissance humanism. In his analysis on visual arts and historiography, Weststeijn provides more examples of similar boundary-crossing experiences. He concludes the chapter by reflecting on a contrast between the Dutch lead in European cultural engagements with China through the seventeenth century and the loss of that legacy in the following eighteenth century.

In Chapter 2, Nikolay Samoylov presents a parallel study on Sino-Russian encounters from the seventeenth to the nineteenth centuries. He first brings forward critical reflections on the four-stage process—*indifferent interaction*, *identification*, *activation*, and *adaptation*—which to him should characterize the increasing contacts between China and Russia over a period of two hundred years. In this process, he highlights the key role of the Russian Ecclesiastical Mission in Beijing, the unofficial embassy of Russia and outpost of the Russian Orthodox Church in China, for transmitting abundant social-cultural information between the two neighboring empires. Samoylov mentions an intriguing example: the Russian missionaries and the Qing Chinese simultaneously adopted Buddhist terminology to identify the country Russia and the Christian religion. It reminds us of a similar appropriation of the Buddhist identity by the first Jesuits in South China in the late sixteenth century. We also see that, despite the claim to present a "real" image of China, the Russian missionaries apparently infused personal opinions and emotions in their works. The prominent Sinologist Archimandrite Iakinf (Bichurin), for example, staged a costume show in the literary salons of St. Petersburg to signal his close association with Confucian intelligentsia, and he created an idealistic, admirable image of China in political, legal, and educational terms. Though the diplomatic twist gradually wore off the spiritual passion of the missionaries, they made noticeable contributions to the growth of early Russian Sinology. Moreover, after a close look at such well-known figures as Alexander Pushkin, Vladimir Odoevsky, and Vissarion Belinsky, Samoylov suggests that missionary Sinologists did not really achieve unanimous support as they had wished. Rather, there appeared diverse and even conflicting perceptions of China among Russian intellectuals. In their works, they did not represent China as it was but as what they expected it to be—a romantic utopia at one time yet a stagnant autocracy at another. As it turned out, China has been consciously reinterpreted as a symbolic mirror image for them to reflect upon the reality in Russia.

Following Weststeijn's and Samoylov's sweeping surveys, David Francis Urrows in his chapter investigates a handful of Ming-Qing sources (and Korean sources in Chinese) on the pipe organ, thus adding a special dimension to the boundary-crossing experience of Western missionaries and late imperial Chinese people. As a cultural commodity, music traveled from early on. Western musical instruments were present when the first Jesuit mission was established in sixteenth-century China, and they were the subject of curiosity and admiration among local Chinese audiences. No instrument better reflected the highest level of Western technology than the pipe organ, the most complex mechanical device in Western culture from antiquity up to the Industrial Revolution. While reading the Chinese accounts on the pipe organ, Urrows affirms that it was precisely the technical and mechanical aspects that excited interest. Aesthetics and music were firmly secondary concerns. In this sense, the pipe organ has been considered a stereotyped icon of Western (Christian) music and in most cases an exotic instrument in the scientific. What is more important, Urrows argues, lies in the fact that Chinese understandings of this Western object did not take any simple form of exoticism or indifference but rather a mixture of diverse transcultural experiences shifting between intellectual openness and ideological resistance. Consequently, it would be natural for some reputed literati, such as You Tong and Zhao Yi, to reinterpret the "wind-*qin*" by using a set of normative ideas in classical Chinese poetry and music. And, we would not be surprised at the self-contradictory "bluff" of the Qianlong Emperor regarding things imported from the West. The intriguing intersection of religion, music, and science brought to light a typical Chinese cultural centricity encountering the *otherness* of Western high culture, from which a new mode of in-between existence emerged along the process of dynamic mutual perceptions and evaluations.

While the first three chapters mainly focus on the endeavors of Catholic and Orthodox missionaries in China over the seventeenth and eighteenth centuries, the remaining four chapters in this volume display a more stimulating picture of the nineteenth century. Featured by more frequent conflicts in political, military, and cultural terms, the century witnessed a significant shift in modern Sino-Western relations.

In Chapter 4, John T. P. Lai presents an illuminative study on how Karl F. A. Gützlaff, a leading Protestant missionary to China in the early nineteenth century, consciously created an idealistic image of Great Britain in two of his novels, *Shifei lüelun* (1835) and *Dayingguo tongzhi* (1834). It is noteworthy that Gützlaff in his narratives employed a series of rhetorical devices to change or redefine the traditional boundaries of Chinese and British cultures. On the one hand, through the voice of a Chinese sojourner who had once lived in Britain for years, Gützlaff put forth his challenging points to counterargue the Sinocentric world order deeply rooted in the imperial Chinese mind. The age-old concept *Hua-Yi zhi bian*, which set geopolitical and ethnical divisions between the civilized Chinese people and the uncivilized barbarians, was refuted in the first place. This was paralleled by a direct challenge to China's long-established tributary system. One could not find any of the alleged devil-like characters among British traders, and instead he would be obliged to admit that they had made great contributions to China's economy and therefore were no inferior tributary subjects of China, or the "Celestial Empire." On the other hand, Gützlaff made great efforts in presenting Britain as the "Supreme Nation," characterized by advanced technology, awe-inspiring military force, efficient legal and parliamentary systems, admirable cultural achievements, and fundamentally, the dominant Christian religion. It is with Lai's careful analysis of these aspects that we can recognize an impressive list of boundary-crossing expressions and thoughts. For example, Gützlaff borrowed conventional Chinese sayings, including the word for the Four Seas and Mencius' statement on an ideal society free of hunger and cold, to describe Britain as a paradise-like nation and a superior overlord of its colonies and tributary states worldwide. The conscious appropriation and exaggeration, Lai argues, aimed to break the boundaries of the old Sinocentric world so that a new model image of the West may be shaped in the Chinese mind. Moreover, Lai points out Gützlaff's omission of some negative aspects, such as King William IV's illegitimate children, social evils, and the opium trade, in order to avoid any Chinese suspicion at the idealistic image of Britain. Motivated by his Eurocentric pride and evangelical zeal, Gützlaff strategically made adaptive and selective reinterpretations on the essential cultural attributes of both countries. The Anglo-Chinese intercourse exhibited a complex destruction–reconstruction process, in which the two-way flow of words and ideas gave shape to one imagined in-between reality to fulfill varied ideological, commercial, and religious motives.

The next two chapters focus on Catholic missions in Liaoning and Shanxi during the late nineteenth century. They arouse no less interest than Gützlaff's symbolic representation of Britain as the "Supreme Nation." In both studies, lower-class Chinese people came to the foreground and played an increasingly decisive role in their negotiations with the Church's religious orthodoxy on the one hand, and the Qing political authority on the other. In Chapter 5, Ji Li first presents a concise survey of the popular devotion to the Sacred Heart of Jesus in France and its introduction to China during the late Qing period. She then analyzes several rarely seen letters, written in 1871 by three Catholic women from a village in Liaozhong County, Liaoning. The letters were addressed to Dominique Maurice Pourquié, a member of the Société des Missions Etrangères de Paris who had worked in Northeast China. Here we come across an exciting case of, perhaps for the first time, rural Chinese Catholic women managing to have their voices heard in Europe. From these original letters, Li detects the underlying sense of feminine piety mingled with the Du women's purposeful borrowing of religious vocabularies to articulate their personal feelings and emotional requests. Such an obvious displacement between the spiritual devotion to Jesus and the sensible attachment to an absent Western priest signifies the new boundary of Christian religiosity being shaped by these village women. When indicating discontent with the institutionalization tendency of another convent, they further played upon subtle sentimental values in the religious discourse by adopting the same spiritual forces of devotion. On this occasion, private writing became an alternative means of self-empowerment for the less privileged Chinese converts to redefine their faith, passion, and collective identity in the turbulent late Qing period.

In Chapter 6, Anthony Clark takes a different angle to explore the drastic change of Chinese views on the Franciscan mission in Shanxi before and after the Boxer Uprising. He makes extensive use of archival sources from late Qing provincial and missionary ecclesial collections to put together a two-sided narrative of what occurred during the fevered pitch of Chinese-Western antagonisms. Compared to the Jesuits' strategic adaptations to Chinese elite culture in the seventeenth century, the Franciscan mission rather followed a not very friendly fundamentalist approach to preaching among lower-class Chinese people. The increased frictions between the God of the West and indigenous Chinese gods finally led to a great conflict in 1900, one that signaled widespread resistance to Western invasion and control over China. From the words of anti-Christian officials and literati, Clark unfolds their willful misreading of Christianity as a heterodox religion, e.g., bearing a rebellious nature, involving black magic, and destroying the five human relations. He is of the opinion that the Franciscan mission in Shanxi at the turn of the century was largely mystified by late Qing political discourses and cultural mores. Ironically enough, right after the occupation of Beijing by the Eight-Nation Alliance, hostile views were radically changed by the new governor of Shanxi, who upheld the exact opposite stance and claimed Christianity to be an orthodox and victimized religion. By carefully tracing the dramatic fast-changing Chinese views, Clark brings to light another vivid example of how the same religious identity might be misread and represented in a sequence of ideologically sensitive exchanges between the *self* and the *other*.

The last chapter, by Melissa Wei-Tsing Inouye, concludes this volume with a critical reflection on the complicated notions of modernity propagated through the flourishing Christian print culture in late Qing and early Republican China. The nineteenth- and early twentieth-century encounter between China and the West, Inouye argues, was far more complex than a one-way influx of "modern" products, ideas, or technologies into China. It carried a distinctively in-between character, as can be seen through bidirectional flows of charisma and cultural exchange. As far as Christian print culture is concerned, Western missionaries had introduced modern print technology to China in the first half of the nineteenth century. This advanced technology was not only a symbol of the scientific ethos of rationalistic modernity, but also a convenient and widely utilized tool for propagating charismatic Christian practices such as prayers for particularistic protection, healing, and ecstatic worship. Those miracle stories appeared side by side with the political, economic, and scientific discourses, in the *Church News*, the *Chinese Christian Intelligencer*, and other nationally distributed Christian publications. The coexistence of technological advancements and supernatural experiences easily gave rise to a paradoxical in-between situation, where multiple expressions of modernity (or "competing modernities" in Inouye's words) could be attached to both old and new ideas frequently crossing the borders of cultural, religious, and material entities. Following her arguments on late Qing Christian printing, Inouye presents further evidence for the overlooked plural form of modernity from yet another angle, i.e., Western missionaries' adoption of the backward-progressive assumption to draw an imagined boundary between the Christian doctrine and Chinese popular religion. According to Inouye, the true motive behind the missionaries' vigorous critique of Chinese popular religion was not a modern scientific agenda to root out irrationality and superstition but rather a traditionalist campaign to police the boundary between acceptable and unacceptable expressions of supernatural belief and practice. Understandably, we come across the ironic juxtaposition of "false" traditional Chinese miracles and "true" Christian miracles, embracing a similar mode of religious efficacy but ending with contradictory appraisals. This, according to Inouye, signals the emergence of a type of in-between space for different and competing ideological paradigms. Through her in-depth analysis of the obvious paradoxes embedded in the late Qing Chinese-Christian encounter, Inouye makes it clear that modernity should not be simply seen as a fixed border between rational/irrational, scientific/superstitious, secular/religious, or other dichotomies. Rather, it involves changeable social-cultural forms, different ways to conceptualize worldly or supernatural experiences, and vital mechanisms that continued to redefine the new boundaries between the *self* and the *other*.

Whether we have already entered into a *glocalized* world remains a subject of considerable discussion and dispute, but the seven studies collected in this volume can give us a glimpse of how the Christian intersection of China and the West in the modern era has undergone a complex process of two-way perceptions, representations, and imaginations. The boundary-crossing words, beliefs, and experiences demonstrated the interactiveness and interdependence of Chinese and Western peoples not only among themselves but also within a larger global community. The distinctive "in-betweenness" of their intercultural exchanges, as these studies suggest, may enlighten further research on the historical formation of today's world and our multiple understandings of it.

1
"Sinarum gentes ... omnium sollertissimae"
Encounters between the Middle Kingdom and the Low Countries, 1602–92

Thijs Weststeijn[1]

The Dutch were adamant that they would gain a foothold in China in their desire to replace the Iberian traders in Asia. Yet throughout the seventeenth century, all their attempts proved failures. Circumventing the Portuguese first involved sailing the so-called Northeast Passage in 1594, which stranded in the arctic ice of Novaya Zemlya.[2] Closer to their goal, a Dutch fleet equipped to besiege Macau in 1622 foundered due to the local Jesuits' skillful marksmanship.[3] Establishing a trading post in Guangzhou was beyond the traders' grasp of the local mandarins' sensibilities.[4] In 1656–66, two costly embassies to the Imperial Court likewise failed to leave a mark beyond the stainless sword presented to the Kangxi Emperor (康熙, 1654–1722), mentioned in his memoirs.[5] And even though the Dutch settlement on Taiwan seemed to develop into a full-fledged European colony, it ended abruptly when a local pirate, Zheng Chenggong

---

1. The author participates in the research project, "The Chinese Impact: Images and Ideas of China in the Dutch Golden Age" at the University of Amsterdam, funded by the Netherlands Organisation for Scientific Research. He owes a debt of gratitude to Song Gang and to the participants of the international symposium, "Strangers and Distant Lands: The West in Late Imperial China," held at the University of Hong Kong on December 7–9, 2012.
2. See J. H. van Linschoten, *Voyagie, ofte schip-vaert, van Ian Huyghen van Linschoten, van by Noorden om langes Noorwegen de Noortcaep, Laplant, Vinlant, Russlandt, de Witte Zee, de Custen van Candenoes, Swetenoes, Pitzora, &c.* (Franeker: Ketel, 1601), and, most recently, J.-J. Zeeberg, *Terugkeer naar Nova Zembla: de laatste en tragische reis van Willem Barents* (Zutphen: Walburg, 2007).
3. See Aad van Amstel, *Barbaren, rebellen en mandarijnen: de VOC in de slag met China in de Gouden Eeuw* (Amsterdam: Thoeris, 2011), 48–56.
4. Admiral Matelief sailed to the islands of Nan'ao and Lantau in 1607; see van Amstel, *Barbaren*, 44–45.
5. Jonathan D. Spence, *Emperor of China: Self-Portrait of K'ang-Hsi* (New York: Vintage, 1988), 67. The missions to Beijing were documented in Johan Nieuhof, *Het gezantschap der Neêrlandtsche Oost-Indische Compagnie, aan den grooten Tartarischen Cham, den tegenwoordigen keizer van China ... Beneffens een naukeurige beschryving der Sineesche steden, dorpen, regeering* (Amsterdam: Van Meurs, 1665), and Olfert Dapper, *Gedenkwaerdig bedryf der Nederlandsche Oost-Indische Maetschappye op de kuste en in het keizerrijk van Taising of Sina: behelzende het tweede gezandschap ... en het derde gezandschap ... beneffens een beschryving van geheel Sina* (Amsterdam: Van Meurs, 1670). For a recent analysis, see L. Hostetler, "Mapping Dutch Travels to and Translations of China: Jan Nieuhof's Account of the First East India Company Embassy, 1655–57," *Horizons* 1/2 (2010): 119–34.

(鄭成功, 1624–62), captured the island in 1662.⁶ Finally, at the end of the century, revived ambitions at an overland route through Central Asia did not proceed beyond the armchair scholarship of *Noord-en Oost-Tartarye* (North and East Tartary, 1692) by the Amsterdam mayor Nicolaes Witsen (1641–1717).

Studying the Dutch encounters with the Middle Kingdom, however, demands our interest because they resulted in the fastest and most efficient route of communication between Europe and East Asia. Western visitors to China, and Chinese visitors to Europe, preferred the ships of the Dutch United East India Company (VOC) for transport and correspondence. The company's voluminous trade in ceramics in particular, which constituted the first exchange of culture on a truly global scale and involved a great measure of artistic imitation and collaboration, served as the material carrier for the exchange of ideas.⁷ An early residue of this cultural encounter occurs in the writings of Qu Dajun (屈大均, 1630–96), who boarded one of the Dutch ships in Guangzhou and recounted his positive impression in his novel *Zhenhai Mansion*. "[The Dutch] clocks, muskets, rapiers, swords, and telescopes are the best in the West"; in light of the frequency with which the visitors were called "red-haired barbarians," this stereotypical image, which the Chinese eventually used in relation to all Europeans, may arguably be based on encounters with the Dutch rather than with the Mediterranean traders.⁸

Due to the intermediary role of the Low Countries in the cultural transfer between East and West, most information is to be found in European sources, which will be the focus point of the present analysis. Even though many historians have pointed out that the Netherlands were "Europe's primary entrepôt for information about Asia" and that the Dutch perception of China has "considerable significance for understanding early modern European culture generally," many aspects of this encounter remain

---

6. John E. Wills, *Pepper, Guns, and Parleys: The Dutch East India Company and China, 1662–1681* (Los Angeles: Figueroa Press, 2005), 49–54.
7. A particular example of the detailed models that Dutch artists provided is kept in the Rijksmuseum, Amsterdam (inv.nr. RP-T-1967-18, Cornelis Pronk, 1734–36, pen in grey and gouache on light brown paper, 19 cm × 16 cm), which was used widely by Chinese potters (e.g., Rijksmuseum, inv.nr. AK-RBK-15939-A, China, Jiangxi Province, Jingdezhen, Qing dynasty, about 1736–38).
8. The term was used throughout the seventeenth century. See van Amstel, *Barbaren*, 33, 43, 44. Cf.: "The red-hair barbarians" have "deep eyes and long noses, with red hair, eyebrows, and beards, with feet longer than a foot and two inches, and huge bodies. But they are not skilled in warfare, and rely on large warships and guns to turn the tide. Their clocks, muskets, rapiers, swords, and telescopes are the best in the West," according to the 1751 account (referring to the seventeenth-century situation) of Yin Guangren (印光任) and Zhang Rulin (張汝霖), *Aomen jilüe* 澳門紀略, modern edition (Macau: Instituto Cultural de Macau, 1992), 126. Cf. the first Chinese eyewitness account of Taiwan, *Taiwan jilüe* (臺灣紀略) by Lin Qianguang (林謙光), a mandarin at Formosa from 1687 to 1691, quoted in L. G. Thompson, "The Earliest Chinese Eyewitness Accounts," *Monumenta Serica* 23 (1964): 179–83. For the modern Chinese edition, see Ji Qiguang 季麒光 and Lin Qianguang 林謙光, *Taiwan zaji, Taiwan jiüe* 臺灣雜記·臺灣紀略, in *Congshu jicheng chubian* 叢書集成初編, 3235 (Shanghai: Shangwu yinshuguan, 1937).

to be explored.⁹ The Dutch Republic was unique not only in the profusion of Chinese ceramics—in contrast to neighboring nations, people from all social backgrounds could afford Chinese-style pottery—but also in the widely shared intuition, probably based on this presence of sophisticated material culture, that Chinese civilization was overall superior. As early as 1602, the political philosopher Hugo Grotius (1583–1645) stated that the Chinese were "very intelligent (*sollertissimae*) in all things";¹⁰ according to the Dutch "Prince of Poets," Joost van den Vondel (1587–1679), the Middle Kingdom itself was a "noble diamond, sparking divinely in the eye."¹¹ Various efforts of early European scholarship on China were products of the Netherlands as well. The earliest illustrated books, printing types, discussions of Chinese history, and adequate translations of Confucius originated in the Low Countries.

This chapter explores how the efforts of individual scholars, linked through networks of trade and correspondence that joined Amsterdam, Antwerp, and Beijing, resulted in cross-cultural exchanges of knowledge. Even though they occurred in the margin of the academic curriculum, they sparked new ideas along four interrelated fronts. The first front focused on the Chinese language and its script. The second one, building on Renaissance practices of philology, involved the translation of Chinese classics into Latin. The third front related to music and the visual arts. Finally, knowledge of Chinese history influenced Biblical criticism, paving the way for the role that China would come to play in the European Enlightenment.¹²

The importance of the Low Countries: Religious and commercial missions to China

The role of the Low Countries depended on a fortuitous combination of factors: the global "Jesuit information network" was complemented with and sometimes catalyzed

---

9. D. Lach and E. van Kley, *Asia in the Making of Europe, Vol. III: A Century of Advance, Book I: Trade, Missions, Literature* (Chicago and London: University of Chicago Press, 1993), 508; E. van Kley, "Qing Dynasty China in Seventeenth-Century Dutch Literature 1644–1700," in *The History of the Relations Between the Low Countries and China in the Qing Era (1644–1911)*, ed. W. F. Vande Walle and Noël Golvers (Louvain: Leuven University Press, 2003), 217–34, 231.

10. H. Grotius, "Sinarum gentes . . . omnium sollertissimas," in *Parallelon rerumpublicarum liber tertius: De moribus ingenioque populorum Atheniensium, Romanorum, Batavorum* (Haarlem: Loosjes, 1802), Vol. 3, 19. Grotius may have based this idea on the acount by Jan Huygen van Linschoten, *Itinerario, voyage ofte schipvaert van Jan Huygen van Linschoten naar Oost ofte Potugaels Indien, 1579–1592* (The Hague: Nijhoff, 1910), Vol. 1, 91. On Grotius's long-distance involvement with China, see now T. Brook, *Mr. Selden's Map of China: Decoding the Secrets of a Vanished Cartographer* (New York: Bloomsbury, 2013), 28ff.

11. "Sina [is] d'eedle diamant, / Die goddelijk in d'oogen flonkert, / En alle uitsteekentheên verdonkert, / Gelijk een onwaerdeerbaer pant," J. van den Vondel, *Zungchin of ondergang der Sineesche heerschappye* (Amsterdam: De Wees, 1667), v, 909–12.

12. From here, the argument follows my analysis in "The Middle Kingdom in the Low Countries: Sinology in the Seventeenth-Century Netherlands," in R. Bod, J. Maat, and T. Weststeijn, eds., *The Making of the Humanities, Vol. II: From Early Modern to Modern Disciplines* (Amsterdam: Amsterdam University Press, 2013), 209–41.

by the interests of the Dutch trading company.¹³ Missionaries traveled on the VOC ships, which also carried their mail; this route was known as the Via Batavica, Via Hollandica, or Via Jacquetrensi. On the way back, Dutch journalism kept the missionaries informed about news from Europe.¹⁴ These contacts helped a small group of Jesuits from the Southern Netherlands, which reached inside the Forbidden City, to become extraordinarily successful. One of them, Ferdinand Verbiest (Chinese name 南懷仁, 1623–88), even became private tutor to the emperor. The missionaries, in turn, provided publishers, scholars, and artists in the Netherlands with firsthand information from their privileged position. Dutch colonial settlements in East Asia sometimes played intermediary roles in this exchange.¹⁵

Linguistic and cultural affinities apparently trumped religious differences; Jesuits could move relatively freely in the Dutch Republic where there was a large Catholic population. Three visits by members of the China mission made a large impact throughout the Netherlands. The first was Nicolas Trigault (Chinese name 金尼閣, 1577–1628) from Douai, who returned from China to the Low Countries in 1614.¹⁶ His edition of Matteo Ricci's (Chinese name 利瑪竇, 1552–1610) papers was translated widely as the first popular source of information on China. This interest was reinforced when, in 1653, Martino Martini (Chinese name 衛匡國, 1614–61) arrived

13. The term "Jesuit information network" is used by Luke Clossey, *Salvation and Globalization in the Early Jesuit Missions* (Cambridge: Cambridge University Press, 2008), title of Chapter 9. For the importance of the interconnected study of the Northern and Southern Netherlands, cf. P. Demaerel, "Couplet and the Dutch," in *Philippe Couplet, S.J. (1623–1693): The Man Who Brought China to Europe*, ed. J. Heyndrickx (Nettetal: Institut Monumenta Serica 1990), 87–120; Karl Davids, "Van VOC-mentaliteit naar Jezuïetenmentaliteit: de Societas Jesu als schrikbeeld, partner en ijkpunt voor de Oost-Indische Compagnie," in M. Ebben et al., *Alle streken van het compas: maritieme geschiedenis van Nederland* (Zutphen: Walburg Pers, 2010), 132–35; and Ronnie Po-Chia Hsia, "China in the Spanish Netherlands: Belgian Jesuits in the Production and Circulation of Knowledge about Ming-Qing China," paper delivered at the conference "Embattled Territory: The Circulation of Knowledge in the Spanish Netherlands," Ghent, March 9–11, 2011.
14. See John E. Wills, "Some Dutch Sources on the Jesuit China Mission, 1662–1687," *Archivum historicum Societatis Iesu* 54 (1985): 267–94. At all times the Portuguese, French, and Italian missionaries were numerically superior. For some numbers, see J. Dehergne, *Répertoire des Jésuites de Chine* (Rome and Paris: Institutum Historicum S.J., 1972), which lists 920 Jesuits of the Chinese mission (who departed for China from Europe, were born in China, or came from the Japanese mission but were relevant to China) in the period 1552–1813. Thirty-eight of them came from the Low Countries, including at least seven born in the Northern Netherlands. One was procurator of the mission (Trigault); two became mandarins (Verbiest and Thomas); another was a visitor for the Chinese mission and rector (Petrus van Hamme, 1651–1727).
15. An example of this was the vital communication between Jesuits from the Southern Netherlands on the Chinese coast, the VOC physician Andreas Cleyer and the minister Theodorus Sas in Batavia, and an Antwerp publisher; see Noël Golvers, *Ferdinand Verbiest, S.J. (1623–1688) and the Chinese Heaven* (Louvain: Ferdinand Verbiest Institute, 2003), 188. To quote Hsia, "China in the Spanish Netherlands": "through [their] proximity to the former northern provinces, which became the independent Dutch Republic, and thanks to the large Catholic population in the north, Belgian Jesuits in China could shift from a Portuguese dominated network to the more efficient Dutch route of communication."
16. Douai, presently part of France, belonged to the Spanish Netherlands at the time and had scholarly connections with the Dutch Republic; see P. Begheyn, "Nederlandse studenten aan de universiteit van Douai (1605–1625)," *Gens Nostra* 55 (2000): 75–78.

in the Dutch Republic from China, accompanied by a Chinese assistant. He stayed in Amsterdam for some time to prepare a set of detailed Chinese maps for the famous publisher Johannes Blaeu (1596–1673). Martini's subsequent visit to the University of Leuven inspired a generation of students to join the mission. Noël Golvers has recently identified over two hundred requests by "Indipetae" from the Low Countries, of which only eight received a positive response. A young teacher of rhetoric, Antoine Thomas (Chinese name 安多, 1644–1709) from Namur, wrote seventeen petitions between 1663 and 1675 before he could finally sail to the East in 1678.[17]

When Martini set out to return to China in 1657, he was accompanied by Philippe Couplet (Chinese name 柏應理, 1622–93) from Mechlin and, from the Northern Netherlands, François de Rougemont (Chinese name 魯日滿, 1624–76) and Ignatius Hartoghvelt (1629–58). In preparing for their expedition, the three young missionaries first stayed in Amsterdam in civilian clothes to preach in the condoned Jesuit mission.[18] After arriving in China, Couplet became a particularly successful strategist, sometimes acting as a political and commercial informer for the Dutch traders.[19] Eventually it was his turn to travel from Beijing to Europe in order to further propagate the importance of the mission. In 1683, he disembarked in Holland, where he worked for some time on an explanation of the writings of Confucius and a text on Chinese chronology, a topic that greatly attracted Dutch scholars.[20] The interest of the Catholic missionaries and the predominantly Protestant traders in their respective activities in the Empire was mutual. The Jesuits from the Southern Netherlands had their Antwerp publisher, Michiel Cnobbaert (active 1662–73), print an unauthorized version of Johan Nieuhof's (1618–72) report of a VOC mission to Beijing, in which they slightly altered the contents for a more favorable view of their own role.[21] Conversely, a wide audience of laypeople in the Dutch Republic was greatly attracted by all writings on China, and the Amsterdam printer Jacob van Meurs (1638–75) made a pirated edition of the relevant Jesuit writings collected by Athanasius Kircher (1602–80), based at the College in Rome. Such interactions ensured that a small group of missionaries hailing from the Low Countries played a remarkably large role in exchanges

---

17. Liam M. Brockey, *Journey to the East: The Jesuit Mission to China, 1579–1724* (Cambridge and London: Harvard University Press, 2007), 228, 227, 222.
18. This was called *Huis de Zonnebloem*.
19. In 1662, a Dutch fleet fought the pirate Coxinga in Fuzhou on behalf of the Qing authorities, hoping for a trade opening. Couplet wrote to them in Dutch. See J. Barten, "Hollandse kooplieden op bezoek bij concilievaders," *Archief voor de geschiedenis van de katholieke kerk in Nederland* 12 (1970): 75–121.
20. Thierry Meynard, ed., *Confucius Sinarum Philosophus (1687): The First Translation of the Confucian Classics* (Rome: Institutum Historicum Societatis Iesu, 2011), 14, 16.
21. See P. Arblaster, "Piracy and Play: Two Catholic Appropriations of Nieuhof's 'Gezantschap,'" in Siegfried Huigen et al., *The Dutch Trading Companies as Knowledge Networks* (Leiden and Boston: Brill, 2010), 129–44. According to Davids, the Dutch trading company's interest in Jesuit scholarship was unique: English and French traders were merely interested in economic information; see Davids, "VOC-mentaliteit," 137–39.

of knowledge.²² In many cases they acted as intermediaries between Rome, Northern Europe, and Beijing. Kircher, for one, depended heavily on an Antwerp Jesuit (Daniël van Papenbroeck, 1628–1714), an Amsterdam publisher, and a collective of artists from the Netherlands to produce his *China Illustrata* (in Latin and Dutch versions), the most popular book on China of the age.²³

"Missionary Sinology," to use Geoffrey Gunn's term, depended on the fact that, from the order's foundation onwards, the Jesuits were geared toward scholarship, as has been amply documented.²⁴ The *Ratio Studiorum* (1599) outlined complete training in the arts and sciences.²⁵ The missionaries from the Low Countries all worked as teachers of humanistic topics—rhetoric and ancient Greek—before leaving for China.²⁶ This background and the strict selection criteria prepared them for the confrontation with the Chinese literati. In their foothold at Macau the Jesuits envisaged introducing the Chinese to the higher truths of Christianity by convincing them of the correctness of Western reasoning in the arts and sciences.²⁷ Liam Brockey has analyzed in detail how the Macanese Jesuits set up an equivalent of the *ratio studiorum* that incorporated indigenous study methods.²⁸

Moreover, the Jesuits used their erudition to legitimize, for a European audience, their costly and intellectually challenging missionary work. The Congregatio de Propaganda Fide, founded in 1622, requested the missionaries report to Rome on a yearly basis. Their letters were often printed, and although officially restricted literature in Protestant countries, these were widely available in pirated editions.²⁹ As we

---

22. Also argued by Hsia, "China in the Spanish Netherlands." The importance of the Low Countries is evident in other activities of the Jesuits as well. For instance, the most productive translator of Jesuit writings in the seventeenth century was Frans de Smidt; others were the Dutchmen Jan Buys and Gerard Zoes. See Peter Burke, "The Jesuits and the Art of Translation in Early Modern Europe," in J. O'Malley et al., *The Jesuits II* (Toronto: University of Toronto Press, 2006), 24–32.
23. On the Dutch translation and the pirated edition by Jacob van Meurs, see I. H. van Eeghen, "Arnoldus Montanus's Book on Japan," *Quaerendo* II (1972): 250–72. The illustrations in Kircher's book are not attributed to individual masters. The extensive collective of engravers working for him included luminaries such as Cornelis Bloemaert (1603–92), Gérard de Lairesse (1640–1711), and Romeyn de Hooghe (1645–1708). Others were Lieven Cruyl (1634–1720), Coenraet Decker (1651–85), Willem van der Laegh (1614–74), Theodoor Matham (1606–76), Jean van Munnichuysen (1654/5–after 1701), Crispijn van de Passe the Younger (1597/8–1670 or after), and Athonie Heeres Sioertsma (b. 1626/7).
24. Geoffrey C. Gunn, *First Globalization: The Eurasian Exchange, 1500–1800* (Lanham: Rowman and Littlefield, 2003), 237.
25. Ladislaus Lukàcs, ed., *Ratio atque Institutio Studiorum Societatis Iesu* (Roma: Institutum Historicum Societatis Iesu, 1986).
26. Trigault taught rhetoric in Ghent for eight years; Couplet taught Greek in Mechlin; Verbiest taught Latin, Greek, and rhetoric in Brussels; Thomas taught rhetoric and philosophy in Douai. In fact, candidates from outside Portugal usually had to wait longer before they were admitted to the mission, which meant that the Netherlanders spent a relatively long period teaching. Brockey, *Journey to the East*, 222.
27. Benjamin Elman, *A Cultural History of Modern Science in China* (New Haven: Yale University Press, 2006), 26.
28. Brockey, *Journey to the East*, 255–63.
29. Lach and van Kley, *Asia in the Making of Europe, Vol. III*, 593. On Jesuit books in Protestant libraries, see also Burke, "The Jesuits and the Art of Translation," 30; Nicolas Trigault, *Rerum memorabilium in regno*

will discuss below, not only did the Jesuits present their own work in the positive light of humanistic scholarship, but they also portrayed Chinese civilization favorably.

It seems that the Jesuits in the Low Countries had an additional incentive for studying China: they expected it would benefit their mission in Protestant Netherlands. The association of the Jesuits with the Chinese was often used to discredit the order in Protestant countries. In practice, however, traders in the Dutch Republic were greatly interested in any information the missionaries could provide about this remote part of the world. When Martini traveled back to Amsterdam from Brussels, his expenses were paid by the magistrates of the Dutch East India Company. Martini, in turn, tried to ensure financial benefits and privileges on the company's ships.[30]

Finally, we should note that, besides the Catholic orders, there were Protestant missionaries in East Asia. As argued below, studying their efforts leads to a full picture of the interwoven scholarly exchanges between the Middle Kingdom and the Low Countries.

Studying Chinese: Guanhua, Sinkan, and Manchu

The year 1600 marks the beginning of the Chinese century in the Netherlands. A Chinese merchant named Wu Pu arrived in Middelburg on a VOC ship and was baptized.[31] A year later, the unloading of the first porcelain cargo in the same city sparked the Dutch fashion for Chinese curios that would soon spread throughout Europe. Chinese books arrived as well in the collections of scholars such as Ernst Brinck (1582–1649), Jacob Golius (1596–1667), Otto Heurnius (1577–1652), Johannes de Laet (1581–1649), Joseph Scaliger (1540–1609), Gerard Vossius (1577–1649), and Bonaventura Vulcanius (1538–1614).[32] Alongside the fascination with exotic objects, many were attracted to speculations about the antiquity of these writings and the nature of the Chinese characters.

Sinae gestarum litterae annuae Societatis Iesu: ad P. Mutium Vitelleschi . . . (Antwerp: Jerome Verdussen, 1625). Trigault's writings in Dutch were *Copye des briefs ghescreven vanden E.P. Nicolaes Trigault, Priester der Societyt Iesu, aenden E.P. Franciscum Fleron, Provinciael der selver societeyt inde Nederlanden. Uut Goa uit Oost-Indien op Kersmis-avont, 1607. Waer in verhaelt wort de vermeerderinghe des Christen gheloof in Indien, Chinen, Iaponien, etc.* (Antwerp: Vervliet, 1609); and *Waerachtich verhael van eenige merckelycke saecken des vermaerts coninckrijcx van Syna* (Den Bosch: Anthoni Scheffer, 1615).

30. Henri Bernard, "Les Sources mongoles et chinoises de l'Atlas Martini (1655)," *Monumenta Serica* XII (1947): 127–44.
31. Wu Pu (also known as Impo or Yppong) acted as a middleman for the Chinese and Vice-Admiral Wybrand van Warwijck (1566 or 1570–1615). See the forthcoming study by T. Weststeijn and L. Gesterkamp in *Netherlands Yearbook for the History of Art* 66 (2016).
32. Some of these books ended up in Leiden University Library, where they have remained. On Brinck's collection containing Chinese curios and texts, see E. Bergvelt et al., *De wereld binnen handbereik: Nederlandse kunst- en rariteitenverzamelingen, 1585–1736* (Amsterdam: Amsterdams Historisch Museum, 1992), 137–38.

Trigault's visit provided a first source of reliable information on the Chinese language. He was among the first missionaries to have excellent knowledge of Guanhua, or Mandarin Chinese, the variant spoken by the elite. At the end of the sixteenth century, the Jesuits had realized that mastering spoken and written Guanhua was essential for being taken seriously by Chinese literati. The missionaries from the Netherlands became particularly active in pleading for the introduction of a liturgy in Chinese rather than in Latin.[33] Trigault (helped by native assistants) translated Catholic theological and philosophical texts, and some of Aesop's fables, while he also assembled an extensive library for the Chinese future instruction that included modern authors such as Erasmus and Lipsius.[34] His efforts culminated in a system of Romanization of Chinese.[35] According to Hsia, this was "the most important lexicon and guide for the learning of Chinese prior to the modern era. The *Xiru ermu zi* (西儒耳目資, A source for the eyes and ears of the Western literati), published in 1626, consisted of a dictionary and language tool with Chinese characters arranged by vowels, consonants, and diphthongs." It remained in use until the nineteenth century.[36]

Trigault's visit to the Netherlands sparked intellectual exchanges on the nature of Chinese writing. In Antwerp, the polyglot Herman Hugo (1558–1629) elaborated the idea that Chinese characters were ideograms that were universally understood throughout East Asia. His *De prima scribendi origine* (Antwerp 1617) repeated some of the missionaries' observations, to which Hugo connected the ideal of a universal script:[37] "When individual letters are qualified to denote not words, but the things themselves, and when all these [letters] are common to all people, then everyone would understand the writing of the various peoples even though each one would call those things

---

33. Nicolas Standaert, ed., *Handbook of Christianity in China. 1: 635–1800* (Leiden and Boston: Brill, 2001), 310. This preference was perhaps related to the missionaries' own affinity with preaching among Dutch-speaking natives, on whom Protestantism exerted a powerful pull. In the winter of 1683–84, shortly after his arrival in Europe, Couplet visited Van Papenbroeck in Louvain in order to solicit support for the Chinese-speaking clergy and liturgy; Van Papenbroeck wrote in support citing many examples from early Church history permitting the use of Slavonic in East European lands. See N. Golvers, "D. Papebrochius, S.J. (1628–1714), Ph. Couplet (1623–1693) en de Vlaamse jezuïetenmissie in China," *De zeventiende eeuw* 14/1 (1998): 39–50, esp. 41–42.

34. Nicolas Standaert, "The Transmission of Renaissance Culture in Seventeenth-Century China," *Renaissance Studies* 17 (2003): 367–91. Cf. André van den Eerenbeemt, "Nederlandsche boeken in de oude bibliotheek van Pé-t'ang in Peiping," *Het Missiewerk* 27 (1948): 174–82.

35. Mark Chang, "The Latin Phoneticization of Chinese Characters of Matteo Ricci and Nicolas Trigault," in *International Symposium in Chinese-Western Cultural Exchange in Commemoration of the 400th Anniversary of the Arrival of Matteo Ricci S.J. in China* (Taipei 1983), 87–97. According to Gunn, Trigault also introduced the Chinese literati to the Latin alphabet. See Gunn, *First Globalization*, 237.

36. Ronnie Po-Chia Hsia, "Language Acquisition and Missionary Strategies in China, 1580–1760," in Charlotte de Castelnau-l'Estoile et al., *Missions d'évangelisation et circulation des saviors XVIe-XVIIIe siècles* (Madrid: Casa Velázquez, 2011), 189–208. See also Brockey, *Journey to the East*, 261.

37. Herman Hugo, *De prima scribendi origine* (Antwerp: Plantin, 1617), 59–62, 88. Hugo also published Latin versions of letters relating to the mission in East Asia.

by very different names."³⁸ In 1635, the first professor of Amsterdam's Athenaeum, Gerard Vossius, formulated the same ambition. He used Trigault's accounts for a statement in *De arte grammatica* (Amsterdam 1635) that "the Chinese and Japanese, although their languages differ just as much as Hebrew and Dutch, still understand one another if they write in this manner. For even if some might pronounce other words when reading, the concepts would nevertheless be the same." Vossius was farther off the mark when he wrote that "for the Chinese, there are no fewer letters than there are words: however, they can be combined together, so that their total number does not exceed 70,000 or 80,000."³⁹ This number was clearly an exaggeration.⁴⁰ In fact, the great number of the characters fascinated Dutch scholars, one of them even rating it at no less than 120,000.⁴¹

Vossius's younger colleague, Jacob Golius, professor of Arabic at the University of Leiden, fanatically collected Chinese books of which, however, he understood nothing. When Martini arrived in 1654, Golius therefore asked his superiors permission to go to Antwerp "in order to speak and confer with a certain Jesuit or a Chinese, both come from China, and thereby to obtain the knowledge of certain characters and secrets of the Chinese language."⁴² They met in the collection of Chinese objects, grandly named "Musaeum Sinense," of the Antwerp city secretary Jacob Edelheer (1597–1657).⁴³ Golius must have been especially excited by speaking in Latin to Martini's "certainly not unlettered" Chinese companion, only known by his first name, Dominicus.⁴⁴ The exchange resulted in Golius's short treatise *De regno Cattayo additamentum*, to be

---

38. "Si singulae literae impositae essent, non vocibus, sed rebus ipsis significandis, eaeque essent hominibus omnibus communes; omnes omninio homines, etiamsi gentes singulae res singulas diversis nominibus appelent, singularum gentium scriptionem intelligerent," Hugo, *De prima scribendi origine*, 60.
39. "[P]rodidit Nicolaus Trigaultius … non pauciores Sinensibus literas esse, quam voces numerantur: eas tamen iter inter se componere, ut LXX, aut LXXX milia non excedant. Imo idem refert, Sinenses & Japanenses, etsi lingua aeque differant, ac Hebraei, & Belgae; tamen, quae sic scribuntur, intelligere … Utcumque enim in legendo alii alia verba pronunciassent: tamen iidem fuissent conceptus. Nempe uti nunc variarum linguarum homines rem eandem conspicientes eandem rem concipiunt: ita idem [sic] rei signum intuentes, eundem haberent conceptum," Vossius, *De arte grammatica* (Amsterdam: Blaeu, 1635), Vol. I, 143. Vossius discusses Chinese writing on pp. 140–43 and 122.
40. The most complete Chinese dictionary of the seventeenth century, Mei Yingzuo's 梅膺祚 *Zihui* 字彙 of 1615, listed 33,179 characters.
41. "Habent [Sinenses] notarum CXX millia, ex quibus mediocriter doctum ad LXXX millia nosse opportet," G. Hornius, *De originibus Americanis libri quator* (Leiden: Vlacq, 1652), 271.
42. Resolution of the University of Leiden dated June 9, 1654, quoted from Duyvendak, "Early Chinese Studies in Holland," *T'oung Pao* 32 (1934): 293–344, esp. 301.
43. Edelheer was a close friend of the printer Balthasar Moretus (1615–74), who published Martini's text *De bello Tartarico*. See Duyvendak, "Early Chinese Studies," 302; on Edelheer's collection, see also N. Golvers, "De recruteringstocht van M. Martini, S.J. door de Lage Landen in 1654: over geomantische kompassen, Chinese verzamelingen, lichtbeelden en R. P. Wilhelm van Aelst, S. J.," *De zeventiende eeuw* 10/2 (1994): 331–50; 348.
44. Duyvendak, "Early Chinese Studies," 322. A handwritten text in Chinese, attributed to this Chinese visitor, remained in Louvain (now in the Royal Library, Brussels), which may be "the oldest Chinese text produced on European soil." See Golvers, "De recruteringstocht," 342.

included in Martini's *Atlas Sinensis* (Amsterdam 1655). Incidentally, this involved the first properly printed Chinese characters in Europe and seems to have established Golius's fame as a Sinologist: Kircher sent him his book on China in 1665 (for which Golius, in exchange, sent the Jesuit some exotic rhubarb seeds).[45] Golius was probably responsible for another discussion of China as well, which was included in 1668 in an account of a Dutch trade mission to Beijing.[46]

Martini presented Golius with additional Chinese books, which made his one of the most important European collections (about eighty volumes). After Golius's death, some of them came into the hands of Adriaan Reland (1676–1718), a famous scholar of Judaism and Islam.[47] His *Dissertationum miscellanearum* (Utrecht 1708) discussed the difficulties of the Chinese language. Echoing Hugo and Vossius, Reland explained how the script was also used for unrelated languages in neighboring countries, which he demonstrated in a glossary of characters and their pronunciation in Chinese, Japanese, and Vietnamese.[48] In his commentary, Reland seized the opportunity to underscore that all these languages originally derived from Hebrew, which he saw as the mother of most languages of Europe, Asia, and Africa, excluding only those of the Americas.

Reland reacted implicitly to a heated debate originating in the 1640s: the philosopher Hugo Grotius (1583–1645) and the linguist Johannes de Laet had discussed the putative Hebrew origin of all languages, including American ones.[49] The debate was touchy because it impacted the validity of the biblical account. Circumventing the issue of Hebrew, the Harderwijk-based professor Georg Hornius (1620–70) argued for an Egyptian origin even for Chinese. He based this idea on the observation, already expressed by Golius, that the ancient forms of the Chinese characters bore some resemblance to Egyptian hieroglyphs.[50]

As I have argued elsewhere, the purported "hieroglyphical" essence of Chinese greatly attracted scholars in Northern Europe. Authors from Hugo and Vossius to Jan Amos Comenius (1592–1670) and John Wilkins (1614–72) used the Chinese

---

45. Duyvendak, "Early Chinese Studies," 300. The Chinese rhubarb seeds came from Leiden University's hortus botanicus. See Golius to Kircher, June 11, 1665, Archive Pontificia Università Gregoriana, Ms 562 f 139.
46. Johan Nieuhof, *Legatio Batavica ad magnum Tartariae Chamum Sungteium* (Amsterdam: Van Meurs, 1668) contains an introduction (absent in the original Dutch book) on Marco Polo, that may have been written by Golius. Golius was also approached to translate Nieuhof's travelogue into Latin, but this was eventually done by Georg Hornius.
47. Reland's works include *Analecta rabbinica* (Utrecht: Appels, 1702) and *De religione Mohammedica libri duo* (Utrecht, 1705).
48. A. Reland, "Tabella vocum, cum pronuntiatione earum Japonica, Sinica et Annamitica," in *Dissertationum miscellanearum* (Utrecht: Broedelet, 1708), Vol. III, 112–16.
49. See J. de Laet, *Notae ad dissertationem Hugonis Grotii De origine gentium americanarum, et observationes aliquot ad melior indaginem difficillimae illius quaestionis* (Amsterdam and Leiden: Elsevier, 1643).
50. According to Hornius, pictograms had traveled from Egypt, via China, to the Americas: "Fateor non unam scribendi penitus apud Mexicanos et Sinenses rationem, nec tamen penitus diversa fuit . . . Cataini scribunt penicillo pictorio et una figura multas literas complectitur ac verbum facit," Hornius, *De originibus Americanis*, 270–71. On Golius, see Duyvendak, "Early Chinese Studies," 326.

characters to discuss the possibility of writing in signs that could be universally understood and its consequences for the philosophy of language. Ultimately, the Chinese script contributed to Gottfried Wilhelm Leibniz's (1646–1716) search for a *characteristica universalis*, a language that could be read without a dictionary.[51] The development of this linguistic discussion, from Trigault's firsthand expertise to fanciful speculations that eventually involved biblical and philosophical questions, typifies how many ideas about China fared during the first century of their European reception: they became *increasingly* stereotypical and fantastic. The discussions about pictographic writing (just like the imaginative illustrations in Kircher's *China Illustrata*) were in many ways more revealing about European preconceptions than about China.

Yet the Protestant mission accompanying the trade expeditions resulted in a few accurate linguistic works. In 1624, the Calvinist minister Justus Heurnius (b. 1587) departed for the Dutch East Indies, where the city of Batavia (modern Jakarta) had a thriving Chinese population. After a few years he had compiled a dictionary "with the aid of a Chinese who understands Latin . . . in which the Dutch and Latin words are placed first and alongside the Chinese characters" (a copy remains in the British Library). This was one of the first of its kind (Trigault had worked on a Portuguese-Chinese dictionary, but the manuscript had disappeared after it was misplaced on the shelves of the Vatican Library).[52] Although he added a synopsis of the Christian religion in Chinese, the minister seems to have had commercial opportunities in mind in particular: "We have taken the trouble to do this, for such Chinese are not often found and it is a work which will be of great usefulness to posterity, as soon as the Chinese trade is opened, as we hope."[53]

Other Protestant missionaries studied the language of Sinkan (新港), a now extinct precursor of the Siraya language spoken in Taiwan. From 1624 onwards, the Dutch in their colony on Formosa (present-day Taiwan) had pioneered the Romanization of the local tongue (in fact an Austronesian language).[54] The minister Daniel Gravius ordered two bilingual books to be published in Amsterdam,[55] written, according

---

51. See my article "From Hieroglyphs to Universal Characters: Pictography in the Early Modern Netherlands," in E. Jorink and B. Ramakers, eds., *Art and Science in the Seventeenth-Century Netherlands: Netherlands Yearbook for History of Art* 61 (2011): 238–81.
52. K. Kuiper, "The Earliest Monument of Dutch Sinological Studies: Justus Heurnius's Manuscript Dutch-Chinese Dictionary and Chinese-Latin Compendium doctrinae Christianae (Batavia 1628)," *Quaerendo* 35/1–2 (2005): 109–39.
53. Letter of Heurnius to the directors of the East India Company (1628), see Duyvendak, "Early Chinese Studies," 318.
54. Gunn, *First Globalization*, 238.
55. Gravius, minister in Formosa 1647–51, published *Het heylige evangelium Matthei en Johannis: Ofte Hagnau ka d'llig matiktik, ka na sasoulat ti Mattheus, ti Johannes appa; Overgeset inde Formosaansche tale, voor de inwoonders van Soulang, Mattau, Sinckan, Bacloan, Tavokan, en Tevorang* (*The Gospels of Matthew and John . . . Translated in the Formosan Language for the Inhabitants of Soulang etc.*) (Amsterdam: Hartogh, 1661). This was followed by the bilingual Declaration of Christianity, *Patar ki tna-'msing-an ki Christang, ka tauki-papatar-en-ato tmaeu'ug tou sou ka makka sideia: Ofte't formulier des Christendoms,*

to the introduction, "in Dutch and Formosan . . . in order to ascertain the successful dispersion of the Dutch language."[56] In 1659, the missionaries founded a college for Formosan youths with Sinkan and Dutch as working languages. As their model they used Comenius's innovative pedagogical work, *Portael der saecken en spraecken* (Gateway to things and languages, Amsterdam 1658).[57]

In regard to China's linguistic varieties, Ferdinand Verbiest's efforts were of a more lasting nature. Even though the Jesuits' main works in Chinese concerned the sciences and scholastic philosophy, his sizeable volumes, which created accurate terminology in Guanhua, were feats of linguistic rigor in themselves.[58] Furthermore, the change from the Ming to the Qing dynasty had meant that the Manchu language had now become the court's official tongue: Verbiest mastered this too, to converse with the emperor. He compiled the first Manchu grammar (*Grammatica Tartarea*, Paris 1676).[59] When his position as court engineer eventually involved casting a great number of cannons for the emperor, inscriptions in Manchu documented that Verbiest was the maker.[60] His successor, Antoine Thomas, found it hard to live up to the standard he had set, lamenting that attempts at handling "the Chinese characters and books" left little time for spiritual matters.[61]

Philology: Publishing the Confucian classics

Traveling on a Dutch ship, Philippe Couplet arrived in Europe to import Chinese knowledge and advertise the mission in papal, aristocratic, and intellectual circles. He brought with him four hundred Chinese Christian books donated by a convert noblewoman with whom he had collaborated closely in Shanghai, Candida Xu

---

met de verklaringen van dien, inde Sideis-Formosaansche tale [door Dan. Gravius] (Amsterdam: Hartogh, 1662).

56. "[B]eyde in Duytsch en Formosaans: het welcke voorwaar sulcken gezegenden voortganck nam, dat'et, by naerstig achtervolgh vry wat groots beloofden: gelijck ick oock t'sedert hebbe verstaan, dat'et oogmerck tot voortplantinge van de Nederduytsche tale aldaar seer geluckelyck wordt bereyckt." See E. L. Macapili and Huang Chun, *Siraya Glossary: Based on the Gospel of St. Matthew in Formosa (Sinkan Dialect): A Primary Survey* (Tainan: Tainan Pepo Siraya Culture Association, 2008).

57. J. A. Comenius, *Eerste deel der schoolgeleertheyd, genoemt het Portael: inhoudende de grondtveste der dingen, en onser wijsheyd omtrent de dingen, als mede der Latijnschen tael met de moedertael* (Amsterdam: Roy, 1658).

58. Cf. Verbiest's fourteen-volume *Yi xiang zhi* was printed by the Jesuits in Beijing in 1673.

59. Printed as "Elementa Linguae Tartaricae," in *Rélations des divers voyages curieux, qui n'ont point esté publiées*, ed. Melchisedech Thévenot (Paris: Moette, 1696). Translation in Pentti Aalto, *The "Elementa linguae Tartaricae" by Ferdinand Verbiest, S.J.* (Wiesbaden: Harassowitz, 1977); see also Golvers, "The 'Elementa linguae Tartaricae' by Ferdinand Verbiest, SJ (1623–88): Some New Evidence," in *Italia ed Europa nella linguistica del Rinascimento: Confronti e relazioni*, Vol. II, ed. Mirko Tavoni and Roberta Cella (Ferrara and Modena: Panini, 1996), 581–93.

60. Giovanni Stary, "The 'Manchu Cannons' Cast by Ferdinand Verbiest and the Hitherto Unknown Title of His Instructions," in *Ferdinand Verbiest (1623–1688): Jesuit Missionary, Scientist, Engineer and Diplomat*, ed. John W. Witek (Nettetal: Institut Monumenta Serica, 1994), 215–25.

61. Brockey, *Journey to the East*, 281.

(許甘第大, 1607–80).⁶² Moreover, he was accompanied by a young Chinese, son of Christian converts from Nanjing, Michael Shen Fuzong (沈福宗, c. 1658–91). Thoroughly educated in the Confucian texts, he was to help Couplet with various literary projects.⁶³ These included the publication in Latin of three of the four Classics attributed to Confucius (*The Great Learning*, *The Doctrine of the Mean*, and *Analects*), in fact, a compilation of translations made by different Jesuits from the sixteenth century onwards.⁶⁴ Couplet finished a lengthy preface to this book, *Confucius Sinarum philosophus, sive scientia Sinica* (Paris 1687), during his stay in the Dutch Republic.⁶⁵

This publication was the missionaries' chief scholarly accomplishment, demonstrating their linguistic and philological skills. The Jesuit involvement with Confucianism had initially been a practical one: they had started translating the *Four Books* for the immediate purpose of teaching the Chinese language to newly arrived recruits. They had recognized that the education of the Chinese elite began with the Confucian texts. Without mastery of at least some of them, the missionaries would fail in converting the literati.⁶⁶ Meynard concludes, however, that by the 1670s, "clearly what [Couplet and De Rougemont] intended was no longer a primer in Chinese language for missionaries, but a manual introducing future missionaries to a certain reading of Chinese thought. The Confucian Classics were called upon to testify to the legitimacy of the Jesuit missionary policy."⁶⁷ The Jesuits hoped to demonstrate that Chinese thought shared some essential tenets with Christianity, on which a project of mass conversion could be based.

Printing this book was no simple matter. Although the missionaries' diaries had found a large audience, publishers apparently hesitated when confronted with this unprecedented and exotic work of Oriental philosophy. It did not help that Couplet, using Shen's expertise, wanted to include the main Chinese terms printed in Chinese characters.

It typifies the interwoven nature of scholarly contacts throughout the Low Countries that the Jesuits first envisaged a Dutch Protestant publisher. Already in the 1670s, they planned on working with Blaeu (who had printed Martini's *Atlas*) for some

---

62. See Philippe Couplet, *Historie van eene groote, christene mevrouwe van China met naeme mevrouw Candida Hiu . . . beschreven door . . . Philippus Couplet . . . ende in onse Nederlandtsche taele door H.I.D.N.W.P. overgheset* (Antwerp: Knobbaert by Franciscus Muller, 1694).
63. T. N. Foss, "The European Sojourn of Philippe Couplet and Michael Shen Fuzong, 1683–1692," in *Philippe Couplet, S.J. (1623–1693): The Man Who Brought China to Europe*, ed. J. Heyndrickx (Nettetal: Institut Monumenta Serica, 1990), 121–42.
64. They used the translations of Confucius by Prospero Intorcetta in particular, who is credited on the title page; Couplet speaks in the introduction in the first person plural to highlight the collaborative nature of his work.
65. Meynard, *Confucius*, 16.
66. Brockey, *Journey to the East*, 243–86. He calls attention to the Jesuits' appropriation of indigenous methods of scholarship.
67. Meynard, *Confucius*, 10.

philosophical texts. He had proven to be an effective patron for the Jesuits and a faithful go-between for letters via the Dutch trading company. Blaeu, for his part, counted on the privilege of being the first in Europe to publish important Chinese sources and studies.[68] For the *Confucius Sinarum philosophus*, De Rougemont again suggested involving Blaeu, the Ypres poet Willem Becanus (1608–83), and the Antwerp architect Willem Hesius (1601–90) to make the frontispiece.[69] Yet the deal fell through, thwarted by Athanasius Kircher who, although confirming the choice for the Dutch Republic, preferred Janssonius in Amsterdam as a printer (with whom Kircher had signed a contract for his own books).[70] In any event, funding for Couplet's idiosyncratic project proved to be a problem. When a different publisher was finally found in Paris in 1687 (a Dutchman recently converted to Catholicism, Daniël Horthemels), he did not want to include the Chinese characters even though the notation numbers for these had already been set in type in the first few chapters.[71]

The book deserves our interest: Couplet's extensive introduction frames the translation as a philological project similar to those dealing with the Latin and Greek classics of Europe. Chapter one establishes the Confucian texts' "First Authorship." It places Confucius in his historical context and laments the difficulty in reconstructing ancient Chinese history due to the paucity of written documents. Another chapter is on additional "Evidence Drawn, Not from the Modern Interpreters, but, as Much as Possible, from the Original Texts." By including comments from other Chinese authors, Couplet highlights that his interpretive work is confirmed by Chinese authorities.

The book's introduction tries to separate the oldest text from all additions made by later commentators.[72] Couplet apparently adheres to the "principle of the oldest

---

68. Prospero Intorcetta had already wanted to print his *Politico-Moral Learning of the Chinese* in the Dutch Republic; see N. Golvers, "An Unobserved Letter of Prospero Intorcetta, S. J., to Godefridus Henschens, S. J., and the Printing of the Jesuit Translations of the Confucian Classics (Rome-Antwerp, 2 June 1672)," in *Syntagmatia: Essays on Neo-Latin Literature in Honour of Monique Mund-Dopchie and Gilbert Tournoy*, ed. D. Sacré and J. Papy (Louvain: Leuven University Press, 2006), 679–98.

69. Meynard, *Confucius*, 12; De Rougemont and Couplet may have become acquainted with Blaeu during their stay in Amsterdam; see N. Golvers, "The Development of the 'Confucius Sinarum Philosophus'" Reconsidered in the Light of New Material," in *Western Learning and Christianity in China: The Contribution and Impact of Johann Adam Schall von Bell, S.J. (1592–1666)*, Vol. 2, ed. R. Malek (Nettetal: Institut Monumenta Serica, 1998), 1141–64, 1144.

70. Janssonius van Waesberghe paid Kircher 2,200 scudi for the publishing rights in the Holy Roman Empire, England, and the Low Countries. See Daniel Stolzenberg, *The Great Art of Knowing: The Baroque Encyclopedia of Athanasius Kircher* (Redwood City, CA: Stanford University Press, 2001), 10. Kicher, after hearing from the "Padri fiamenghi" in China on their projected publication, was uncompromising: "non vorria io che il Blaeu le [i.e., the manuscripts] trattenesse," Archive Pontifica Università Gregoriana, Misc. Epist. Kircher, 560, f. 79r. As early as 1671, Kircher wrote to Janssonius proposing that he would publish some of the Confucius translations; in 1672 Van Papenbroeck became involved too. See Golvers, "Confucius," 1145–46, 1149.

71. The numbers can still be seen in copies of the first edition. According to Golvers, the choice for Horthemels was inspired by Couplet's being "attracted to his Flemish-Dutch countrymen," Golvers, "Confucius," 1160.

72. Meynard, *Confucius*, 101.

source" in philology even though he uses stylistic and biographical arguments rather than those of stemmatic philology.[73] For one, he attempts to explain differences in style by connecting them to different periods in Confucius' life.[74] This leads to the hypothesis that the sage himself had planned writing an elucidation, but his death had prevented this. "Such ancient obscurity and such obscure antiquity!"[75] Couplet portrays the later Daoists and Buddhists as bad interpreters of Confucius because they failed to use the right sources in the right manner; their false religious assumptions apparently derived from false philological practices.

To back up his approach, Couplet quotes Chinese writers who have themselves criticized the corrupt Buddhist interpreters. This enables him to argue that *Confucius Sinarum philosophus* presents pure Chinese thought. He highlights not only that the interpretation of Chinese philosophy should depend on the oldest Chinese sources but also that the Chinese themselves are the best interpreters of Chinese philosophy:[76]

> I assure you that the most learned Chinese Doctors . . . have always shared the same opinion: we missionaries should not pay any attention to the commentators of the ancient books, but should adhere only to the ancient texts.[77] We should work on the basis of the ancient texts alone, and if we find something unclear, hopefully we will be able to find among the Chinese . . . some men of prime erudition and authority who can explain to us the most difficult passages.

The ideal missionary apparently excels in linguistic prowess and philological rigor:

> A prudent man . . . [w]hen he has reached the region where he wants to convert the natives to Christ, if that people has many records of literature and wisdom inherited from their ancestors, then he should not decide for or against them by a quick and rash decision, nor should he blindly condemn or approve the interpreters, whether foreigners or locals, of their ancient books. . . . [B]esides asking for God's support, he should first try to carefully master their language and literature. Then, he can continually read the most important books as well as their interpretations, and examine and evaluate them thoroughly. Meanwhile, he can zealously investigate whether the sincerity and truth of the ancient text is confirmed, or, on the other hand, whether it has been corrupted by the mistakes and negligence of the later interpreters. He can investigate again whether those who work as interpreters have steadily followed the steps of their ancestors or whether they

---

73. Rens Bod, *De vergeten wetenschappen: een geschiedenis van de humaniora* (Amsterdam: Bakker, 2010), 195.
74. For instance, Couplet sees the *Yijing* as a less authentic text without the status of a classic, arguing that "though these poems have great authority, the style is quite difficult and obscure because of their always-laconic shortness, of their usual metaphorical style and also because of their ornamentation with very old proverbs," Couplet, 'Proemialis Declaratio', quoted from Meynard, *Confucius*, 101.
75. Couplet, 'Proemialis Declaratio', quoted from Meynard, *Confucius*, 102.
76. Meynard, *Confucius*, 217.
77. This was a true statement: the rejection of modern interpretations of Confucius was a Chinese tradition; see David. E. Mungello, *Curious Land: Jesuit Accommodation and the Origins of Sinology* (Honolulu: University of Hawai'i Press, 1985), *Curious Land*, 262.

have distorted their teaching and twisted it to fit their errors ... Finally he should judge whether it was the unanimous mind and doctrine of all, or whether they contradicted themselves and fought each other.[78]

By presenting his book emphatically as a work of philology, Couplet intends to legitimize the Jesuit missionary work as something grounded on a sound basis in the European humanities. Apparently, only the philological search for the oldest sources can uncover the hidden, yet fundamental relations between Christian and Confucian texts. Couplet's reasoning depends implicitly on an invalid syllogism: "All Christian books are pure; Some Chinese texts are pure; therefore some Chinese texts are Christian texts." This cross-boundary reasoning allows the author to call on the authority of the Chinese themselves to plead for the similarities between Confucius' original writings and Christianity. He concludes that every missionary should focus on those elements in the Chinese texts that correspond to Christian teaching:

> if [the missionary] realizes that nothing firm and true can be found in the above mentioned books and records, he should not touch them and should not make mention of them. But if on the contrary the kings and teachers of the ancients, led by nature, have reached many things which are not opposed to the light and truth of the gospel, but are even helpful and favorable so that it seems that they open the way for the early dawn of the Sun of Justice, then surely the preachers of the gospel ... will not despise these things at all but shall use them regularly, so that they can instill in the tender minds of the neophytes, the foreign ambrosia of a heavenly teaching with the original sap of native teaching.[79]

This stress on philology seems to have been directed not just at prospective missionaries themselves, but rather at the Republic of Letters in Europe. By claiming that philology had allowed him to unveil Christian elements in Chinese philosophy, Couplet gave Confucius the same status as some of the Greek and Roman authorities had. Humanists in Europe would have recognized this procedure: it was identical to how pagan antiquity had been incorporated in Christian scholarship. As had been argued, some pagan texts had even prophesied the New Testament. Allegedly, the authors had had knowledge of *prisca philosophia*, primeval Christian wisdom before Christ's actual birth. Confucius, now, could be given a place in the same typology, on a par with the Hebrew prophets or, more radically, with the pagan Sibyls, the female soothsayers from places outside the Middle East who had preceded Moses.[80]

---

78. Couplet, 'Proemialis Declaratio', quoted from Meynard, *Confucius*, 222.
79. Couplet, 'Proemialis Declaratio', quoted from Meynard, *Confucius*, 223.
80. Kircher had already interpreted Egyptian wisdom in this manner and used this approach as the basis for his Chinese studies. The French Jesuit Joachim Bouvet (1656–1730) was most explicit in linking Egyptian proto-Christianity to the ancient Chinese wisdom, using the hieroglyphical origin of Chinese writing as an argument. His main work was translated into Dutch: *'t Leven en bedrijf van den tegenwoordigen keizer van China* (Utrecht: Schouten, 1699).

Even though Couplet himself did not explicate these ultimate conclusions,[81] it is clear that he tried to fit Confucius into the scholarly framework that linked the philological principle of the oldest source to the quest for the most ancient wisdom. In fact, Couplet's most original addition to standard humanistic practices in Europe was not his search for proto-Christian elements but his stress on the Chineseness of his account. This latter emphasis was obviously a central tenet of his visit to Europe, staged as a display of authenticity with its cargo of Chinese books, Shen Fuzong's presence, and his ambition to print Chinese characters.

Unsurprisingly in the light of the Low Countries' engagement with China, what purported to be a vernacular version of the *Analects* appeared first in a Dutch translation. Pieter van Hoorn (b. 1619), who had chaired a trade mission to Beijing in 1665, met Father Couplet in China, who may have shown him a manuscript of the *Confucius Sinarum philosophus*. Twelve years before the Latin book appeared, Van Hoorn published his translation in Batavia: *Eenige vorname eygenschappen van de waren deugdt, voorsichticheydt, wysheydt en volmaecktheydt, getrocken uyt den Chineschen Confucius* (Various outstanding properties of true virtue, wisdom, and perfection drawn from the Chinese Confucius, 1675). It was later followed by similar works in French and English.[82] All three works were not literal translations: they presented the *Analects* as a series of moral truisms, without the stress on philological and linguistic integrity that marked Couplet's edition. Yet lettered circles in Amsterdam were confronted with a serious scholarly reaction to Chinese thought in December 1687, when the monthly journal *Bibliothèque universelle et historique* published a 68-page review of Couplet's book. The Amsterdam-based Calvinist scholar Jean le Clerc (1657–1736) gave a precise summary of Confucius' views, including passages translated from the Latin into French. In striking contrast to Couplet's view, Le Clerc interpreted Confucius' role as one of transmitter rather than as primary author.[83]

Even though Couplet's efforts did not have the wide impact on the Western humanities that he may have expected, his visit did not fail to impress scholars throughout

---

81. Couplet provides the framework for Bouvet's "Hermetic" arguments. pointing out that "the holy Writers and Fathers ... familiar with pagan testimonies remote from human reason but revealed by God, such as the prophesies of the Sibyls or the statement by Trismegistus ... or the image of Serapis which is thought to show an image of the Most Holy Trinity," in Meynard, *Confucius*, 216.
82. Pierre de la Brune, *La Morale de Confucius, philosophe de la Chine* (Amsterdam: Pierre Savouret, 1688); *The Morals of Confucius, A Chinese Philosopher, who Flourished above Five Hundred Years before the Coming of Our Lord and Saviour Jesus Christ, Being one of the Choicest Pieces of Learning Remaining of that Nation* (London: Randal Taylor, 1691). The English translation seems to be made from the French, as De la Brune is again named as the author. Couplet himself also envisaged making a French translation, which did not materialize. See Golvers, "Confucius," 1163.
83. The review fills pp. 387–455 of the December 1687 issue; the statement on Confucius is on p. 400. The citations from the *Analects* are on pp. 441–50. Other reviews appeared in *Basnage histoire des ouvrages des sçavans* (Rotterdam, September 1687) and *Journal des sçavans* (January 5, 1988), probably by Pierre-Sylvain Régis. See Mungello, *Curious Land*, 289–91.

Europe. Arriving in Paris in 1686, Couplet and Shen aided Melchisédech Thévenot (c. 1620–92) in putting together a *clavis sinica* ("key to Chinese") and in describing Chinese books in Louis XIV's library. Shen then left France for England in 1687, where he sat for Rembrandt's pupil Godfried Kneller (1646–1723) and catalogued the Sinica in Oxford's Bodleian Library.[84] Robert Boyle (1627–91) interrogated the foreign guest on the nature of the Chinese script and its characters, which fascinated Protestant scholars so much as they pondered the possibility of a philosophical language.[85] Furthermore, Couplet himself eventually inspired "Proto-Sinologists" in Germany and England: Christian Mentzel (1622–1701), Andreas Müller (1630–94), Andreas Cleyer (1634–c. 1698), and Thomas Hyde (1636–1703).[86]

In the Netherlands, Couplet was a special source of information for Nicolaas Witsen, a former student of Golius, who had been appointed governor of the United East-India Company. Witsen had already spoken to a traveler from China in Amsterdam in 1670 to discuss a topographical question.[87] In 1683 he met Couplet in Amsterdam, apparently in order to confirm the details of his book, *Noord-en Oost-Tartarije* (Amsterdam, 1692).[88] The former mayor also seems to have envisaged continuing the work on translating Confucius. For this, he arranged a subsequent meeting with the traveling Chinese doctor Zhou Meiye (周美爺) in 1709, who stayed for six weeks in the Dutch Republic and reportedly spoke "Dutch as well as a Dutchman," before returning to China.[89]

---

84. The painting is now in the British Royal Collection.
85. See Jonathan Spence, "When Minds Met: China and the West in the Seventeenth Century," Jefferson Lecture in the Humanities, May 20, 2010, Washington, DC. Available at: http://www.neh.gov/whoweare/Spence/lecture.html. Accessed on November 15, 2011.
86. For instance, Couplet provided Latin translations from Chinese medical books for Cleyer's *Specimen medicinae sinicae, sive opuscula medica ad mentem Sinensium* (1682). See P. Begheyn, "A Letter from Andries Cleyer, Head Surgeon of the United East India Company at Batavia, to Father Philips Couplet, S.J.," *Lias* 20 (1993): 245–49. Couplet himself sent his *Confucius* to Mentzel and others in "England and Holland"; letter to Mentzel of November 17, 1687. See Golvers, "Confucius," 1164.
87. Witsen (Amsterdam) to Vossius (London), November 6, [1670], "hebbe hier met een persoon gesprooken, die uit Sina of Katai komt welke des menings mede is als myn Heer" on a topographical question. Leiden University Library, UBL Ms Bur F11, fol. 160r.
88. Golvers, *Ferdinand Verbiest and the Chinese Heaven*, 191.
89. The doctor accompanied Johan van Hoorn, Governor-General of the Dutch East Indies, to the Netherlands. Archival documents are kept in the KITLV library, Leiden ("Aantekeningen van de Chinese arts Thebitia," DH 269) and the library of the University of Amsterdam (from Witsen's collection), including two drawings of an arm, relating to the Chinese doctrine of the circulation of blood. See Leonard Blussé, "Doctor at Sea: Chou Mei-Yeh's [*sic*] Voyage to the West (1710–1711)," in *As the Twig is Bent . . . Essays in Honour of Frits Vos*, ed. Erika de Poorter (Amsterdam: J. C. Gieben, 1990), 7–30; the quotation about the doctor's Dutch, which he had learned in Batavia, is from F. Valentijn, *Oud en Nieuw Oost-Indien* (Dordrecht and Amsterdam, 1724–26), Vol. I, 2, 254.

Theories on music and visual arts

From Matteo Ricci's work onwards, translated sayings by "ancient saints and sages" of the West had played a role in attempts to convert the Chinese.[90] These editions were facilitated as in contrast to the other missionary territories; the Chinese had a thriving indigenous printing industry. Moreover, the Jesuits combined their publications with the arts of spectacle, including music and painting.

Verbiest's writings in Chinese, which greatly contributed to the introduction of Western learning in China, reflect these activities at the imperial court, where he held a special position with more than a hundred Chinese pupils.[91] His sizeable books for the emperor included excerpts (now lost) from Kircher's *Musurgia* (Treatise on music, Rome 1650), optical and acoustical theories, and explanations of mathematical perspective and the camera obscura.[92] Musical theory returned in the writings of Verbiest's successor, Antoine Thomas, likewise recruited from the Low Countries.[93] We should understand these books, some of which were carefully illustrated, not simply as aimed at humanistic exchange but rather as elucidations of the instruments and other curios that the Jesuits imported from Europe as gifts, the organs and bell chimes they made for the court, and the paintings in their chapels.[94]

The China mission exploited innovative techniques to impress the native audience. Verbiest demonstrated projection devices to the Kangxi Emperor, giving him "insight into opticks by making him a present of a semi-cylinder of a light kind of wood; in the middle of its axis was placed a convex-glass, which being turned towards any

---

90. Standaert, *Handbook*, 604–8.
91. Verbiest's was "the most ambitious project in the field of sciences and (natural) philosophy," according to Nicolas Standaert, "Jesuits in China," in *The Cambridge Companion to the Jesuits*, ed. T. Worcester (Cambridge and New York: Cambridge University Press, 2008), 169–85, 179; Libbrecht confirms that "[o]ne of the most important facts in the introduction of European and [sic] Chinese astronomy in the seventeenth century was . . . the building of the new instruments for the observatory in Peking by the Flemish Belgian Jesuit Ferdinand Verbiest." U. Libbrecht, "What Kind of Science Did the Jesuits Bring to China?" in *Western Humanistic Culture Presented to China by Jesuit Missionaries (17th–18th Centuries)*, ed. F. Masini (Rome: Institutum Historicum S.I., 1996), 221–34, 221.
92. Ferdinand Verbiest, *Astronomia Europaea sub imperatore Tartaro-Sinico Cám Hý appellato ex umbra in lucem revocata à R.P. Ferdinando Verbiest Flandro-Belga e Societate Jesu Academiae Astronomicae in Regia Pekinensi Praefecto anno M.DCLXVIII* (Dillingen: J. C. Bencard, 1687), documents the author's presentation of Western music and optical devices at the imperial court. Verbiest also expanded on Giulio Aleni's effort to explain the European system of disciplines in the arts and sciences to the Chinese; see Standaert, *Handbook*, 606. F. Verbiest, *Kunyu tushuo* [Illustrated explanation of the entire world, 1674] has many illustrations derived from Netherlandish and German engravings; see Standaert, *Handbook*, 810.
93. Robert Halleux, Carmélia Opsomer, and Jan Vandersmissen, eds., *Geschiedenis van de wetenschappen in België van de Oudheid tot 1815* (Brussels: Gemeentekrediet/Dexia, 1998), 289.
94. The respective specialists were Filippo Grimaldi and Tomé Pereira. The Jesuits sent at least four artists from the Low Countries to China. Albert Brac (b. 1622) from the Dutch Republic and Ignatius Lagot (1603–51) and Henri Xavier (b. 1608) from the Southern Netherlands all worked as painters in Macau. The Maastricht-born artist Henrik van Vlierden (b. 1608) departed for China in 1644. See Dehergne, *Répertoire des Jésuites de Chine*.

object, painted the image within the tube to great nicety." The new invention of the "Magick-Lanthern" was particularly effective: a "machine which contained a lighted lamp, the light of which came through a tube, at the end whereof was a convex-glass, near which several small pieces of glass painted with divers figures were made to slide."[95] These same devices were used in Europe to showcase the Jesuit mission. Martini illuminated the Netherlands' understanding of China by projecting slides.[96] Most of these images, intended at ephemeral display, do not survive; we do have, however, various *Vue d'optique* images (colored engravings viewed through a convex lens for a seemingly three-dimensional scene) based on Dutch drawings of Chinese scenes.[97] In China and in Europe, the Jesuits apparently staged their mission as a visual spectacle of knowledge.

Even though the Jesuits saw the arts of spectacle as essential to proselytizing, they failed to appreciate Chinese music and painting. Trigault wrote that "the whole art of Chinese music seems to consist in producing a monotonous rhythmic beat as they know nothing of the variations and harmony that can be produced by combining different musical notes."[98] In regard to the visual arts, Ricci's authoritative criticism had a long afterlife (extending to the nineteenth century).[99] Even the Dutch trade missions to Beijing, which in one case included an artist, Johan Nieuhof (1618–72), to document China visually, repeated Ricci's view that the Chinese "do not understand how to make shadows... and how to temper their colors with oil. This is the reason why their paintings appear very dead and pallid, and look more like dead corpses than like living figures."[100] Supposedly, the Chinese had attained competence only after the Jesuits taught them working with the oil medium.[101]

This failure to appreciate Chinese art mirrored the Chinese scholars' point of view. The Jesuits confronted them with prints from the Netherlands and oil paintings, but the Chinese (unlike the Japanese) remained unimpressed. To quote one of the literati,

---

95. J. B. du Halde, *The General History of China Containing a Geographical, Historical, Chronological, Political and Physical Description of the Empire of China* (London: Watts, 1741), 72–75.
96. Golvers, "De recruteringstocht," 331–50.
97. For instance, Georg Balthasar Probst after P. van Blankaert after Johan Nieuhof, *Vue d'optique of the interior of the Imperial Palace in Beijing*, 1766–90, the Getty Research Institute, Los Angeles. Image in M. Reed and P. Demattè, eds., *China on Paper: European and Chinese Works from the Late Sixteenth to the Early Nineteenth Century* (Los Angeles: Getty Research Institute, 2007), 12.
98. Standaert, *Handbook*, 856, referring to P. M. d'Elia, ed., *Fonti Ricciane* (Rome: Libreria dello Stato, 1942–49), Vol. I, 32, 130.
99. Gauvin Alexander Bailey, *Art on the Jesuit Missions in Asia and Latin America: 1542–1773* (Toronto: University of Toronto Press, 1999), 88. See also Nicolas Trigault, *De christiana expeditione apud Sinas* (Cologne: Bernardus Gualterus, 1618), 22–23, and d'Elia, *Fonti Ricciane*, 31–32.
100. "Tot de Schilderyen en Schilderkunst, die zy doorgaans veel in hunne kunsten gebruiken, toonen deze volken een groote genegentheit en begeerte: doch mogen evenwel in't maken van eenige uitmuntende kunststukken tegen d'Europers geensins op; want eensdeels verstaanze zich noch niet op 't maken van schaduwen, en ten andre wetenze de kleuren niet te temperen en met olie te mengen. Dit is d'oorzaak waarom hunne Schilderyen zeer doots en bleek zich vertoonen, en veel meer na dode lijken dan levendige beelden zwemen," Nieuhof, *Het gezantschap*, Part II, 30. Cf. Dapper, *Gedenkwaerdig bedryf*, 504.
101. Nieuhof, *Het gezantschap*, Part II, 30; Dapper, *Gedenkwaerdig bedryf*, 504.

"Students of painting may well take over one or two points from [Europeans] to make their own paintings more attractive to the eye. But these painters have no brush-manner whatsoever; although they have skill, they are simply artisans and cannot consequently be classified as painters."[102] In short, the literati regarded naturalistic art as mechanical and trivial, while the Jesuits had a blind spot toward calligraphy. Both factors limited the Jesuit artistic venture in China.[103]

The only Western scholar who formulated a positive view of Chinese art was Isaac Vossius (1618–89), son of the Dutch Republic's literary "emperor," Gerard Vossius.[104] He did not visit China but knew its paintings and applied art through the many imports in Dutch households; it is probable that he himself collected Chinese art.[105] Isaac's uncompromising enthusiasm for China has been said to surpass even Marco Polo's.[106] In any event, it inspired him to criticize European painting for its dependence on dark tones and praise the Chinese for their clear drafting ability:

> Those who say that Chinese paintings do not represent shadows, criticize what they actually should have praised.... The better the paintings, the less shadow they have; and in this respect they are far superior to the painters from our part of the world, who can only represent the parts that stand out by adding thick shadows. The [European painters] obey in this matter not nature, nor the laws of optics. For these laws teach that when any object is put in diffuse light, so that no shadows catch the eye, the aspects that are most close at hand and stand out must be shown with rather clear lines, but those aspects that are farther away and recede must be shown less distinctly. When someone obeys this rule of painting, his art will emulate nature, and the more outstanding parts will appear to come forward even without conspicuous shadows.[107]

---

102. The court artist Zou Yigui (鄒一桂, 1686–1772) is quoted in Michael Sullivan, *The Meeting of Eastern and Western Art* (revised ed.) (Berkeley: University of California Press, 1997), 80. Cf. Baily, *Art on the Jesuit Missions*, 82.
103. This becomes clear from the fact that the main Chinese Jesuit artist, Wu Li (吳歷, or Simon de Cunha, c. 1632–1718), who instigated a completely new genre of Sino-Christian poetry, remained true to the style of the literati in his paintings. Wu accompanied De Rougemont on one of his mission tours in the Guangzhou area.
104. Vossius is called "Emperor" in Franciscus F. N. Junius's introduction to G. Vossius, *De quator artibus popularibus* (Amsterdam: Blaeu, 1650), no pagination.
105. See my article "Vossius's Chinese Utopia," in *The Challenger: Isaac Vossius (1618–1689) and the European World of Learning*, ed. E. Jorink and D. van Miert (Leiden and Boston: Brill, forthcoming).
106. Virgile Pinot, *La Chine et la formation de l'esprit philosophique en France (1640–1740)* (Genève: Slatkine Reprints, 1971 [orig. Paris: 1932]), 202.
107. "Cum vero inquiunt umbris fere carere Serum picturas, carpunt quod laudare debuerant. Parce admodum sunt illi in exprimendis umbris, & quidem quanto meliores sunt picturae, tanto minus umbrantur; in quo longe peritiores sunt nostri orbis pictoribus, qui non nisi additis densis umbris partes magis exstantes norunt repraesentare. Qua quidem in re nec naturae, nec optices observant leges; illae nempe docent, si quod corpus aequale fere lumine aspergatur, ita ut nullae conspicuae sint umbrae, partes magis vicinas aut exstantes distinctioribus lineamentis, recedentes vero & remotiores minus distincte esse exhibendas. Hanc si quis in pingendo observet rationem, erit pictura naturae aemula, & etiam absque umbris conspicuis magis extantes apparebunt partes," I. Vossius, "De artibus et scientiis Sinarum," in *Isaaci Vossii variarum observationum liber* (London: Scott, 1685), 69–85; 79.

Vossius was unique among early modern Europeans in praising the Chinese for their failure to represent shadows. In his view, spatiality should not be constructed with exaggerated contrasts that are not found in nature, but only with subtly fading contours. We should note that, in such a boundary-crossing reinterpretation, he would understand Chinese art by using a central dichotomy of Western artistic theory: line versus tone (or design versus color). This division was particularly relevant in seventeenth-century Netherlands, where painters of strong chiaroscuro were pitted against those who preferred a clear language of classical forms.[108]

Vossius stated that the Chinese were in fact superior to the Europeans in almost all arts and sciences—they needed the West only for mathematics and astronomy. He concluded that China was better not only at painting, sculpture, architecture, and music but also at medicine, botany, pharmacology, and technical inventions (such as the compass, the manufacture of gunpowder, and the art of printing). Vossius's main contribution to the Western appreciation of the Middle Kingdom, however, related not to art but to history.

The impacts of Chinese history

A key element of Western interest in China was the suspicion that the country had older written documents than the European ones. The philologists' search for first sources and the fascination with *prisca philosophia* made this an irresistible source of speculation. Moreover, humanists in the Netherlands had already been studying chronology ever since Joseph Scaliger had realized that biblical history could not accommodate the antiquity of Egyptian accounts.[109] Dutch interest in China was therefore automatically interwoven with calculations of the origin of the world, a serious matter in which historians, theologians, and astronomers held stakes.

Duyvendak has traced the earliest discussion of the Chinese calendar to three scholars based at Leiden: Scaliger, Golius, and Claudius Salmasius (1588–1653). They had come across the Chinese system of identifying certain years with the names of certain animals.[110] Yet the chronology's full extent was only disclosed by Martini's visit. He had read Chinese sources such as the official *Annals* that documented an uninterrupted Chinese civilization from 2900 BCE onwards. This feat planted a seed that would blossom in the climate of philosophical and religious skepticism fostered by Dutch Cartesianism from the 1650s onwards. After all, sacred history could not accommodate Chinese texts and monuments that were apparently untouched by the Flood (which, according to the Hebrew Bible, occurred in the year 2349 BCE).

---

108. Weststeijn, "Vossius's Chinese Utopia."
109. Anthony Grafton, *Joseph Scaliger: A Study in the History of Classical Scholarship, Vol. II, Historical Chronology* (Oxford: Clarendon Press, 1993), 405–7.
110. Duyvendak, "Early Chinese Studies," 293–95.

Isaac Vossius came to the radical conclusion that the biblical text was unreliable, as he argued in *De vera aetate mundi* (The Hague 1659).[111]

Unsurprisingly, more orthodox scholars were appalled, first among them Georg Hornius (whose musings on the Chinese script we have mentioned above). His own *Dissertatio de vera aetate mundi* (Leiden 1659) pointed out the danger of Vossius's theory, which implied "that until now no church in the West has admitted a true version of the Holy Scriptures."[112] Taking aim at Vossius's preference for exotic authorities, he asked: "What do we think of the Seres, commonly called Chinese, whose precise chronology antedates the Flood by seven or eight centuries? . . . We think that their chronology is false, even though they speak about the eternity of the world and about Panzonis and Panzona, Tanomus, Teiencomus, Tuhucomus, Lotzizanus, Azalamus, Atzionis, Usaonis, Huntzujus, Hautzibona, Ochentejus, Etzomlonis." China's antiquity was apparently "contaminated by monstrous fables."[113] Yet this altercation only seems to have strengthened Vossius's belief in the superiority of Chinese scholarship. Afterwards he even developed a utopian vision of Chinese society, a political and ideological unity starkly contrasting with Europe—no less than a realization of the Platonic Republic.[114] Vossius's stance that connected China to radical thought would soon become commonplace among philosophers of the early Enlightenment (inspiring, for instance, Pierre Bayle's identification of Spinoza with Confucius).[115] By that time, the assumption of primeval wisdom shared by the ancient Chinese and the Hebrew prophets was replaced by another argument, foregrounding natural religion—shared by all rational human beings—as more important than revealed doctrine.

Whether Vossius's Sinophilia was merely a cover for his libertine ideas or whether he was inspired by genuine interest in a foreign culture is a moot point. Jonathan Israel, studying Vossius in the context of Spinozism in the Dutch Republic, calls his remarks a rhetorical ploy for promoting a radical agenda. As I have argued elsewhere, this may be only partly true.[116] In any account, Vossius's writings made clear once and for all that Western scholars should take China seriously. It was probably in reaction to his heretical ideas that Philippe Couplet decided to add a discussion on chronology to

---

111. In fact, Vossius prefers the Greek Septuagint, which states that the world was 1,200 years older than the Hebrew Bible suggests. The Septuagint states that the world was created in the year 5200 BCE, the Vulgate in the year 4004 BCE; the deluge was computed to have happened in the years 2957 and 2349 BCE; see Jack Finnegan, *Handbook of Biblical Chronology* (Princeton: Princeton University Press, 1964), 191, 184.
112. "[C]onsequitur in nullis hactenur Ecclesiis occidentalibus veram Sacram Scripturam versionem receptam fuisse," *Georgii Hornii dissertatio de vera aetate mundi, qua sententia illorum refellitur qui statuunt natale mundi tempus annis minimum 1440. vulgarem aeram anticipare* (Leiden: Elsevier and Leffen, 1659), 3.
113. Hornius, *Dissertatio*, 34, 50. Hornius identified the Flood with a natural disaster in the time of the Yao Emperor and proceeded to associate Chinese rulers with figures from the Old Testament.
114. See Weststeijn, "Vossius' Chinese Utopia."
115. See my article "'Spinoza sinicus': An Asian Paragraph in the History of the Radical Enlightenment," *Journal of the History of Ideas* 68/4 (2007): 537–61.
116. Weststeijn, "Vossius' Chinese Utopia."

the masterpiece of Chinese learning in Latin, the *Confucius Sinarum philosophus*. This *Tabula chronologica monarchiae Sinicae* (1686) was a 109-page chronology listing all Chinese emperors from the mythical Huangdi (the Yellow Emperor) to 1683.[117] The text, which Couplet finished during his stay in the Dutch Republic, defended the orthodox view of sacred history and highlighted similarities between the Chinese chronology and calculations based on the Septuagint.

Conclusion

There were strikingly similar developments in both the European humanities from the late sixteenth century onwards and seventeenth-century Chinese civilization. To quote Standaert, "The means of reproduction of knowledge were more or less similar."[118] Both areas witnessed an increasing flood of printed books. In China and Europe, vigorous intellectual discussions, backed by a well-established educational system, took place in public meetings at academies, where scholars greatly respected classical learning, books, and antiquities.[119] Yet this chapter has tried not just to point out such parallels but rather to analyze the explicitly cross-cultural efforts established by the seventeenth-century scholars themselves.

It is particularly noteworthy that, within decades of the first European attempts to master the language of the Chinese literati, the ideals of Western humanism in "defending the text" and establishing the original source were applied to Chinese studies. In the field of comparative linguistics, however, the search for origins gave rise to misguided theories about a Hebrew or even an Egyptian provenience for Chinese. When it came to the visual arts, Western and Eastern scholars formulated their mutual incomprehension, though influences on both sides were to take place in the next century. It seems that biblical history and criticism ultimately benefited the most from confrontation with the Chinese accounts.[120]

The Low Countries deserve special attention when analyzing this cultural engagement. The area was obviously a cradle of European "Chinoiserie" as the visual imagery, imported porcelain and its imitations in particular, determined Chinese themes and

---

117. "Tabula Chronologica Monarchiae Sinicae" (1686), bound with *Confucius Sinarum Philosophus* (Paris: Horthemels, 1687). The text ranges from Huangdi to Kangxi's campaign to pacify the western Mongols in 1683. According to Meynard, *Confucius*, 14, Couplet finished the text in 1683, during his stay in Holland. He first published it as an independent work entitled *Tabula genealogica* (Paris, 1686); see Golvers, "Confucius," 1153.
118. Standaert, "Transmission of Renaissance Culture," 369.
119. Cf. John E. Wills, "Brief Intersection: Changing Contexts and Prospects of the Chinese-Christian Encounter from Matteo Ricci to Ferdinand Verbiest," in *Ferdinand Verbiest (1623–1688): Jesuit Missionary, Scientist, Engineer and Diplomat,* ed. John W. Witek (Nettetal: Institut Monumenta Serica, 1994), 383–94. On the Chinese respect for books in particular, see Standaert, "Transmission of Renaissance Culture," 370–72.
120. Vossius's ideas contributed to a respected English school of biblical criticism; see David S. Katz, "Isaac Vossius and the English Biblical Critics 1670–1689," in *Scepticism and Irreligion in the Seventeenth and Eighteenth Centuries,* ed. R. H. Popkin and A. Vanderjagt (Leiden: Brill, 1993), 142–84.

styles in the applied arts throughout Europe—so much so that the words "Dutch" and "Chinese" were eventually used interchangeably.[121] Something similar held true albeit in a less evident manner, in the domain of learning and literature. The traders' unique infrastructure and their hunger for information on China, paired with the scholarly ambitions of the Netherlandish missionaries as relatively independent from Portuguese and French doctrines, certainly made possible many "firsts" in printing, translation, and interpretation—at least for individuals who were able to benefit from their mediating position like Trigault, Couplet, and Verbiest. Combined with the willingness of a scholar such as Isaac Vossius to explode accepted European opinions, this could result in the radical Sinophile stand that would become commonplace in eighteenth-century France, Germany, and England.

At the turn of the century, however, it became clear that the Low Countries' essentially intermediary role meant that interest in China had not taken root. In 1689, the greatest Sinophile philosopher of the age, Leibniz, formulated the ideal of a mutually beneficial exchange of knowledge between Europe and the Middle Kingdom, "a commerce of doctrine and mutual light" which inspired his own extensive interest in China.[122] The groundwork for this notion had been laid by older scholars: Leibniz depended on Verbiest and Vossius.[123] Yet this legacy was soon forgotten in the eighteenth-century Dutch Republic itself. Witsen's projected continuation of the Confucian texts came to nothing. When François Noël (1651–1729) eventually finished translating the last of the four Chinese Classics, *Mencius*, in 1711, he had to find a publisher in Prague.[124] After Vondel, Van Hoorn, and Van der Goes, no one continued writing in Dutch on Chinese topics in a serious manner.[125] Whereas the end of the seventeenth century saw information on China being discussed increasingly in the context of specialized academies such as the Parisian Académie Royale des Sciences and the Royal Society of London, no such institution was founded in

---

121. Two examples: the Countess of Arundel's "Dutch" cabinet in London contained Chinese porcelain, and August the Strong built a "Holländische Palast" in Dresden to house his East Asian ceramics. By 1638, the Dutch had imported over three million pieces of Chinese porcelain, and Amsterdam had become "the hub for the accumulation and dispersal of knowledge about the non-European world," according to D. Odell, "Porcelain, Print Culture and Mercantile Aesthetics," in A. Cavanaugh, et al., *The Cultural Aesthetics of Eighteenth-Century Porcelain* (Farnham, Surrey: Ashgate, 2010), 141–58; 142.
122. "Commercia inquam doctrinae et mutuae lucis," Leibniz to Giovanni Laureati, November 12, 1689. See G. W. Leibniz, *Leibniz korrespondiert mit China* (Frankfurt am Main: Klostermann, 1990), 11.
123. For Verbiest and Leibniz, see Gerhard Strasser's chapter in the present volume. Part of Verbiest's *Astronomia Europaea* is included in Leibniz's *Novissima sinica* (1697). For Leibniz and the chronological issues sparked by Vossius, see Li Wenchao, "Leibniz, der Chronologiestreit und die Juden in China," in D. J. Cook et al., *Leibniz und das Judentum* (Stuttgart: Steiner, 2008), 183–208. Van Papenbroeck informed Leibniz on the publication of *Confucius Sinarum philosophus*. See Mungello, *Curious Land*, 287.
124. *Sinensis imperii libri classici sex* (Prague: Kamenicky, 1711). The manuscript is presently in Arras library. Noël was born in Hestrud in the Spanish Netherlands.
125. China was treated in a satirical manner by Jacob Campo Weyerman and others; see A. Pos, *Het paviljoen van porselein Nederlandse literaire Chinoiserie en het westerse beeld van China, 1250–2007* (PhD diss., University of Leiden, 2008).

the Low Countries.[126] As Duyvendak concludes, scholars "failed to take advantage of the enormous lead given to the Dutch by the excellent exchange of information in the seventeenth century."[127]

For reasons that merit additional research, "Holland had lost its interest in China."[128] As a final note, we may again point out a Chinese parallel. In the Middle Kingdom, the initial interest in European learning waned outside the emperor's close circles. Hsia speaks of the Confucian literati's "disenchantment" with the West in the late seventeenth century.[129] In 1692 the Kangxi Emperor, under Verbiest's guidance, had issued an edict of toleration of Christianity. Yet when Charles-Thomas Maillard Tournon (1668–1710) brought forth the papal order to denounce the Jesuits' Sinophile stance in 1707, he annulled the edict and took steps to restrict and finally ban the Christian missions in his empire. A century of mutual exchange drew to a close.

---

126. Louis XIV sent six Jesuits to Beijing as correspondents for the Académie Royale des Sciences (while the Académie des Inscriptions et Belles Lettres studied the Chinese language); the Royal Society proposed to include the Jesuits in China among their correspondents in 1667; the Imperial Academy of Sciences in Saint Petersburg maintained links with the French missionaries. See Standaert, *Handbook*, 892–93. In 1732, Naples saw the foundation of a specialized Collegio dei Cinesi.

127. Duyvendak, "China in de Nederlandse letterkunde," 13. Over time, this even resulted in the Amsterdam-born philosopher Cornelis de Pauw (1739–99) refuting all previous positive images of China in *Recherches philosophiques sur les Egyptiens et les Chinois*, 2 vols. (Berlin, Amsterdam, and Leiden: Vlam and Murray, 1773).

128. Duyvendak, "China in de Nederlandse letterkunde," 13. This was obviously related to the decline of the Dutch East India Company. See Lach and van Kley, *Asia in the Making of Europe, Vol. III*, 506. After 1678, the Dutch concentrated their direct trade on Java and relied for contacts with China on Chinese and Portuguese intermediaries, whereas European commercial interest in East Asia became increasingly focused on the large-scale production of certain products for export; see Wills, *Pepper, Guns, and Parleys*, 261–64.

129. Ronnie Po-chia Hsia, "The Catholic Mission and Translations in China, 1583–1700," in *Cultural Translation in Early Modern Europe*, ed. P. Burke and R. P. Hsia (Cambridge: Cambridge University Press, 2007), 39–51. According to Wills, *Pepper, Guns, and Parleys*, 264, by 1700 "[b]oth sides in the Sino-Western trade were reasonably content with their profits, and the eighteenth century passed with little political contact between Europeans and Chinese."

2
Russian-Chinese Cultural Exchanges in the Early Modern Period

Missionaries, Sinologists, and Artists

Nikolay Samoylov

Introduction

Sino-Russian cultural interaction can be safely characterized as having a long-standing tradition. Today, numerous studies on Sino-Russian relations exist. However, it should be noted that the majority of books and articles on this subject concentrate on the history of political relations. They particularly address the signing of major treaties and agreements, as well as the establishment of borders between the two neighboring states. Russian-Chinese economic relations, and specifically cultural connections, have been analyzed to a much lesser degree. They frequently engage in sweeping generalizations and do not utilize new methodological approaches. Taking the field of research into account, it appears imperative to conduct a full-scale survey on the process of sociocultural interaction between Russia and China from a historical approach. This type of analysis should highlight the importance of interaction between the two inherently different societies and cultures.

Sino-Russian cultural interactions are more complex than a simple bilateral pattern of cultural contacts. In this case, historians face dynamic and constantly flowing social, ideological, and cultural exchanges between China and Russia. The encounter of a variety of different concepts, ideas, and behaviors gave rise to diversified modes in the interaction process, which was closely tied with the social-cultural developments of native Chinese and Russian communities.

Sociocultural interaction represents a process of concrete parameters, ramifications, and requirements of cultural, social, and historical components, as well as external influences by way of global trends. Putting together these interrelated factors, we can structure a general four-stage development for the historical encounters between cultures.

In the first stage of sociocultural interaction, each society tends to show little interest in its counterpart. The mutual indifference may last for a long time till social shifts or cultural requirements create favorable conditions for a breakthrough toward rapprochement. Often in a specific situation a series of subjective factors—cultural, ethnic, political, ideological, or personal—are present. This first stage can be characterized as a stage of *indifferent interaction*. Sporadic contacts between the representatives of different societies and cultures may take place, but as a whole these types of contacts do not affect the general character of the initial interactions.

In the next stage, a process of recognition of the *other* culture takes place. Close political, diplomatic, and economic relations lead to an increasing need for a better understanding of the differences and similarities between one's own culture and the *other* culture. It occurs spontaneously without prior schemes and often leads to certain unorganized accumulation of information and unguarded infiltration of elements from one culture into another. Gradually, the *other* culture with which a society chooses to interact is identified and conceptualized by means of collective representations, often expressed in certain stereotyped narratives and images. This stage of sociocultural interaction may be called the *identification* stage.

After the *identification* stage, there comes the period of increased interests in the *other* culture. The accumulation of data and knowledge shifts from a casual, incidental style to a purposeful and, under certain conditions, institutionalized project. Some cultural elements are adopted by both parties, a definite consequence of deliberation and development of stable and active trade relations. Sociocultural interactions begin to cover wider spheres of culture and various aspects of daily life. In this stage, cultural adoption may certainly be localized in a geographical sense, or within a specific social class. This adoption and expansion may be characterized as the *activation* stage.

When sociocultural interactions in a historical continuum become entrenched more deeply into the new spheres of a society, it may lead to active adoption of achievements from the *other* culture. This does not necessarily happen to all interactions between societies and cultures. When it does occur, it is referred to as the *adaptive* stage. Ultimately, in active adoption of cultural achievements from each other, there often appears a process of *cultural synthesis* between the encountering societies.

The stage of *indifferent interaction* in the history of Russian-Chinese relations should be traced to a period before the seventeenth century. During that time, contacts between Russians and Chinese were sporadic, and few stable communication channels existed. There were unofficial, inconsistent, and mostly trade-focused stimuli for communication.

The *identification* stage can be traced to the seventeenth century. The first Russian embassy/envoy sent to China was Ivan Petlin's mission of 1618, and from that moment, the cultural distinctions between the two countries became present.[1] Though subsequent missions in the next few decades failed due to Sino-Russian confrontations

---

1. Vladimir S. Miasnikov, *The Ch'ing Empire and the Russian State in the 17th Century* (Moscow: Progress Publishers, 1985), 64–70.

on territorial control, the Russian envoys did serve as intermediaries in transmitting substantial messages between two essentially different sociocultural systems.²

The foundation of cultural intercourse and scientific research of China was laid during the reign of Peter the Great (1672–1725). On June 18, 1700, he issued an edict considered to be the first decree on Russian studies of Asian languages. In 1716, the first Russian Ecclesiastical Mission, established according to Peter the Great's edict, arrived at Beijing. The missionaries stayed and worked through the next three centuries. Apart from their political and religious activities, members of the mission's staff figured prominently in advocating Sino-Russian cultural exchanges in various aspects. More remarkably, it is largely owing to the Ecclesiastical Mission in Beijing that Russian Sinology began to take shape. The mission is considered to have served as a major channel for communication and transmission of cultural concepts and ideas between Russia and the Qing Empire.

The influential 1727 Treaty of Kyakhta brought the *identification* stage to an end. The significance of the treaty is now readily admitted by Russian, Chinese, and many Western historians due to its emphasis on Russian-Chinese trade as a major communication channel for sociocultural interaction. Precisely, trade promoted mutual distribution of elements of Chinese and Russian material culture. Kyakhta should be recognized as the focal point of the initial sociocultural interaction.

Members of the Russian Ecclesiastical Mission in Beijing brought substantial contributions to the spread of knowledge about the Qing Empire and the formation of an idealized image of China in Russia. Sino-Russian interactions by this point entered the *activation* stage, and the role of Russian missionaries in this process was very important.

The Russian Ecclesiastical Mission in Beijing

The Russian Ecclesiastical Mission operated in China for about three centuries. The staff slowly established a small Orthodox Christian community in Beijing. They endeavored to translate liturgical books into Chinese and Manchu, as well as translate Chinese books about the Qing Empire into Russian. More noticeably, members of the mission carried out various diplomatic assignments, and since 1917 they began to focus on the spiritual care and moral support of a large group of Russian exiles due to the October Revolution and the Civil War in Russia.

Nowadays there is still the need to further explore the history of the Russian Ecclesiastical Mission in developing sociocultural ties between Russian and Chinese peoples. Some key issues deserve more serious study and analysis: (1) the place of Russian Orthodox Christianity in the religious exchanges between Russia and China, (2) the importance of Russian and Chinese works written by Russian missionaries in

---

2. Nicolas Standaert, ed. *Handbook of Christianity in China, Volume One: 635–1800* (Leiden: Brill, 2001), 367–68.

the interaction process, and (3) the role of the Russian Ecclesiastical Mission in the formation and transformation of multilayered cultural images in Russia and China. Based on in-depth analysis of these issues, we will get a comprehensive understanding of the crucial role of the Russian Ecclesiastical Mission in the Russian-Chinese cultural dialogues in the modern era.

The Russian Ecclesiastical Mission in Beijing had a clear goal to disseminate knowledge between Russia and China. Eight groups of missionaries were dispatched in turn during the mid-Qing period, i.e., the eighteenth century, and their activities clearly suggested a remarkable three-in-one role: (1) fulfilling diplomatic assignments from the Russian imperial government, (2) studying Chinese language, history, and culture for practical and intellectual purposes, and (3) preaching Orthodox Christianity. Due to the diplomatic twist, the Orthodox missionaries often fell short of evangelical enthusiasm. Their religious function was largely confined to serving Christian members of the Albazin community in Beijing during the first hundred years of their missions. However, the direct contacts between these missionaries and the Chinese people provided a nice opportunity for the latter to know more about Russia and Russian culture. It is interesting to note that the term *Luocha* (羅剎 a category for demons in Buddhism) was adopted for the country name of Russia, and it became increasingly popular in mid-Qing Chinese sources. Ironically, the Russian missionaries themselves played a role in this conscious appropriation and misidentification because they did not bother to use the term *Fo* (佛 Buddha) to refer to the Christian God and another term, *Lama* (喇嘛 a guru in Tibetan Buddhism), to refer to their Christian identity.[3]

The Russian Ecclesiastical Mission also made contributions to the cause of teaching the Russian language in China. On March 24, 1708, during the reign of the Kangxi Emperor (1661–1722), the first school of Russian language was founded in Beijing. This was approved by the imperial court. At that time, there were "68 people who have the intention to study the Russian language."[4] However, the first classes in this school were conducted very irregularly. At the beginning the Russian language teachers were merchants, who arrived in Beijing with trade caravans. When the merchants left with caravans, the classes stopped. In a few years, students from the school were taught by some representatives from the Albazin community. A new stage in Russian language teaching came with the start of the Russian Ecclesiastical Mission. After the Yongzheng Emperor's (1723–35) ascension to the throne, there was a reorganization of the school, which in 1716 was renamed the School of Russian Language at the Imperial Chancellery. After the emperor's edict, two priests from the Orthodox Mission were invited to teach Russian in the school. From then on, priests from

---

3. Standaert, *Handbook of Christianity in China*, 372.
4. Su Fenglin 宿豐林, *Istorija kul'turnyx otnoshenij Kitaja s Rossiej do serediny 19 veka* [History of cultural relations between China and Russia until the mid-19th century] (Vostok-Zapad: Istoriko-kul'turnyj al'manax: M.: Vostochnaja literature, 2002), 75.

the Russian Ecclesiastical Mission were actively engaged in teaching. They not only introduced students to the basics of Russian but also acquainted young Chinese and Manchu people with important and useful aspects of Russian culture and daily life. In so doing, the Orthodox missionaries managed to maintain a vital component for their cross-cultural dialogues with the Chinese people.

P. E. Skachkov suggested that the first teachers from the mission's staff were cleric Osip Dyakonov, who died in Beijing in 1736, and Ierodiakon Philemon. A student for the mission, Luka Voyeikov brought to Beijing *The Russian Grammar* by Meletij Smotritsky (1578–1633), which was well-known in Russia. Later, it was translated into Manchu by Illarion Rossokhin (1717–61) together with the Manchu Fulahe, a teacher of the school. While Rossokhin became a leading teacher in the Russian Language School, he translated a number of essential Chinese and Manchurian historical works into Russian, including *Zizhi Tongjian Gangmu* (資治通鑑綱目) by the well-known Song Neo-Confucian Zhu Xi (朱熹, 1130–1200).[5]

The multilingual expertise enabled Rossokhin and other Sinologists to shift easily between two cultural traditions for different purposes, including a political one. In 1757, at the request of the Senate of the Russian government, Rossokhin began to translate the history of the Qing dynasty in collaboration with Aleksei Leont'ev (1716–86), a probationer of the Russian Ecclesiastical Mission in Beijing from 1743 to 1755. Two decades later, Leont'ev published their sixteen-volume work, titled *A Detailed Description of the Origins and Conditions of the Manchu People and Their Army, Consisting of Eight-Banners* (1784). Moreover, Leont'ev followed the order of Catherine II (Yekaterina Alexeevna, 1729–96) to translate several official legal works of the Qing Empire. Apparently, the ruling elite in Russia expressed this special interest not for a genuine admiration of China's alleged superiority over all other nations but for the pragmatic intent to reinforce their enlightened monarchical order by using China as a convenient parallel example.[6]

In the first half of the nineteenth century, members of the Russian Ecclesiastical Mission became reputed Sinologists and made notable contributions to Russian intellectuals' research on Chinese culture, history, and language. They acted as interpreters of Chinese culture, as well as its original chroniclers in the Russian language, thereby promoting the formation of what was essentially a new mode of Sino-Russian interaction. At a time when Russian people's knowledge about China largely depended on the reports of the Jesuit missionaries in China and various secondhand texts from Europe, the endeavors of these early Russian Sinologists opened an alternative channel, though

---

5. Vladislav Sorokin, "Two and a Half Centuries of Russian Sinology," in *Europe Studies China: Papers from an International Conference on the History of European Sinology*, ed. Ming Wilson and John Cayley (London: Han-Shan Tang Books, 1995), 111–12.
6. Susanna Soojung Lim, *China and Japan in the Russian Imagination, 1685–1922: To the Ends of the Orient* (London and New York: Routledge, 2013), 42–61.

often twisted by some nonacademic interests, for the growing inflow of multilayered cultural representations of Russia's eastern neighbor.

Archimandrite Iakinf and the rise of Russian Sinology

Among members of the mission whose scholarly achievements won wide recognition, there were Archimandrite Iakinf (Bichurin, 1777–1853), Archimandrite Peter (Kamensky, 1765–1845), Archimandrite Palladiy (Kafarov, 1817–78), and Vasiliy Vasiliev (1818–1900). They studied the history of the Qing dynasty, Manchu Army, the relations between China and neighboring countries, and they endeavored to translate many Chinese and Manchu historical sources into Russian.

Archimandrite Iakinf (Nikita Yakovlevich Bichurin), a prominent Russian Sinologist and head of the Ninth Russian Ecclesiastical Mission in China (1807–21), played a leading role in awakening interest in China and creating a positive image of China among the Russian intellectual elite. Upon his return to Russia, Archimandrite Iakinf became a frequent guest of the literary salons of St. Petersburg, for example, "the Saturday Club" organized by a prominent philosopher and romantic writer, Vladimir Odoevsky (1803–69), in his house. There he met with many Russian writers and artists. Apparently to keep in dear memory of his life in Beijing, Archimandrite Iakinf often dressed like a Chinese scholar, held a Chinese tea cup in hand, and talked about the government, education, philosophy, and customs of China.[7] Many Russian cultural elite were honored to talk with this highly educated man, who was also a professional Sinologist. Under his influence there appeared several works by Russian authors who have tried to understand general and particular aspects in the development of Russia and China and think about the common historical destiny of the two nations.

In 1829, Alexey Olenin (1763–1843), the director of Imperial Public Library, asked the minister of education to include Archimandrite Iakinf in the staff of honorary librarians to describe books in Chinese and Manchu. It took place in the public library where Archimandrite Iakinf met with a number of famous Russian writers and scholars, including Russia's best-known fabulist, Ivan Krylov (1769–1844), the director of the Asiatic Museum Christian, Martin Frähn (1782–1851), the orientalist, popular writer and professor of St. Petersburg University, Osip Senkovsky (1800–1858), as well as François Bernard Charmoy (1793–1869), who served in the Russian Foreign Ministry and professor of St. Petersburg University. All of them were honored librarians in the Imperial Public Library.

A talented scholar with a truly encyclopedic knowledge, Archimandrite Iakinf played a decisive role in the development of Sinology as the most important area of Oriental Studies in Russia. He wrote more than one hundred works, including

---

7. Li Weili 李偉麗, *Ni-Ya-Biqiulin ji qi Hanxue yanjiu* 尼・雅・比丘林及其漢學研究 [Bichurin and his sinology] (Beijing: Xueyuan chubanshe, 2007), 142.

scholarly studies as well as translations of Chinese historical and geographical texts. His name and scholarly works became well-known not only in Russia, but also in Western Europe. In 1828, he was elected a member of the Russian Academy of Sciences in literature and antiquities of the East. In 1831, on the proposal of French Orientalists, he was elected a member of the Paris Asia Society.

In the writings of Archimandrite Iakinf, especially those published in the 1840s, we can find a panoramic picture of Chinese geography, ethnography, history, and culture, as well as detailed analysis of the social, economic, and religious systems of Qing China. It is interesting to note that his descriptions and comments revealed an explicit tendency to create an idealistic, admirable image of China. For example, in his 1840 book *China, Its People, Customs, Habits, Education*, Archimandrite Iakinf wrote that Chinese people enjoyed pervasive equality in social, economic, and legal terms, while the emperor's personal power was limited by law despite the autocratic nature of the government. As for Chinese schools and Civil Service Exams, he was of the opinion that Confucian ethics lay at the center of such a sophisticated education system, so much so that Confucian classics (especially the Five Classics and the Four Books) became the key in developing a high standard of morality. Their importance to the Chinese people may be comparable to that of the Holy Bible among Christians.[8]

Archimandrite Iakinf also made contributions in the linguistic aspect. In 1831, he initiated the foundation of the Kyakhta Chinese language class, which was converted into a special school in 1832. He composed the training program that marked the beginning of new methods in teaching Chinese in Russia, and he was the author of *Chinese Grammar*, the first of its kind published in Russia.

In his intellectual circle in St. Petersburg, Archimandrite Iakinf maintained friendly relations with the famous Russian poet Alexander Pushkin (1799–1837). He carefully affirmed his respectful position as a Sinologist by presenting Pushkin with his works on Chinese culture, for example, the *Description of Tibet*, with the inscription: "To Dear Sir Alexander Pushkin from the translator as a sign of true respect. April 26, 1828," and the Russian translation of *Sanzijing* (三字經 *Three Character Classic*), with the inscription "To Alexander Pushkin from the translator."

Pushkin always spoke with reverence about the scientific works and deep knowledge of Archimandrite Iakinf, in particular in his book *History of Pugachev*. Under the influence of Archimandrite Iakinf, Pushkin became more and more interested in China, so much so that he even cherished a dream to visit China. He had the dream after reading Voltaire's "The Orphan of China" ("L' Orphelin de la Chine"), in which there was nothing of the Chinese. Bearing this regret in mind, Pushkin wanted to write "a Chinese drama" in order to "annoy the spirit of Voltaire." On January 7, 1830, Pushkin sent a formal request to Alexander von Benkendorff (1781?–1844), executive

---

8. Iakinf, *Kitaj, ego zhiteli, nravy, obychai, prosveshhenie* [China, its people, customs, habits, education] (St. Petersberg: Izdanie gospozhi Micikovoj; Tipografija imperatorskoj akademii nauk, 1840), 30–35.

director of the Third Section of the Imperial Chancellery, in which he mentioned his desire to visit China: "I would ask permission to visit China to go there as a member of the Embassy staff." In fact, Pushkin had in mind the Eleventh Russian Ecclesiastical Mission to Beijing, headed by Archimandrite Veniamin (Morachevich), and the scientific expedition to the borders of China headed by Archimandrite Iakinf and Baron Pavel Schilling (1786–1837). Largely due to Pushkin's disgraced status as an exiled poet for years, his request was rejected by Tsar Nicolas I (1796–1855).[9]

In St. Petersburg salons, educated celebrities were attracted by Archimandrite Iakinf's works and stories about China, and they wanted to be more acquainted with the achievements of Chinese culture and thought. Not surprisingly, there emerged a series of new images of China in their works, at times in parallel with or in contrast with Russia as its counterpart. Vladimir Odoevsky, for example, wrote a futuristic novel *The Year 4338: Petersburg Letters* (1835). The protagonist was a young Chinese man, who came to Russia to study various arts and sciences. He was favorably described as a popular foreign sojourner in St. Petersburg society, and his letters to the other students constituted the main body of the novel. In the same work, Odoevsky consciously depicted a marvelous future world dominated by the alliance of China and Russia, the two most advanced countries in the fifth millennium, and in particular their united efforts to prevent the catastrophic collision of the earth with another planet. As a result, there appeared a friendly representation of China and its people for the Russian audience of the time.[10]

While Odoevsky, under the obvious influence of Archimandrite Iakinf, reinforced a popular mode of utopian perception of China in the early nineteenth century, it met strong criticisms from intellectuals who would promote a nationwide campaign of Westernization in Russia. Vissarion Belinsky (1811–48), a well-known literary critic, was among this group of Westernizers. Targeting Archimandrite Iakinf's works, as well as many other eulogistic writings on China, Belinsky bluntly argued for the opposite by equating Chinese imperialism with primitive despotism and by claiming China as one typical example of a stagnant society. His perception of China was clearly on negative side, as he considered the words "kitaism" (Sinologism) and "kitayschina" no other than the synonyms of "conservatism," "sanctimony," and "hypocrisy." Bearing a Eurocentric world order in his mind, Belinsky believed that the mythical and secluded Chinese empire was undoubtedly against the modern progression and advancement of Western nations, hence a symbol of stagnation and backwardness. As one of the most radical critics of the Russian autocracy, Belinsky consciously spoke out the true motive behind his words. Provoking criticism and ridicule at the idealized portrait of China made by Archimandrite Iakinf and contemporary Sinophiles, he intended to create

---

9. Alexander Lukin, *The Bear Watches the Dragon: Russia's Perceptions of China and the Evolution of Russian-Chinese Relations since the Eighteenth Century* (Armonk, NY: M.E. Sharpe, 2003), 14–15.
10. Lukin, *The Bear Watches the Dragon*, 62.

an alien image of China, morally corrupt and ideologically dangerous, that could be projected onto the gloomy reality and disorder of his homeland.[11]

In the first half of the nineteenth century, China gradually became a metaphor in Russian literature. No matter under the influence of Archimandrite Iakinf or his opponents, the image of China was characterized by a mixture of both realistic and imaginary depictions, romantic at one time but derogatory at another. Objective observation was mixed with subjective judgment; factual knowledge coexisted with intuitive conceptualization: China became more a symbol than a reality. Whether good or bad, China was not faithfully depicted as it was but as what the Russian writers expected it to be, thereby creating a mirror image for them to reflect on the conditions in Russian society (or Europe in a broad sense). This trend, embedded with a subtle self-other paradox, has continued to evolve in later decades.

Archimandrite Iakinf became a phenomenal milestone in the course of Sino-Russian cultural interactions. The extent of his personal influence on Russian writers and thinkers was truly enormous. His marvelous stories on China inspired many young people to start to cherish a dream of becoming Sinologists. Moreover, his introduction of the history, philosophy, and geography of China and other Asian countries opened new ground for Russian intellectuals to develop varied types of in-between experiences, which from time to time redrew the boundaries of two different cultures.

Mission through translations, book collections, and medical practices

Archimandrite Peter (Kamensky), the chief of the Tenth Ecclesiastical Mission (1821–30), was another outstanding Sinologist of that time. As a student from the Eighth Mission in Beijing (1794–1807), he actively studied Chinese and Manchu and translated many texts into Russian, focusing on historical treatises and writings on social and economic issues. In Beijing, he started to compile a Sino-Mongolian-Manchurian-Russian-Latin dictionary. In 1819, he was elected a corresponding member of Russian Academy of Sciences for the category of literature and antiquities of the East, as well as a member of the Paris Asia Society, the Royal Society of Northern Antiquities at Copenhagen, and the Free Society of Science and Arts.

At that time, Archimandrite Peter distinguished himself not only as an outstanding researcher of China, but also as a talented organizer of Chinese studies and student training. None of the previous missions presented Russia with such a large group of skilled Sinologists ready for scientific and practical activities. Of the nine members of the student body, seven employed knowledge of Chinese and Manchu languages in their future works and became professional Sinologists.

During these years, a former student of the Eighth Ecclesiastical Mission, Stepan Lipovtsov (1770–1841), published his translation of the Gospel in Manchu. It was

---

11. Lukin, *The Bear Watches the Dragon*, 17–18.

actively used by the staff of the Russian Ecclesiastical Mission and other Russian missionaries. This translation has been highly regarded in Europe. It was published in London by the London Missionary Society, but was printed in St. Petersburg, because at that time Russia possessed the best Manchurian font in Europe, made by Baron Schilling.

In the 1820s, Zakhar Leontevsky (1799–1874), a member of the Tenth Ecclesiastical Mission in Beijing, translated into Chinese the *History of the Russian State* by the famous Russian historian Nikolay Karamzin (1766–1826). Leontevsky presented four copies of his translation to St. Petersburg University (now kept in the library of the Faculty of Asian and African Studies), the Public Library, the Asian Department of the Foreign Ministry, and the Asian Museum. Available data suggest that the stationery copy of the translation was presented to the Daoguang Emperor (1782–1850). For this work, the Russian Sinologist was awarded the title of *guoshi* (國師 state mentor), and was revered as the *zuoshizhe* (作史者 historian).[12] The Russian Emperor Alexander I (1777–1825) even awarded him a diamond ring. To show the Chinese people that Russians respectfully refer to the rituals associated with ancestral worship, Leontevsky translated a description of the burial ceremony of Alexander I into Chinese.

The Russian Ecclesiastical Mission played a central role in accumulating Chinese book collections and spreading knowledge about China in Russia. Gradually, the mission became the main supplier of Chinese and Manchurian books for these collections.

The eighteenth century witnessed the creation of the main collection of Chinese books in the Library of the Russian Academy of Sciences. Later, a book collection in the Asiatic Museum was also founded. The contribution of the mission to these collections was very significant. In 1741, Rossokhin, who had been a student in the Second Mission, brought to the Russian Academy of Sciences twenty books from China. After his death, his widow sold his personal collection of books and xylographs to the Academy of Sciences. These books were used for teaching Chinese and Manchu.

In 1747, the building of the academic library and Kunstkamera was badly damaged by fire. In 1753, Franz Jellachich was sent to China to restore books lost in the collection. He had a list of books prepared by Rossokhin, and brought forty-two books. Subsequently, the academic library was constantly replenished by new arrivals from the former missionaries who needed to sell their books in order to make ends meet, or after their death.

The start of a library in the mission itself was put forth by the monk Sophronius (Gribovsky, archimandrite between 1796 and 1807). Later, it was gradually enriched and had a considerable collection of Oriental books. The composition and size of the mission library can be revealed in the catalog compiled by Hieromonk Alexy

---

12. P. E. Skachkov, *Ocherki istorii otechestvennogo kitaevedenija* [Essays on the history of Russian Sinology] (Moscow: Nauka, 1977), 136.

(Vinogradov, 1845–1919), who wrote that the library was well equipped with books on history, philosophy, theology, and church organization.

An essential element in the development of intercultural dialogue between Russia and China was the spread of natural sciences and, above all, medical knowledge. Interest in Chinese medicine appeared in Russia in the eighteenth century. Russian medical knowledge was introduced to China with the advent of Russian physicians among the staff of the Russian Ecclesiastical Mission in Beijing. First among them was Osip Voytsehovsky (1793–1850), who was sent to China as a member of the Tenth Ecclesiastical Mission. At first, the Chinese were skeptical about the techniques of European medicine, but after seeing the effectiveness of the treatment, they were drawn to the Russian doctor. His credibility especially increased after he cured a relative of the emperor. Voytsehovsky also fought very successfully against the cholera epidemic that raged in Beijing in 1820–21.

On November 14, 1829, shortly before his departure from Beijing, Voytsehovsky received a present from his grateful Chinese and Manchu patients. It was a commemorative plaque with words of gratitude and appreciation. Hieromonk Veniamin (Morachevich, archimandrite between 1830 and 1840) wrote in his report about the contributions of Voytsehovsky in creating an image of advanced Russian culture and science in China.[13]

Artistic representations of China by Russian artists

A unique role in the development of cultural dialogues between Russia and the Qing Empire was played by the artists from the Russian Ecclesiastical Mission in Beijing. From 1830 to 1864, on the recommendation of the president of the Imperial Academy of Fine Arts, the ecclesiastical missions continually recruited professional painters. The first among them was Anton Legashov (1798–1865), who spent ten years (1830–40) in Beijing. He graduated from the Academy of Fine Arts. His main focus lay in painting nature, demonstrating a detailed, true-to-life picture of Chinese life, and in focusing on ethnographic features of the Chinese. He was also instructed to learn the secret concoction and application of Chinese paints, which were known for their durability and brightness. Legashov was commissioned to paint portraits of notable people for the purpose of enhancing mutual contacts between the two countries. In total, he painted more than forty oil portraits, which depicted both the notables and commoners of Beijing.

The instruction that Anton Legashov received from the Academy of Fine Arts before his departure (this instruction is deposited in the State Historical Archive in St. Petersburg) said that the artist must draw people, clothing, household items, musical instruments, weapons, houses, animals, plants, and flowers. All this must be

---

13. Skachkov, *Ocherki istorii otechestvennogo kitaevedenija*, 196.

realistic. He should abandon academic samples of Greek statues and preserve the peculiar character of the Chinese. In the portraits of young and older Chinese painted by Legashov we may see some influence of Chinese painting, but it is not so obvious. Legashov's popularity in Beijing was pointed out by Avvakum (Chestnoj), the monk of the Russian Ecclesiastical mission and a Sinologist.[14]

Three other artists who followed him as members of the mission were Kondratii Karsavin (twelfth mission in the 1840s), Ivan Chmutov (thirteenth mission in the 1850s), and Leo Igorev (fourteenth mission in the 1860s). Their Chinese landscapes, genre paintings, and portraits of Chinese nobles and common people (including Beijing beggars) played an important part in creating and introducing the image of nineteenth-century China in Russia. Photography being unavailable in that period, the influence of realistic painting on people's minds was as great as that of a visual image sequence in modern mass media. In their turn, the Chinese could become acquainted with Russian arts through the works of these painters. Ivan Chmutov's drawings *On a Street in Beijing* and watercolor *Behind the Walls of Beijing* became very popular among the Russian public, because people considered them to be influenced by a Chinese painting style. The artist also illustrated the book *Travel to China* (1853) by the famous Russian traveler and diplomat Yegor Kovalevskiy (1811–68). Thanks to their sketches, one can visualize a picture of Chinese life at that time through Beijing's buildings, household utensils, and other aspects. The Chinese and their daily life were seen through the eyes of Russian people. Russian artists also studied the production of Chinese ink and paints, and investigated their compositions. They played a very special role in the construction of a new image of China and Chinese in Russia.

Conclusion

The Chinese historian Chen Kaike considers the contacts of the mission staff, Russian physicians, and artists with Beijing people to be very active, and they matched the spirit of a "people's diplomacy." He notes that, by the mid-nineteenth century, "the views of ordinary Beijing residents of the Russian Ecclesiastical Mission have changed significantly. The former distrust of the Chinese people to the Russians has gradually changed to a friendly relationship."[15]

From the eighteenth to the nineteenth centuries, the Russian Ecclesiastical Mission and its staff played a crucial role in promoting cultural dialogues between Russia and China. Through their activities and scholarly works, the Russian public for the first

---

14. A. Chestnoj, *Nasha kitajskaja missija polveka nazad: Pis'mo A. Chestnogo iz Pekina* [Our mission half a century ago: A letter written by A. Chestnoj from Beijing] (Russkij arxiv, 1884), 55.
15. Chen Kaike 陳開科, *Kontakty chlenov rossijskoj duxovnoj missii s zhiteljami Pekina v duxe narodnoj diplomatii (pervaja polovina 19 veka)* [Contacts between members of the Russian Ecclesiastical Mission and Beijing residents in the spirit of public diplomacy (the first half of the 19th century)] (Razdvigaja gorizonty nauki: k 90-letiju akademika S. L. Tihvinskogo; Moscow: Pamjatniki istoricheskoj mysli, 2008), 237.

time learned about China, Chinese history, and culture, while Chinese people in the Qing Empire began to obtain substantial knowledge about Russian culture and Orthodox Christianity. The mutual exchanges constituted a complex process in which they found ways to redefine the cultural boundaries, promote expedient means of interpersonal and intercultural adaptations, and assume a kind of in-between thinking and way of life.

3
The Wind Qin

Hearing and Reading Chinese Reactions to the Pipe Organ

David Francis Urrows

Late in the year of 1600, with only a few months to live, a Chinese official by the name of Wang Linheng (王臨亨, 1548–1601) put his brush to paper and wrote of an almost fantastic voyage. His story was an account of his visit the previous year to a place on the fringe of late Ming China, an enclave of "barbarians" called *Amagao*. Wang found there to his surprise that these strangers, who had been occupying and trading on the narrow peninsula for nearly a century, were adept at many things of a technical nature. He wrote of the novelties he found there in an approving tone, and remarked that

> The foreigners in Macau are good craftsmen, and they have constructed well-made objects such as the organ and the carillon. They made a case with hundreds of pipes inside (or with hundreds of 'strings'). It is operated by a machine: when one person blows the bellows, then all pipes will sound. When one person plays the machine, then all tones will sound. The music is well-moderated, and can be heard from afar. The carillon is made of copper metal; it rings at noon, and then it rings every two hours, twelve times in a day.[1]

This description is notable as the first Chinese description of a Western pipe organ. It points to a number of things, but above all to the idea that musical instruments—quite apart from their intended functions—are forms of technology. As a result of their movement around the globe, as evinced by this account, they are therefore potential vectors of technological transfer as well as cultural and artistic interchange. In this account we can begin to see the elements of a nascent, if then a generally unperceived, global cultural exchange. Wang, it could be said, found this in a space somewhat "in-between" two exclusive domains.

Wang was writing for a Chinese readership of literati about a curio he had encountered in the strange world of Macau. He mentioned the pipes (by "hundreds" he meant, colloquially, "lots") and then immediately made an analogy with "strings." He was

---

1. Wang Linheng, *Yue jian bian* 粵劍編, ch. 3 (1600). This can be found in *Yuan-Ming shiliao biji congkan* 元明史料筆記叢刊 [Series of historical sources and writings in Yuan-Ming Period] (Beijing: Chung Hwa Book Co., 1987), 92.「澳中夷人，飲食器用無不精鑿。有自然樂、自然漏。制木一櫃，中真笙簧數百管，或琴弦數百條，設一機以運之，一人扇其竅，則數百簧皆鳴；一人撥其機，則數百弦皆鼓，且疾徐中律，鏗然可聽。」

not, I think, referring here to a tracker mechanism (as later writers will, when describing the "strings" or "threads" in a pipe organ) but wanted to make clear that the pipes are the sounding part of the instrument, just as strings are the sounding part of the great majority of Chinese musical instruments.

The mechanical nature of the organ was uppermost in his mind: it is an instrument which is made to sound "by a machine," and implicitly requires two people to operate. This signal difference, between the uninterrupted personal, tactile contact with indigenous Chinese instruments, was set by Wang in contrast to a curious invention from the West. Moreover, the organ is an instrument for "well-moderated" music; that is, it is neither too loud nor too soft, too fast nor to slow. The tonal power of the instrument, a recurring theme in these accounts, is his final point of information. These salient points—size, mechanical complexity, and power—are given here for the first time in Chinese by Wang. He hardly alluded at all to the polyphonic music performed, which would have been incomprehensible to him.

Wang was the first Chinese writer to discuss the pipe organ, but this was not the first pipe organ in China. In 1599–1600, the very first Western pipe organ in China had been constructed in Macau for Matteo Ricci's second embassy to Beijing. In truth, Ricci's small positive organ might have been constructed as little more than an elaborate toy, an amusement. It was not intended for actual use as a pipe organ within a liturgical context, but rather as a gift for the Wanli Emperor (1563–1620), thus a sample of technology, an instrument in the scientific as well as the musical sense. Nevertheless, this pipe organ appears to have been an instrument similar in size to the one seen by Wang Linheng.

Unfortunately for Ricci, the positive was slow to be completed and never made it to Beijing. It eventually reached Nanjing at the end of 1600, where for about sixteen years it was used by the Jesuit mission, and thus became—for a time—a liturgical instrument in spite of its origins. In the "Nanjing Incident" in the years 1616–18, the foreign missionaries in China became subject to general persecution instigated at both national and local levels. In April 1617, the vice-minister of rites, Shen Que (沈㴶), had all the foreign Jesuits arrested and sealed their house. An inventory was made of their possessions around April 25, 1617, in which Shen's staff listed in the Jesuit residence a "wind qin" (*fengqin* 風琴, organ) and a "foreign qin" (*fanqin* 番琴, harpsichord).[2] If in fact these instruments were sold, then it seems likely that they would have gone to a person of means in Nanjing. Thus the first pipe organ in China may have become the property of a mandarin or other wealthy citizen, someone who unknowingly took a very early step in cross-cultural interchange by allowing the foreign "wind *qin*" into his home and into his musical and intellectual life.

---

2. See Adrian Dudink, "The Inventory of the Jesuit House at Nanjing made up during the Persecution of 1616–1617," *Bibliotheca Instituti Societatis Iesu* 49 (1996): 119–57. This inventory is contained in the *Nangong shudu* (南宮署牘) of 1620.

Ricci died in 1610, and by the time of his funeral in 1611 there was an organ at the Zhalan compound in Beijing though we know nothing about it other than it existed and that it was probably built by the Jesuits on the spot.³

During the last years of the Ming dynasty several Western missionaries, writing in Chinese, brought the pipe organ to the attention of Chinese literati. Chief among these was Giulio Aleni (1582–1649), who seems to have published the first detailed account of a Western pipe organ in Chinese (in his *Zhifang waiji*, 職方外紀, Notes on the foreign lands) of 1623), and then further described the instrument in his *Xifang dawen* (西方答問, Questions and answers on the western territories) of 1637. This description provided a source for many later writers, such as Ferdinand Verbiest (1623–88), who copied it almost wholesale in his *Xifang yaoji* (西方要紀, Notes on the western territories) of 1669. Aleni may even have had a pipe organ at his mission in Sanshan, Fujian Province. On May 8, 1631, a "western *qin*" (*xiqin* 西琴) was displayed and played for a group of Chinese visitors by Aleni's colleague, the Lithuanian Jesuit Andrzej Rudamina (1596–1631). After the performance a Catholic convert, the scholar Li Jiubiao, declared that "it was quite amazing, and made us raise a cheer in admiration."⁴

No Chinese accounts of pipe organs seem to have survived from the middle decades of the seventeenth century. The years in which the Qing replaced the Ming as rulers of China led to immense difficulties for the Catholic missions, and so it is not surprising that we hear next to nothing until things had calmed down. In 1670, a Qing literary scholar, Qu Dajun (屈大均, 1630–96) described an organ at Macau, this time in the church of Madre de Deus (St. Paul's):

> There is an organ in the church, which is stored in a leather [*sic*] case. Inside are many pipes lined up like teeth, with a bellows outside; when air is blown in, sounds come out from the case The music [played] is fast and complex, especially when all the stops are drawn ["if all eight tones sound."] It is suitable for accompanying the liturgy, making good music.⁵

---

3. For more (speculative) details of this instrument, see my article, "The Music of Matteo Ricci's Funeral: History, Context, Meaning," *Chinese Cross Currents* 9 (2) (2012): 104–15; and my chapter, "The Pipe Organ of the Baroque Era in China," in *China and the West: Music, Representation, and Reception*, ed. M. Saffle and Yang Hon-lun (Ann Arbor: University of Michigan Press, forthcoming).
4. It is not clear if this *xiqin* (西琴) was really an organ or a harpsichord. The editor of the English translation of the *Kouduo richao* (口鐸日抄) calls it a "clavichord." See Erik Zürcher, *Kouduo richao: Li Jiubiao's Diary of Oral Admonitions: A Late Ming Christian Journal*, ed. and trans. Li Jiubiao (Sankt Augustin: Institut Monumenta Serica, 2007), 263.
5. Qu Da-jun, *Guangdong Xinyu* 廣東新語:「寺有風樂, 藏革櫃中, 不可見。內排牙管百餘, 外按以囊, 噓吸微風入之, 有聲嗚嗚自櫃出, 音繁節促, 若八音然, 宜合經唄, 甚可聽。」 Roderick Ptak's translation, in his "Notes on the Kuang-Tung Hsin-Yu" (*Boletim do Insituto "Luís de Camões,"* XV (1/2) (1981): 140) misread much of this. He interpreted the single character for "tooth/teeth" (牙) as "elephant tusk" (象牙), giving rise to an erroneous but much-repeated idea that the pipes were made of *ivory*, and not of either wood or metal. What Qu meant by this simile is that the pipes in the façade looked to him "like a mouthful of teeth" (perhaps because of the tapering feet of the metal (?) pipes). Ptak also misunderstood the remark about the "eight tones." The eight tones (八音) are the classical

At the beginning of the eighteenth century, two Chinese writers described organs in St. Paul's. In the first account, written by the famous scholar Wang Shizhen (王士禎, 1634–1711) around 1701, he observed that:

> In the church [of St. Paul's] there is an organ; all sorts of different timbres are produced through [its] metal pipes. The machine is stored in a wooden case; the pipes are connected with strings [trackers] and wheels [rollers]. One person operates the machine, and is able to play all of the tones.[6]

Slightly later, the writer Liang Di (梁迪, dates unknown) described an organ in the church, which was probably similar to, if not the same as, the one described by Wang Shizhen. "The Western organ is like a *sheng* [笙]," he wrote,

> which has two wings on either side, like the [wings of the] phoenix. The pipes are made of metal (bronze) and are lined up in order from long to short. A wooden case is used instead of a gourd, the bellows are made from leather, which is compressed and released to circulate the wind. The reeds (pipes) sound when the air moves [through them]; striking the keys ["toothpicks"] causes the sound to come crashing down. [While] music is being played in St. Paul's, the sound can be heard at a very great distance ["from a hundred *li*"].[7]

In all three of these accounts from the late seventeenth and early eighteenth centuries, we begin to see the same common themes emerging. First, a description of the physical mass of the organ, with the pipes lined up inside. Then, the fact that it is a kind of machine, and requires air to operate, usually provided by a bellows pumped by someone other than the player. Finally, the full organ was the best appreciated part of the spectacle. Perhaps there is not enough evidence here to draw any meaningful conclusions. Even so, there is a very apparent intellectual openness in the accounts, and a certain fascination, expressed simply as the description of a space occupied by observer and observed. That the technical details of the organs described here were occasionally "misread" is unimportant.[8] Already Liang Di tried to map the Western pipe organ onto

---

Chinese formulation for all the timbral and instrumental types in Chinese music. By analogy, Qu undoubtedly meant here the *organo pleno*.

6. The passage can be found in *Chibei outan* 池北偶談, ch. 21 (published 1701); see *Wenyuange Siku Quanshu* 文淵閣四庫全書 (http://v3.skqs.com/skqs/download/):「寺有風琴，其琴銅絃，彈之以和唄，並管簫諸樂器，藏機木櫃，聯以絲繩，輪牙相錯，一人轉機，則諸音並奏。」
7. Liang Di 梁迪, *Xitang ji: Waiguo zhuzhici* 西堂集：外國竹枝詞 [Collection of Xitang: Poems on foreign countries], in Tao Yabing 陶亞兵, *Ming-Qing jian de Zhong-Xi yinyue jiaoliu* 明清間的中西音樂交流 [Sino-Western music exchanges in the Ming-Qing period] (Beijing: The Eastern Publishing Co., 2001), 111–13. Note the interesting "deconstruction" of the organ into the constituent parts of the *sheng*.「西洋風琴似鳳笙，兩翼參差作翅形。青金鑄管當偏竹，短長大小遞相承。以木代匏囊用革，一提一壓風旋生。風生簧動眾竅發，牙簽戛擊音砰訇。奏之三巴層樓上，百里內外咸聞聲。」
8. A semiotic analysis of these texts would likely find itself in disagreement with my assertion that these "misreadings" are unimportant. The cultural value of the read (or misread) sign would be so overwhelming as to render these descriptions (which are written, and therefore ultimately also only *signs* of an encounter with the pipe organ) barely plausible as epistolary accounts of reality, if we were to follow the logic of

his understanding of both musical instruments and machines. In doing so, he created a space where *inter*action could occur.

Although not strictly a Chinese writing, a Korean visitor to Beijing, Kim Ch'ang-ŏp (김창업／金昌業, 1658–1721), wrote in 1712 of his encounter with an organ originally built by the Jesuit Tomás Pereira (1645–1708) in the Nantang (南堂, South Cathedral). This four-rank organ, rebuilt in 1703–11 by Pereira and his colleague and protégé, Leopold Liebstein (1667–1711), was attached to an automatic player mechanism, and was able to play Chinese, Western, Manchu, and Mongolian tunes by itself:

> Barely had the peals of bells [from Pereira's clock-carillon, built in 1677] died down when suddenly the sound of a gust of wind emerged from the inside of the arch by the [south-] east door. It sounded like many wheels moving together. Then music was played, it was [like] the sound of string and wind instruments. I didn't know where it was coming from. The official who interpreted said that it was Chinese music. After a long while it stopped, and then another melody was played. This was like the one I heard while paying obeisance and offering congratulations to the Emperor. [The interpreter] indicated, "This is Manchurian music." It stopped after a considerably long time, and then yet another piece with a fast beat was played, and the interpreter pointed out, "This is Mongolian music." The music then stopped completely and the six ranks [of pipes][9] shut [down] automatically on their own.

After this, someone played the organ in the normal manner:

> The sound of a sudden gust of wind and the moving of wheels was caused by the channel [wind trunk] which was physically connected to the bellows, which blew into it air, as if blowing by mouth. And when player started playing, the wind entered the channels, the trackers rolled, and the reed tongues [*sic*, pipes] opened.

Roland Barthes as elaborated in his 1970 classic, *L'Empire des Signes*. Barthes would have rightly pointed out just how much we, the readers, contribute to the reconstruction of reality in these cases. On top of that, I am reading and discussing English translations of the original Chinese and Korean accounts here with all the problems to which that predisposes analysis. However, my feeling is that these accounts are all we have left; we have no material culture to study. It is possible, with the right training and insight, to decode some if not all of the "mis"-readings; and further, we must use our imagination to get around logical difficulties in scholarship.

9. Pereira and his colleagues referred to the 1680 organ as a four-rank instrument, and it was probably enlarged in the 1703–11 rebuilding. However, one of the "ranks" consisted of a series of bird and animal sound effects ("traps"); in this case, Kim was probably counting three flue ranks, and three different traps, making six in all. See my chapter on "The Organ of the Baroque Era in China," and "Highly Applauded, as Novelties Are: Science, Politics, and the Pipe Organs of Tomás Pereira, s.j.," in *History of the Catholic Church in China: From Its Beginnings to the Scheut Fathers and the 20th Century: Unveiling Some Less Known Sources, Sounds and Pictures* (Leuven: Ferdinand Verbiest Institute, Catholic University of Leuven, 2015), 99–124. 「俄見日影到其方位，則臺上大小鍾，各撾四聲。中央大鍾，撾六聲。鍾聲纔止，東邊虹門內，忽有一陣風聲，如轉眾輪，繼以樂作，絲竹管絃之聲。不識從何而來，通官言此中華之樂，良久而止。又出他聲，如朝賀時所聽，曰：此滿州之樂也，良久而止。又出他曲，音節急促，曰：此蒙古之樂也，樂聲既止，六扉自掩。」

All these openings [of pipes] were making sounds together. Regarding the design of the bellows, the material is a fabrication of five calfskin hides, smooth like a silk bag. Like a huge bell, it [the bellows] was suspended by a large, thick velvet rope from the beam of the room['s ceiling.] Two persons needed to grasp the rope tight, jumping up in the manner of sailors hoisting a sail. And then they stepped onto the bellows and made it compress. And the middle [of the bellows] would become swollen, filled with air, and [the air] was then forced out [of the bellows] into the channels [wind trunk]. The next step was to press the keys to shut [*sic*] the openings; the air had nowhere to escape but struck with pressure the mouths of the flue pipes. One after another of them were [thus] struck, and all [then] produced music. Today, I can describe a little of it, yet I still cannot tell the whole picture of its subtle magic. If this can be funded by the government, perhaps it can be made [here in Korea].[10]

The poet You Tong (尤侗, 1618–1704) was moved to include a reference to Pereira's 1680 organ and clock-carillon in his *zhuzhici* (竹枝詞), "Europe":

> Beautiful chimes from the open cathedral,
> Organ and bells high and low resound;
> Roses in bloom past the gates of the city,
> To the honor of Ricci, wine (was) poured on the ground.[11]

Nearly eighty years later, a much-rebuilt version of Pereira's organ at the Nantang, as well as the carillon, were still very much in working order and attracted the attention of the poet Zhao Yi (趙翼, 1727–1814). In his essay, "The Western Telescope and Musical Instruments," Zhao described being introduced to the organ by Augustin von Hallerstein (1701–74), the Jesuit director of the Chinese astronomy bureau from 1746 to 1774. "This organ," wrote Zhao in 1759,

---

10. Kim Ch'ang-ŏp's account is seen in his *Yenjing Diary* 燕行日記／연행일기, *Yŏnhaeng ilgi*, and cited in a record of a visit to Beijing in 1780 by Pak (Park) Chi Won (박지원／朴趾源, 1737–1805) in his *Jehol Diary* 熱河日記／열하일기, *Yŏrhailgi*. This can be accessed in the *Database of Korean Classics*, http://db.itkc.or.kr/itkcdb/mainIndexIframe.jsp. By this date (1780), the Nantang of Pereira's day had burned down (on the night of February 13/14, 1775) and the organ destroyed. From Pak's account, however, we can theorize that the bellows and the pinned barrel for the automatic playing mechanism were placed on the ground floor level, below the chamber in the southeast tower where the organ was installed, and near the "arched doorway."「忽有一陣風聲如轉衆輪者，爲地道宛轉相通，而皷橐以達氣如口吹也。繼以樂作者，風入城道，輪囷輾輵而簧葉自開，衆毅嗷噪也。其皷橐之法，聯五牛之皮，柔滑如錦袋。以大絨索懸之樑上如大鐘，兩人握索奮躍，懸身若掛帆狀，以足蹈橐，橐漸蹲伏。而其腹澎漲，虛氣充滿，驅納地道。於是按律掩竅，則無所發洩，乃激金舌，次第開展，所以成衆樂也。今吾略能言之，而亦不能盡其妙。如蒙國家發帑命造，則庶幾能之云。」

11. This is the second half of Yu's poem; the versification is my own. You Tong (尤侗), *Ouluoba zhuzhici* (歐羅巴竹枝詞) [Poems on Europe], in Tao Yabing, *Zhong-Xi yinyue jiaoliu shigao* 中西音樂交流史稿 [A historical study on Sino-Western music exchanges] (Beijing: Encyclopedia of China Publishing House, 1994), 73.「天主堂開天籟齊，鐘鳴琴響自高低。阜城門外玫瑰發，杯酒還澆利泰西。」 "Outside the Fuchengmen gate" refers to the Zhalan compound and the site of Ricci's tomb, which lay in what was then a western suburb.

is in the upper part [tower] of the building, and is placed on top of a wooden case. A man with a beard sits there and plays the [organ].You hear the sounds of all musical instruments, of *sheng*, *xiao* [簫 end-blown flute], *qing* [磬 a stone chime], *di* [笛 traverse flute], *zhong* [鐘 bells], *gu* [鼓 a drum], *nao* [鐃 hand bells], *zhuo* [鐲 a small bell, used in the army for signaling]. Tens of lead pipes are suspended [*sic*] from the case. The foot of [each of] the [façade] pipes is several inches from the ground. Two wooden panels [slider and table] are bored with holes, which match up with the pipe holes [top board]. At the south-eastern corner a man is pumping the bellows for air to pass through the pipes. Each pipe is connected by a copper thread [pull-down wire] to a string [tracker] inside the instrument. If these strings [trackers] are pulled, then the instrument produces sounds of different pitches. The lead pipes are of different sizes and qualities of timbre. Thus when someone plays the organ, and all the pipes are sounding, you can hear the sounds of all musical instruments . . . solemn, stirring, powerful . . . It is truly astonishing. There is also a bell [Pereira's clock-carillon of 1677] which sounds all by itself. It rings automatically at times, along with the sounds of the organ and various instruments . . . the 'harp' sounds like a cold spring, the '*pipa*' sounds like snowflakes floating through the air . . . When I go up to the [organ] loft, I am astonished to see only one old man [Florian Bahr, SJ, 1706–71] is sitting there and playing. It seems as though a hundred people are making music . . . the bellows breathes, [rising and falling] like the morning and evening tide . . . This, too, is wonderful . . . there are so many intelligent people in the world, and we should broaden our horizons . . . Knowledge is not limited to the Confucian school. I lingered and enjoyed so much as to forget to go home. I was not aware it was already eight in the evening, and the city gate would be closed. Arriving back home, I have to record what I have heard and seen today, and write it down [reclining] on my pillow.[12]

What, then, can we learn from these writings about how (in these rather specialized instances) China and the Chinese viewed and understood these Western visitors to China and their musical technology in the late Ming and Early Qing eras? How can (or, should) we summarize Chinese reactions to these "wind-*qin*"? Working though our chronological journey, we see that, at their most positive, literati such as You Tong and Zhao Yi were generous and open-minded about these Western novelties. They interpreted them, naturally, from a position of Chinese-cultural centricity: the imagery of classical Chinese poetry and prose was brought into play, and the organ was explained with reference to normative ideas about Chinese musical instruments, to which their

---

12. Zhao Yi 趙翼, *Yanpu zaji* 簷曝雜記 [Jottings of Yanpu], in Yu Sanle 余三樂, *Zhong-Xi wenhua jiaoliu de lishi jianzheng* 中西文化交流的歷史見證 [Historical witness of Sino-Western cultural exchanges] (Guangzhou: Guangdong People's Publishing House, 2006), 246–48. 「一人在東南隅，鼓鞴以作氣。氣在夾板中盡趨於鉛管下之縫，有縫直達於管。管各有一銅絲繫於琴絃。蚰須彖撥絃，則各絲自抽頓，其管中之關捩而發響矣。鉛管大小不同，中各有竅竅，以象諸樂之聲，故一人鼓琴而衆管齊鳴，百樂無不備，真奇巧也。又有樂鐘，並不煩人挑撥，而按時自鳴，亦備諸樂之聲。」 A further description of the instrument, possibly based on Zhao's book, was given by Wu Changyuan 吳長元 in his *Chenyuan shilue* 宸垣識略 (Beijing, 1788), by which date this organ no longer existed.

Chinese readership would be able to relate. The pipe organ is presented as a kind of *sheng*; it has the winged appearance of a phoenix (*feng* 鳳);[13] the timbres of the different ranks are described with reference to indigenous instruments (*pipa* 琵琶, *qin* 琴, *gu* 鼓, *zhong* 鐘). The fact that the sound-producing parts of the instrument (the pipes) are physically separated from the player's fingers is a recurrent theme, as are its volume and tonal force, particularly as they are under the control of a single performer (or two, if you count the calcant who pumped the bellows). Far from rejecting the pipe organ, or taking a confrontational approach or tone, all of these writers were receptive to it. Nonetheless, its oddity limited its potential usefulness to the Chinese. As Zhao Yi said: "[While] it might not be able to play the traditional songs of China,[14] it is still [an instrument] of very good quality. This instrument, originating outside of China is [itself] amazing and intelligent. Despite the long history of civilization in China, we still have not developed such an instrument." In this we can understand that, while reception is almost always balanced by the need to preserve a sense of self-identity, it leads to a newly defined space—and aesthetic space, in this instance—between *self* and *others*.

The open-mindedness revealed here has larger ramifications, beyond purely music historical and musicological enquires. It is part of a larger topic, on which scholars such as Johanna Waley-Cohen and Julia Lovell have recently written, and one that continues to analyze the practical and political reception of Western science and technology in China from the time of Ricci onwards.[15] This reception was greatly aided at the time by the Jesuits' liberal "cross-cultural communication" approach[16] and by the presence of the missionaries during the reign of the Kangxi Emperor (1661–1722), a period described as one of "Qing multiculturalism."[17] The mindset (having in part anti-Jesuit origins) which arose in the late seventeenth century, and which took hold in the eighteenth and nineteenth centuries, of Chinese "indifference" to things Western, particularly technology, is still sometimes encountered today. But as Waley-Cohen has succinctly put it, while it is true that

> the Chinese, and their rulers, have uniformly displayed a powerful reluctance to surrender authority or autonomy to any outsider or even to take a chance of doing

---

13. One the resemblance of the *sheng* to the phoenix (*feng*), see Xiao Jun, "The Golden Phoenix: The Classical Sheng," *Chinese Music* 33 (1) (2010): 1–6.
14. This was probably due to the fixed Western scale of the keyboard, and the organ's temperament, which Zhao (and other Chinese writers) felt was incompatible with Chinese music. 「雖難繼韶護，亦頗諧皦繹。白翎調漫雄，朱鷺曲未敵。奇哉創物智，乃出自蠻貊。緬惟華夏初，神聖幾更易。」
15. See Johanna Waley-Cohen, "China and Western Technology in the Late Eighteenth Century," *American Historical Review* 98 (5) (1993): 1525–44; and her *The Sextants of Beijing* (New York: Norton, 1999) for more on this point of view.
16. In this connection, see Ian Rae, "The 'Cross-Cultural Communication' Approach of the Early Jesuit Missionaries in China," *RC: Review of Culture*, Ser. 2, Vol. 21 (1994): 121–32.
17. See Peter C. Allsop and Joyce Lindorff, "Teodorico Pedrini: The Music and Letters of an 18th-Century Missionary in China," *Vincentian Heritage Journal* 27 (2) (2007): 43–59.

so ... [t]his attitude must be distinguished from the isolationism, the hostility to innovation, especially when of foreign origin, and the immutable sense of superiority for which it has often been mistaken.[18]

Comments, then, such as those of You Tong, Zhao Yi, Liang Di, and others cited here contribute to the body of evidence that any perceived "indifference" had its origins in political control issues, such as those which led the Qianlong Emperor (1711–99) to famously declare to George Macartney (1737–1806) in 1793, "we have never valued ingenious articles, nor do we have the slightest need of your country's manufactures."[19] However, I cannot resist observing that Qianlong had at least two, and perhaps more, positive organs built and installed in the imperial palace, as well as an 18-piece Western-style chamber orchestra, which had been trained by the Jesuits, and who performed in Beijing incongruously garbed in the periwigs and tailcoats of European court lackeys.

To do that—calling, in short, Qianlong's bluff—is to enter into part of another chapter of the story of the pipe organ in China, one that can only be summarized here. By the beginning of the nineteenth century, imperialistic expansion in full flood, the pipe organ was no longer treated as a novelty. Vastly improved transportation links, and a growing globally interdependent economy, led to the demise of the homemade pipe organs of the early traders and missionaries. Pipe organs were imported to China from the Spanish-controlled Philippines as early as 1678, but the mid-nineteenth-century importation from Europe or North America became the universal norm. The last—and greatest—of the localized efforts to build pipe organs was made by a group of Jesuits in Shanghai, who, under the leadership of Fr. François Ravary (1823–91) and Br. Léopold Deleuze (1818–65), established a workshop for making organs with bamboo pipes at Zikawei (Xujiahui 徐家匯) in 1856. This, however, was set up only as a direct response to the arrival of a Gray and Davison pipe organ for the Anglican Church in Shanghai (Holy Trinity) in the same year, and it marked both a high point and an end to local manufacture.[20] From the 1840s on, the Chinese were also far more likely to encounter the harmonium than the pipe organ when they encountered it at all; and local builders in cities such as Shanghai (Moutrie) and Beijing (the *Imprimerie des Lazaristes* at the Beitang) began to manufacture harmoniums for sale in China, as well as for a wider Asia-Pacific market. By the end of the nineteenth century, harmoniums were also being imported from all over, including France (Kasriel), the United States (Mason and Hamlin), and Germany (Mannborg).[21]

---

18. Waley-Cohen, "China and Western Technology in the Late Eighteenth Century," 1528.
19. Ibid., 1525. Also see Joyce Lindorf, "Burney, Macartney and the Qianlong Emperor: The Role of Music in the British Embassy to China 1792–1794," *Early Music* 40 (3) (2012): 441–53.
20. For a comprehensive look at the story of the Zikawei organ workshop, see my article "The Bamboo Organs of Nineteenth-Century Shanghai," *Nineteenth-Century Music Review* 11 (2014): 113–34.
21. In the early years of my research on this topic (1989–91), I encountered examples of these very harmoniums in various churches in China, as well as Chinese-manufactured harmoniums still displayed for sale in music shops in Shanghai and Guangzhou.

From this point on, in a decaying, late Qing political environment, the successors to the cordial and intellectually open literati such as Zhao Yi had little interest in such things as the pipe organ and had quite understandably adopted a hostile political attitude toward the missionaries in most cases. In addition, the whole examination system that had produced the scholar-officials whose mutually respectful accounts I noted earlier, had degraded by the early nineteenth century to the point that

> [E]ven after a student ventured to attempt the lowest of the three rungs of the imperial examinations . . . the odds were stacked against success. During the Qing, around two million candidates sat for the lowest, country level examinations . . . only 1.5 percent passed . . . No more than 5 per cent [of these] would succeed at the next, provincial stage, and less than 1.5 made it past the final metropolitan rung . . . As a result, late-imperial China was increasingly saddled with an ageing population of academic failures.[22]

After 1800, accounts of pipe organs from the Chinese side, then, are mostly anecdotal accounts from ordinary people, committed to the historical record from recollections or interviews, of which the following is typical:

> Most of the people who went to the Church of St. Louis [in Tianjin] were from Western countries . . . using a circular staircase, you walked up to the organ loft. There stood a Western classical pipe organ. The red copper [*sic*] pipes, which reached to the roof, were lined up along the wall. When it was played, the sound was very loud, robust, and harmonious. The power of the organ was very great. When the organ was playing and the choir was singing, the atmosphere was very solemn. It was said that when the organ was playing in the silence of midnight, the sound of the organ carried for more than ten *li*.[23]

These comments, compiled in the 1960s and '70s from residents of Tianjin, could almost have been written by Wang Linheng or Liang Di. The circularity of the accounts points to a common experience, however. When unimpeded by political resistance, or supervening animosities, a cautious interest in and approval of the Western pipe organ has always been evident. There was a challenge, of a sort, offered to China by the pipe organ, but it was a challenge not taken up until recently: it was only in 1988 that a pipe organ[24] was commissioned and installed in China under Chinese administration.

---

22. Julia Lovell, *The Opium War: Drugs, Dreams and the Making of China* (London: Picador, 2011), 44–45. The low pass rates were a fact of life in the late Ming era as well, and it is possible that the interest displayed by many literati toward the Jesuits in particular may have been a reaction to their exclusion from higher office.
23. These accounts are summarized in *Tianjin lao jiaotang* 天津老教堂 [Old churches in Tianjin] (Tianjin: People's Publishing House, 2005).「舊時到紫竹林教堂進行宗教活動的多為歐美各國僑民。……沿螺旋式樓梯攀上唱經樓，西洋古典管風琴赫然聳立，紫銅音管靠牆排列，直向屋頂。演奏時，聲音宏大豐滿，圓渾和諧，音域寬廣，和伴唱詩班的歌聲時，神聖而莊嚴。據說在夜深人靜的時候演奏，方圓十里以外都可以清晰地聽到。」
24. Rieger-Kloss Op. 3164, Beijing Concert Hall.

In a sense the pipe organ, with its powerful iconic properties pointing to Christianity, has remained a stereotype of Western (religious) music. The installation of about twenty-five pipe organs in China in the past three decades have mostly been carried out in civic buildings (many of them concert halls connected with the Poly Group), and less often churches or conservatories, with the anomalous effect of putting a potent religious symbol in a thoroughly nonreligious environment. However, the mere desire to emulate the Western concert hall visually has won out over any atheistic scruples; and sadly this can be seen in the rapid deterioration of these organs in China's concert halls within a year of installation. In my experience, they almost all suffer from a uniform lack of climate control, few performers are invited to play (leading to further deterioration through disuse), and consequently there are limited opportunities to develop an audience for organ repertory. There they remain, but only as extremely expensive bits of furniture.[25] The challenge to indigenize the pipe organ is still very much an open question, as it was over four centuries ago when Wang Linheng wrote the very first account of the instrument in Chinese. For the time being, it still occupies that in-between space first articulated in the words of a dying scholar in 1600.

---

25. The few instruments installed in the past decade in two or three music schools, and a few in churches in Beijing, Qingdao, Shanghai, Nanjing, and Tianjin, have fared somewhat better. Also, an organ "museum" now exists in Xiamen but with a variety of redundant instruments bought overseas and shipped to China for modern reinstallation.

4
"Supreme Nation"

The British Image in Karl Gützlaff's Novels Shifei lüelun *and* Dayingguo tongzhi[*]

John T. P. Lai

Introduction

Among nineteenth-century Protestant missionaries to China, Prussia-born Karl Friedrich August Gützlaff (1803–51)[1] emerged as the most prolific missionary novelist for the publication of more than ten novels within his large corpus of Chinese works on Christianity, ranging from catechisms, evangelical tracts, to biographies of biblical figures.[2] Unlike most of his novels focusing on the discussion of Christian thought and Chinese religions,[3] *Shifei lüelun* (是非畧論, Brief discussion of right and wrong, 1835; hereafter *Right and Wrong*)[4] and *Dayingguo tongzhi* (大英國統志, General

---

[*]   The work described in this chapter was substantially supported by the General Research Fund from the Research Grants Council of Hong Kong Special Administrative Region, China (Project no. CUHK447510: "Chinese Christian Novels in Late Qing China [1807–1911]: An Interdisciplinary Study of Religion and Literature").

1. For the life and work of Gützlaff, see Jessie Gregory Lutz, *Opening China: Karl F. A. Gützlaff and Sino-Western Relations, 1827–1852* (Grand Rapids, MI: William B. Eerdmans Pub. Co., 2008), and Charles Gützlaff, *Journal of Three Voyages along the Coast of China, in 1831, 1832 & 1833* (London: Frederick Westley and A. H. Davis, 1834).

2. For the list of Gützlaff's works in Chinese, see Alexander Wylie, *Memorials of Protestant Missionaries to the Chinese: Giving a List of Their Publications and Obituary Notices of the Deceased* (Shanghai: American Presbyterian Mission Press, 1867), 56–63.

3. Most of Gützlaff's novels use the *zhanghui* (章回) genre, a type of traditional novel, each chapter headed by a couplet giving the gist of its contents. Heavily indigenized, many stories portray Chinese society, culture, and customs in the Ming and Qing dynasties, the characters being mainly Chinese officials, literati, and merchants. It is also worth noting that Gützlaff's works frequently quote or paraphrase from vernacular Chinese novels, for example, *Romance of the Three Kingdoms*, and Confucian classics, for instance, *The Book of Mencius*, as aesthetic and hermeneutical strategies for a better understanding and reception of Christian messages. For a brief introduction of some of Gützlaff's novels, see Patrick Hanan, *Chinese Fiction of the Nineteenth and Early Twentieth Centuries* (New York: Columbia University Press, 2004), 61–70. For a collection of Gützlaff's novels, see John T. P. Lai, ed., *Shuzui zhi daozhuan: Guo Shilie Jidujiao xiaoshuo ji* 贖罪之道傳：郭實獵基督教小說集 [The doctrine of redemption: The collected Christian novels of Karl Friedrich August Gützlaff] (New Taipei: CCLM Publishing, 2013).

4. In the six-chapter *Right and Wrong*, Chen Zeshan (陳擇善), a Qing dynasty Guangzhou merchant who returned from London, discusses the British affairs with his friend, Li Jinbing (李金柄). Dissuading Li from despising foreigners as "barbarians" or "red-haired devils," Chen discusses the British commercial activities in China and the trading restrictions imposed by the Qing court. Chen also talks about a wide variety of topics, including British economy, military power, monarchy, territories, cultural activities, religious lives,

records of Great Britain, 1834; hereafter *Great Britain*)⁵ place great emphasis on constructing the image of Britain as the "supreme nation" (*Wushang zhi guo* 無上之國). From the perspective of Chinese migrants returning from Britain, the protagonists of both *Right and Wrong* and *Great Britain* display to their compatriots a kaleidoscope of the cultural, social, and political landscape of Great Britain of the early nineteenth century.⁶

Both works are similar in genre, subject matter, and publication period, so an integrated study will offer a more comprehensive and in-depth examination of Gützlaff's depiction of British society and culture prior to the Opium War (1839–42). Taking a textual-historical approach, this study presents a critical analysis of the two novels with a focus on their strategies of dispelling several traditional Chinese misconceptions: regarding Westerners/British as "barbarians," trading between the West and

---

and so forth. The version used in this article is Ai Han Zhe 愛漢者 [Lover of the Chinese/philosinensis] [Karl Gützlaff], *Shifei lüelun* 是非畧論 (Malacca: Anglo-Chinese College, 1835). For an introduction of *Right and Wrong*, see Wu Yixiong 吳義雄, *Zai zongjiao yu shisu zhijian: Jidujiao Xinjiao chuanjiaoshi zai Huanan yanhai de zaoqi huodong yanjiu* 在宗教與世俗之間：基督教新教傳教士在華南沿海的早期活動研究 [Between religion and the secular world: A study on the early activities of the Protestant missionaries in the coastal regions of south China] (Guangzhou: Guangdong jiaoyu chubanshe, 2000), 399–405.

5. *Great Britain*, a five-chapter story, begins with Ye Duhua's (葉犢花) journey to Britain, followed by the events that happened after Ye returns to his hometown in the wake of a twenty-year stay in Britain. Ye meets his compatriots and tackles their biases toward the British by means of his knowledge and admiration of Britain. Ye gives an account of the British society and culture, including the geography, population, education, marriage, political system, legal system, and military strength. On religious topics, Ye talks about the baptism of children and grandiose churches. With a visit of his friend Guo Zhang (郭帳), Ye goes on to mention Scotland and Ireland, including the style of housing and the scale of cities. By listing the colonies of the British Empire, Ye concludes the novel by suggesting the ideal of "uniting all peoples from the Four Seas into one." The version used in this article is [Karl Gützlaff], *Dayingguo tongzhi* 大英國統志 (s. l.: s. n., 1834). For an introduction of *Great Britain*, see David K. Y. Chng 莊欽永, "*Wushang*" wenming guguo: Guo Shilie bixia de Daying「無上」文明古國：郭實獵筆下的大英 ["Supreme" civilized ancient country: Great Britain in Karl Gützlaff's works] (Singapore: SIM University and Global Publishing, 2015); Xiong Yuezhi 熊月之, "Yapian Zhanzheng yiqian Zhongwen chubanwu dui Yingguo de jieshao: jieshao *Dayingguo tongzhi*" 鴉片戰爭以前中文出版物對英國的介紹：介紹《大英國統志》[An introduction of Britain in the Chinese publication before the Opium War: Introducing *General Records of Great Britain*], *Anhui shixue* 安徽史學 1 (2004): 52–58; Zou Zhenhuan 鄒振環, *Xifang chuanjiaoshi yu wan Qing Xishi dongjian: yi 1815 zhi 1900 nian xifang lishi yizhu de chuanbo yu yingxiang wei zhongxin* 西方傳教士與晚清西史東漸：以 1815 至 1900 年西方歷史譯著的傳播與影響為中心 [Western missionaries and the eastward spread of Western histories in the late Qing period: With a focus on the dissemination and influence of translated works of Western history from 1815 to 1900] (Shanghai: Shanghai guji chubanshe, 2007), 338.

6. For the historical background and political tension between China and Britain behind *Right and Wrong*, see David K. Y. Chng 莊欽永, "Dujin niaolong li de nahan: Guo Shilie zhengzhi xiaoshuo *Shifei lüelun* xilun"「鍍金鳥籠」裡的吶喊：郭實獵政治小說《是非略論》析論 [Yells in the "Gilded Bird Cage": An analysis of the political novel *Shifei lüelun* (A brief comment on right and wrong) by Karl Gützlaff], in *Xixue dongjian yu Dongya jindai zhishi de xingcheng he jiaoliu* 西學東漸與東亞近代知識的形成和交流 [The eastward spread of Western learning and the formation and exchanges of knowledge in modern East Asia], ed. National Research Centre of Overseas Sinology, Beijing Foreign Studies University and Chinese Modern News Publication Museum (Shanghai: Shanghai renmin chubanshe, 2012), 259–90.

China as "tribute paying" (*jingong* 進貢), and Christianity as the "heresy of Western barbarians" (*Xiyi yiduan* 西夷異端). Gützlaff's discourse will be examined against the historical, political, and religious contexts of Anglo-Chinese intercourse in the early nineteenth century. This study aims to enhance our understanding of the textual strategies employed for rendering the British image acceptable and appealing to the Chinese readers and the underlying factors behind such a purposeful portrayal.

Westerners/British, not 'barbarians'

Viewing China (*Hua* 華) as the center of the world differentiated from the cultural or ethnic barbarians (*Yi* 夷), Sino-centrism, or the so-called "Sino-barbarian dichotomy" (*Hua-Yi zhi bian* 華夷之辨, the distinction between Hua and Yi), took root as the fundamental worldview and diplomatic mentality of imperial China.[7] According to the "Royal Regulations" (*Wangzhi* 王制) of *The Book of Rites* (*Liji* 禮記), the Chinese empire occupied the heart of civilization, while the peripheral tribes and nations from four directions, Eastern *Yi* (東夷), Western *Yong* (西戎), Southern *Man* (南蠻), and Northern *Di* (北狄), were less civilized, if not barbarians.[8] While emperors of China were heralded as the "Sons of Heaven" in the "Celestial Empire" (*Tianchao* 天朝), other nations were relegated to tributary states. This mentality was explicitly exhibited in the Qing Qianlong Emperor's (1711–99) cold-shouldered response to George Macartney (1737–1806), the British envoy to China in 1793 for the establishment of free trade and equal diplomatic relationship, that "the Celestial Empire, ruling all within the four seas, simply concentrates on carrying out the affairs of Government properly, and does not value rare and precious things."[9] This self-important and self-contented attitude rendered it superfluous for the importation of goods from the world outside the "Celestial Empire."

It was also commonplace for the official documents and correspondences to address the Westerners as "barbarians" or "foreign barbarians." Deng Tingzhen (鄧廷楨, 1776–1846), governor of Guangdong and Guangxi Provinces, reported the movements of British ships in his 1837 memorial to the throne that there were designated

---

7. For the formation of this worldview, see Lydia H. Liu, *The Clash of Empires: The Invention of China in Modern World Making* (Cambridge, MA: Harvard University Press, 2004), 31–69.
8. "The people of those five regions—the Middle states, and the Zung, I (and other wild tribes round them)—had all their several natures, which they could not be made to alter. The tribes on the east were call I. They had their hair unbound, and tattooed their bodies. Some of them ate their food without its being cooked. Those on the south were called Man. They tattooed their foreheads, and had their feet turned in towards each other. Some of them (also) ate their food without its being cooked. Those on the west were called Zung. They had their hair unbound, and wore skins. Some of them did not eat grain-food. Those on the north were called Ti. They wore skins of animals and birds, and dwelt in caves. Some of them also did not eat grain-food." See James Legge trans., *Li Chi: Book of Rites, An Encyclopedia of Ancient Ceremonial Usages, Religious Creeds, and Social Institutions* (New York: University Books, 1967), 229.
9. J. L. Cranmer-Byng, ed., *An Embassy to China: Being the Journal Kept by Lord Macartney during His Embassy to the Emperor Ch'ien-lung, 1793–1794* (London: Longman, 1962), 340.

sites for the ships of "foreign barbarians" (*Waiyi* 外夷) to drop anchor.[10] The "foreign barbarians" were frequently further degraded as the "red-haired" (*Hongmao* 紅毛) or "foreign devils" (*Fangui* 番鬼). In the Ming dynasty, Wang Linheng (王臨亨, 1548–1601), an officer of the Ministry of Justice, gave an account on the arrival to southern China of a "maritime barbarian" (*Haiyi* 海夷) tribe of more than two hundred people, called "red-haired devils" (*Hongmao gui* 紅毛鬼).[11] In 1755, the provincial authorities of Zhejiang recommended to the Qing court that the ships of the British merchant James Flint should be received "with compassion" as the ships of the "Red Hair," the nickname for the English and the Dutch.[12] Against the context of anti-Christian incidents in Guangdong Province in the 1890s, Zheng Xianchen (鄭獻琛) declared the vicious activities of Westerners as "the foreign devils have sent accomplices to China to drop poison."[13]

The aforementioned deep-rooted Chinese worldview and Western image, specifically toward the British, are manifested in *Right and Wrong* and *Great Britain*. The former novel reveals its basic tone by the opening remarks of Li Jinbing (李金柄), a non-Christian character, who calls Britain a place of the "red-haired foreign devils" (紅毛番鬼) (p. 2), while foreigners are perceived by Chinese officials as "barbarians" (*Yiren* 夷人) possessing "deceitful and eccentric traits" (*qiqing guijue* 其情詭譎) (p. 5). Similarly in *Great Britain*, Li Quande (李全德), a non-Christian character, looks down upon the British by asserting that "[t]he red-haired are barbarians," and that they are merely "beast-like," "godless," "kingless," and "without any ethics" (ch. 1, p. 3). These comments reflect the negative image of the British people as "barbarians," "foreign devils," and "red-haired" commonly held among contemporary Chinese people, and the Qing court is accused as the chief culprit for intensifying such a despicable and xenophobic attitude.

With a view to reconstructing the British image, *Right and Wrong* refutes the erroneous perceptions through the mouth of Chen Zeshan (陳擇善), the Christian protagonist. Claiming the Chinese impression of the British as absurd and groundless, Chen argues that it is vulgar and antagonistic to address the British people as "foreign devils" (pp. 2–3) and challenges the underlying rationale of calling the British "barbarians." He maintains that "barbarians," according to traditional Chinese records, are

---

10. Wen Qing 文慶 et al., *Chouban yiwu shimo: Daoguang chao* 籌辦夷務始末：道光朝 [The beginning and end of making preparations for the barbarian affairs: The reign of the Daoguang Emperor] (Taipei: Wenhai chubanshe, 1970), 85.
11. Wang Linheng 王臨亨, *Yue jian bian* 粵劍編 [Swords of Guangdong Province], in *Xuanlan Tang congshu xuji* 玄覽堂叢書續集 [Continuation of the collected works of Xuanlan Tang], Vol. 19 (Taipei: National Central Library, 1985), 175–76.
12. Immanuel C. Y. Hsü, *The Rise of Modern China* (6th ed.) (Oxford: Oxford University Press, 2000), 140.
13. Zheng Xianchen 鄭獻琛, "Guangdong Jieyangxian jietie" 廣東揭陽縣揭帖 [A notice of Jieyang county of Guangdong Province] (1892), in *Jiaowu jiao'an dang* 教務教案檔 [Archives on church affairs and missionary cases], Part 5, Vol. 4, ed. Institute of Modern History, Academia Sinica (Taipei: Institute of Modern History, Academia Sinica, 1977), 2202.

confined to the uncivilized tribes within the boundary of the Chinese empire, while the British territories fall completely outside the domain of China. In other words, the British people are not "barbarians" by the traditional definition of the Chinese worldview. The novel also speaks highly of the talents and virtues of the British who are "richly endowed with gifts and skills, unparalleled under heaven" (pp. 3–4), far from "deceitful and eccentric" as perceived by the Chinese (p. 6). Adopting a similar textual strategy, the protagonist of *Great Britain* does not conceal his admiration of the high cultural achievements of the British: "Those foreigners in Canton manifest the dignity of their home countries . . . they compose poems and prose in their own languages, which is comparable to the scholarship of the Chinese" (ch. 1, p. 3).

During the early nineteenth century, both the Qing court and most common people embraced an entrenched Sinocentric worldview of the "Celestial Empire" and a perception of "barbarians" and "foreign devils." As a direct response to this negative imagination and political discourse, *Right and Wrong* and *Great Britain* challenge the presiding Chinese prejudice toward the Western nations and Westerners, particularly the British. In so doing, the two works attempt to pave the way for an equal trading and diplomatic relationship between Britain and China.

Trading, not "tribute paying"

Closely associated with the "Sino-barbarian dichotomy" is the deep-rooted conception of imperial China on trading and foreign relations. Traditionally, China gave priority to stability in its intercourse with foreign nations, only allowing foreigners to pay tribute to the Chinese court or conduct limited trading activities. This Chinese mindset on foreign trade was typically demonstrated in a document of Gu Yanwu (顧炎武, 1613–82), an early Qing dynasty official: "In the early reign of the Jiajing Emperor (1507–67), Portugal dispatched an envoy to pay tribute (*laigong* 來貢)."[14] In other words, China considered the trading activities of Westerners a kind of tribute paying, and the allowance of the exportation of Chinese goods an act of benevolence on the part of the "Celestial Empire." This attitude was clearly reflected in the Qing official Lu Kun's (盧坤, 1772–1835) memorial in 1834: "The allowance for foreign barbarians to carry out trading activities was bestowed out of the solicitude of the Celestial Empire (*Tianchao tixu* 天朝體恤) . . . In breach of the regulation, William John Napier, chief of English barbarians, sailed their warships into the inner rivers. The barbarian traits were crafty and deceitful (*Yiqing jiaohui* 夷情狡獪), solely bent on profit (*weili shitu* 惟利是圖)."[15]

---

14. Gu Yanwu 顧炎武, "Tianxia junguo libing shu" 天下郡國利病書 [The advantages and disadvantages of all prefectures and countries under heaven,], in *Xuxiu Siku Quanshu* 續修四庫全書 [Continuation of the complete library in the Four Branches of Literature], Vol. 597 (Shanghai: Shanghai guji chubanshe, 1995), 584.
15. Tingfu F. Tsiang 蔣廷黻, *Jindai Zhongguo waijiao shi ziliao jiyao* 近代中國外交史資料輯要 [A collection of essential sources of Chinese modern diplomatic history] (Shanghai: Shanghai shudian, 1990), 13.

The increasing trading activities between the West and China in the eighteenth century deepened the Chinese anxiety toward the encroaching Western influence in China. In 1720, Chinese merchants in Canton formed their own monopolistic guild called the Cohong (公行) to control foreign trade and regulate prices. In 1754, these merchants were ordered by the Qing court to ensure the foreign crews' good behavior and payment of transit dues.[16] In an effort to tighten its regulation on foreign traders, the Qing government issued a decree in 1759 to make Canton the only port open to foreign commerce and hence instituting the Canton Trade System, or the so-called Cohong System, which lasted until 1834. As the intermediary between the Qing court, Chinese traders, and foreign traders, Cohong was an institution with the official permission to manage, if not monopolize, foreign trade in Canton, and exercised both commercial and diplomatic functions.[17] Meanwhile, a set of regulations against foreign barbarians (*Fangfan waiyi guitiao* 防範外夷規條) promulgated by Li Shiyao (李侍堯, ?–1788), the governor of Guangdong and Guangxi Provinces, in 1759 underwent many subsequent revisions and additions to restrict the activities of the "foreign barbarians" and their contacts with the Chinese. For instance, foreign traders were not allowed to bring their wives or remain in Canton after the trading season but had to return home or go to Macau. Also, they might not communicate with Chinese officials except the Cohong.[18] Under the Canton Trade System, in essence a protectionist or seclusion policy, Canton was the single port opened for foreign trade, and Westerners were not granted access to the inland areas out of the concern for national security.

Taking the perspective of contemporary Chinese people, *Right and Wrong* demonstrates the common misconception on foreign trade and negative attitude toward foreign merchants: "Isn't Great Britain paying tribute to our country?" (p. 21), and "Thanks to the great benevolence of the Celestial Empire (*Tianchao hou'en* 天朝厚恩), foreigners are bestowed with trading rights in our country. Isn't that a magnanimous gift of benevolence?" (p. 13). Some Chinese characters in the novel cast doubt on the social and economic value of the commercial activities with foreign merchants on the grounds that a small number of merchants could hardly bring benefit to such a huge Chinese population. On the contrary, British merchants are thought to have snatched commercial gain from China while generating no tax revenue to China (p. 14).

---

16. Jonathan D. Spence, *The Search for Modern China* (2nd ed.) (New York and London: W. W. Norton & Company, 1999), 120.
17. For the history of the Canton Trade System, see Immanuel C. Y. Hsü, *The Rise of Modern China*, 139–67; Frederic Wakeman, "The Canton Trade and the Opium War," in *The Cambridge History of China, Volume 10 Late Ch'ing, 1800–1911, Part I*, ed. J. K. Fairbank (Cambridge: Cambridge University Press, 1978), 163–71; and Peter C. Perdue, "Rise & Fall of the Canton Trade System," at http://ocw.mit.edu/ans7870/21f/21f.027/rise_fall_canton_01/pdf/cw_essay.pdf. Accessed on April 29, 2013.
18. See Immanuel C. Y. Hsü, *The Rise of Modern China*, 150–51.

To counter these accusations, *Right and Wrong* highlights the immense profits that China may be able to make in the process of trading with Britain. It states that the two-century Anglo-Chinese trade has brought a massive increase of tax revenue for China, amounting to millions of taels of silver annually. The novel also argues that Anglo-Chinese trade has succeeded in creating ample job opportunities for tens of thousands of Chinese tea farmers, thousands of coolies, and hundreds of merchants who make a living from the exportation of tea and manufactured goods, and in turn contribute to the prosperity of China as a whole (pp. 14–15). *Right and Wrong* also expresses sympathy toward the dire situation of the Chinese merchants who are oftentimes falsely prosecuted as traitors, being punished, tortured, or even executed in prison (p. 15). In fact, even though the Qing officials claimed that the "Celestial Empire" did not take into account the tax revenue generated from foreign trade, they failed to deny the fact that the termination of foreign trade would jeopardize the livelihood of hundreds of thousands of people in the coastal regions, who made their living on the trading activities with foreign countries.[19] Some statistics show that the custom collected at Canton was as high as 855,000 taels of silver per annum.[20] Though the figures on the tax revenue and job opportunities might well be exaggerated within a literary framework, Gützlaff's arguments in his novels are, in fact, not altogether groundless.

Instead of addressing the misconception on the unequal trading relationship, *Great Britain* remarks that the commercial activities have introduced a large variety of foreign resources to China. With reference to the Anglo-Chinese trade in 1834, the work gives a laundry list of detailed figures of the British export of manufactured goods to China, including cloth, steel, and frankincense, with a total value of $23 million (ch. 3, p. 11), while the Chinese export to Britain amounts to $20 million (ch. 3, p. 13). The novel arrives at the conclusion that "the scale of English trade is unparalleled in the world" (ch. 3, p. 9) and "how thriving is the English trading enterprise!" (ch. 4, p. 13). The conscious use of meticulous trading statistics and financial revenue, regardless of their credibility, to some extent renders Gützlaff's constructed British image more convincing and appealing to his Chinese readers.

Toward the late nineteenth century, many Chinese still held fast to their belief that Western merchants and missionaries served as foreign spies to secure intelligence of China under the disguise of trading and preaching, as commonly accused in anti-Christian material, for instance: "The rebellious barbarians and bandits of the cult deceive the Chinese in the name of commercial activities . . . those preachers go from place to place as spies for the invaders."[21] Along with such a mindset, *Right and Wrong*

---

19. Wen Qing et al., *Chouban yiwu shimo: Daoguang chao*, 39.
20. Chang Te-Ch'ang, "The Economic Role of the Imperial Household in the Ch'ing Dynasty," *The Journal of Asian Studies* 31 (2) (February 1972): 258.
21. Institute of Modern History, Academia Sinica, ed., *Jiaowu jiaoan dang*, 918.

depicts the Chinese anxiety on the trading activities of the Western countries which might enable the foreigners to spy on Chinese intelligence and expose China to the threat of being conquered (pp. 7–8). For the purpose of alleviating these misgivings, *Right and Wrong* takes Britain as an example of the gracious treatment toward foreign merchants, who were granted free access and movement within the British territory. While foreign trade brought great wealth to the nation, interaction with foreign merchants helped to broaden the horizons of the British nationals (p. 30).

The disparate ideas held by China and Britain on trading intensified their tensions and conflicts on trading in the 1830s, culminating in the Opium War. Against this historical background, *Right and Wrong* makes efforts to dispel the Chinese misconception of trading as tribute paying, and renounce the unfair and restrictive regulations imposed on foreign traders. By depicting Britain as a global trading power, *Great Britain* attempts to prove that China has made great profits in the process of trading with Britain. Both works strive to rid Britain of the tributary status and advocate an equal trading relationship with China. Claiming Britain as the "supreme nation" constitutes a crucial textual strategy for the achievement of this objective.

Britain: The "Supreme Nation"

Britain has been heralded by *Right and Wrong* as the "supreme nation" on the grounds of its impressive technological development, strong military power, and solid cultural foundation. The novel demonstrates some major new advancement in British technology after the Industrial Revolution, especially the improvement of steam engines that push forward manufacturing industries, and the steamships that motivate navigation, international trade, and the expansion of the British Empire. While *Right and Wrong* depicts the operation of steam engines that could substitute the labor of almost fifty people (p. 31), *Great Britain* mentions that steam engines enable sewing and machines to work automatically (ch. 3, p. 8). Both novels also highlight the military might of the British Empire. Other than describing the various forces in the British army, *Right and Wrong* portrays the equipment of the soldiers who employ "guns, swords instead of bows, arrows and shields," while different classes of British warships are equipped with powerful cannons (p. 23). *Great Britain* goes into minute detail on British military power, including the exact number of gunboats and soldiers on gunboats, and claims that the British troops, including those stationed in tributary states, reach 800,000 (ch. 2, p. 7). Though its accuracy may well be questionable, the meticulous account of weaponry and troops would give an impression of precision and clarity of presentation and hence enhance the persuasiveness of the image of Britain as a military powerhouse in the eyes of the Chinese readers who had not experienced the Industrial Revolution.

Apart from constructing a towering image of a technologically advanced and militarily powerful Britain, *Right and Wrong* attempts to justify Britain's superiority as the "supreme nation" by signaling its control over a great number of colonies and tributary states, including Hindustan, Ceylon, Burma, New Holland, Selat Island (present-day Singapore), Penang, Malacca, and so forth. It remarks that "[t]he King of Great Britain rules over billions of people, and unites the Four Seas (*Sihai* 四海) into one family" (p. 20). *Great Britain* also gives a list of the British colonies in the Mediterranean, the two Americas, Africa, and India, then comments that "[t]he Great Britain rules over the Four Seas," and that "God the Father, the creator of the world, treats all peoples as one family, different tribes as one clan, and unites all peoples from the Four Seas into one" (ch. 5 p. 22). The "Four Seas," a classical Chinese phrase with a long history, traditionally refers to four bodies of water that metaphorically made up the boundaries of the ancient Chinese empire. The phrase was often alluded to by Chinese writers, for instance, Jia Yi (賈誼, 201–169 BCE), who wrote that the Qin dynasty had succeeded in "rolling up the empire like a mat, enveloping the entire universe, pocketing all within the Four Seas."[22] A popular folk song of the Han dynasty sings praises that "within the Four Seas, we are all brothers, and none be taken as strangers!"[23] According to the discourse of *Right and Wrong* and *Great Britain*, the British Empire has already stretched over different oceans and continents of the world, i.e., the "Four Seas." By employing the expression "uniting the Four Seas into one family," Gützlaff not only aims to redefine the traditional Chinese concept of "Four Seas" but also to reshape the Chinese worldview and challenge the deep-rooted Sinocentrism. In other words, it was the British Empire, in lieu of the "Celestial Empire", which took the center stage of the world and exercised control over the "Four Seas."

In line with the Confucian background that attaches great importance to education and culture, both novels maintain that the well-established cultural foundation of Britain was on a par with the foundation of Chinese culture and that the quality of the British nationals and social institutions might even supersede the Chinese counterparts. *Right and Wrong* remarks that "[t]he government of Great Britain pays great attention to the cultivation of talents, the transformation of customs, and the establishment of schools" (pp. 32–33). The novel also underscores the relationship between education and family ethics by pointing out that the British girls have an equal right to receive education because the well-being of a family depends on female education, while mothers assume a vital role in the education of the young (pp. 35–36). Furthermore, women are said to have taken up teaching positions in various kinds of schools and academies (p. 33). On the topic of female education, *Great Britain* points out that "girls not merely acquire needle work, but also read classics extensively" (ch. 3, pp. 4–5). Both novels foreground the British emphasis on education to the extent

---

22. Charles Holcombe, *A History of East Asia: From the Origins of Civilization to the Twenty-First Century* (New York: Cambridge University Press, 2011), 48.
23. Chang Chun-shu, *The Rise of the Chinese Empire: Nation, State, and Imperialism in Early China, ca. 1600 B.C.–A.D. 8* (Ann Arbor: University of Michigan Press, 2007), 263.

of establishing a comprehensive educational system, with institutions of higher education established all over the country. The lavish illustration of British priority on education conforms to the Chinese cultural tradition, and the depiction of universal education, particularly female education, might likely be inspiring, if not revolutionary, to Chinese readers of the early nineteenth century.

The well-established legal, judicial, and parliamentary systems are given due importance as the cornerstone of the stability and prosperity of the "supreme nation." While *Right and Wrong* maintains that not even imperial edicts could hinder the legal procedure and the verdicts would be made public immediately, rendering any bribery impossible (p. 32), *Great Britain* highlights the paramount importance of the rule of law instead of the rule by individuals, as stipulated in the constitution of Great Britain (ch. 2, p. 5). The portrayal of the impartiality of the British judicial system might function as Gützlaff's subtle protest against the widespread phenomenon of bribery in China, where many foreign merchants were victimized in the process of Sino-Western trade.[24] With regard to the British parliamentary system, *Right and Wrong* gives an elaborate account of the election, formation, and legislative procedures of the British Parliament, which comprises the "Upper House" (*Shangjia* 上家) and the "Lower House" (*Xiajia* 下家) (p. 23). *Great Britain* points out that "the national budget must obtain the approval of the Parliament, without which no tax could be collected. Even the prime minister was not able to dictate his own will" (ch. 1, p. 7). Gützlaff illustrates the pillars of "supreme nation," particularly the ways in which the British Parliament may check and balance the power of the government, and common people may participate in politics through election, and the British people show their solemn respect of the national constitution. The kaleidoscopic display of the British legal and parliamentary systems might not only offer an alternative but serve as a challenge to the longstanding political orders of imperial China.

The conscious construction of an ideal image of the "supreme nation," however, involves a noticeably exaggerated depiction on the part of Gützlaff. Notably, the English King William IV (1765–1837) is portrayed in *Right and Wrong* to have "immersed people with benevolence, disciplined people with righteousness" (*jianmin yi ren, momin yi yi* 漸民以仁，摩民以義) (p. 21). Gützlaff employs these classical expressions to portray the ideal of a virtuous ruler in the Confucian tradition for underscoring the good governance of the British monarch. In order to consolidate the image of a virtuous king, *Right and Wrong* also makes deliberate attempts to conceal some of the private life of William IV, "The King William (*Weiyan* 威嚴) of Great Britain, aged 67, and his 44-year-old queen Adelaide (*Dilaidi* 帝賚苐), fathered six princes and four princesses" (p. 21). Historically, King William IV of England was also the head of the Kingdom of Hanover and Adelaide of Saxe-Meiningen (1792–1849) as

---

24. Kuo Ting-yee 郭廷以, *Jindai Zhongguo shigang* 近代中國史綱 [A short history of modern history] (Vol. 1) (Hong Kong: Chinese University Press, 1986), 34–36.

his queen. The ten children of William IV, however, were not born of the queen but of his mistress, Dorothea Jordan (née Bland, 1761–1816).²⁵ By calling these illegitimate sons and daughters "princes" and "princesses," Gützlaff has beautified the image of the British monarch by concealing the historical facts, most likely out of the consideration of the negative impact of revealing the dark side of the British royal family while singing high praises of the British nation.

To illustrate the wealth and prosperity of the British people, *Right and Wrong* makes an explicit reference to *The Works of Mencius* for the portrayal of an ideal society: "The elderly wear silk and eat flesh, and the masses suffer neither from hunger nor cold" (p. 22).²⁶ Similarly, the "Ten Odes to London" (*Landun shi yong* 蘭墩十詠) in *Great Britain* eulogize London as an earthly paradise where citizens sing and dance to extol the golden age, everybody enjoying stability and affluence (ch. 3, pp. 5–7). This rosy picture, however, exhibits a gross exaggeration of early nineteenth-century British society, if a comparison is made with some realistic contemporary English novels, such as Charles Dickens' *Oliver Twist*, which depicts an array of social problems in Britain, including orphans, child labor, and juvenile gangs. Such a great disparity in the portrayal of the British society may be explained by the differences of targeted readers and authorial intention. British writers, like Dickens, were not reluctant to expose the social reality in a bid to awaken the English readers' concern of the social evils and garner support for the reform movements. Gützlaff, in contrast, purposefully conceals the dark side of British society and publicizes its bright aspects in order to render the "supreme nation" more appealing to his Chinese readers. This textual strategy aims to put forth a more underlying religious discourse of the image of Britain as the upholder of orthodoxy.

Britain upholding the orthodoxy

Gützlaff's positive, and often exaggerated, portrayal of Britain is closely related to his own position on religion and identity as a missionary. The image of Britain was intimately connected, if not overlapping, with Christianity in the eyes of most Chinese people in the nineteenth century. Inheriting the anti-Christian sentiments and discourses from the late Ming and early Qing periods, late Qing intellectuals like Wei Yuan (魏源, 1794–1857) retained the commonly held perceptions of Christianity. One of the typical examples was the widespread rumor that Catholic priests plucked out

---

25. See Alison Weir, *Britain's Royal Families: The Complete Genealogy* (revised ed.) (London: Vintage, 2008), 303–4; Philip Ziegler, *King William IV* (London: Collins, 1971), 296; Simon Jenkins, *A Short History of England* (London: Profile Books, 2011), 240.
26. Mencius' original statement is rendered "persons of seventy wearing silk and eating flesh, and the black-haired people suffering neither from hunger nor cold." See James Legge, trans., *The Chinese Classics, with a Translation, Critical and Exegetical Notes, Prolegomena, and Copious Indexes* (Vol. II) (Hong Kong: Hong Kong University Press, 1960), 132.

the eyeballs of Chinese converts.²⁷ This kind of criticism was even more acrimonious in *Bixie jishi* (辟邪紀實 True records of extirpating heresy, 1871), an anthology of anti-Christian articles from the Ming and Qing periods: "The sect of Jesus indulges in the fantasy of eternal bliss and suffering. The acts of its believers are a billion times more absurd and illusory than those of Buddhism and Daoism."²⁸ These two representative materials point to the fact that Christianity was widely perceived as an absurd and threatening heresy in the late Qing era.

Most of Gützlaff's novels attempt to deal with the Chinese hostility toward Christianity, especially the image of Christianity as the "heresy of Western barbarians." In Gützlaff's longest novel, *Shuzui zhi dao zhuan* (贖罪之道傳 Doctrine of redemption, 1834), Christianity is condemned by a Chinese intellectual as the "teaching of the barbarians" and a "heresy" to be rejected.²⁹ Another novel, *Zheng xie bijiao* (正邪比較 Orthodoxy and heresy compared, 1838), illustrates the contempt of a non-Christian character toward Christianity: "Heresies must be banished as robbers and thieves . . . the believers of the heretical sect of Jesus gang up to rebel against the country."³⁰ In fact, this viewpoint constitutes an explicit response and reinforcement to the official ideology of the Qing court issued by the Kangxi Emperor, *Shengyu guangxun* (聖諭廣訓 Sacred edict),³¹ its seventh chapter, "Extirpate heresy and exalt orthodoxy" (*chu yiduan yi chong zhengxue* 黜異端以崇正學), stipulating "banish these heretical sects as you would stop the progress of robbers, thieves, torrents and flames" (*binchi yiduan, zhiru daozei shuihuo* 擯斥異端，直如盜賊水火), and "the sect of the Western Oceans which honours Tianzhu [Lord of Heaven] also ranks among those who are corrupt"³² (*Xiyangjiao, zong Tianzhu, yi shu*

---

27. Wei Yuan 魏源, *Haiguo tuzhi* 海國圖誌 [Atlas and annals of overseas countries] (Vol. 2) (Changsha: Yuelu shushe, 2011), 882.
28. Tianxia diyi shangxin ren 天下第一傷心人, ed., *Bixie jishi* 辟邪紀實 (s. l.: s. n., 1871), preface, 1.
29. Ai Han Zhe 愛漢者 [Karl Gützlaff], *Shuzui zhi dao zhuan* 贖罪之道傳 (s. l.: s. n., 1834), 40.
30. Shan De 善德 [Admirer of virtue] [Karl Gützlaff], *Zhengxie bijiao* 正邪比較 (Singapore: Jianxia shuyuan, 1838), 2.
31. For the proclamation and circulation of *Shengyu guangxun* in the Qing dynasty, see Wm. Theodore de Bary and Richard Lufrano, comp., *Sources of Chinese Tradition* (2nd ed.) (Vol. 2) (New York: Columbia University Press, 2000), 70–72, 125–26; Wang Erh-min 王爾敏, "Qing ting *Shengyu guangxun* zhi banxing ji minjian zhi xuanjiang shiyi" 清廷《聖諭廣訓》之頒行及民間之宣講拾遺 [*The Sacred Edict* on the civilian teachings for good conduction and the mass propagation by the local officials and scholars preaching periodically in everywhere in Ch'ing China], *Bulletin of the Institute of Modern History, Academia Sinica* 中央研究院近代史研究所集刊 22 (Part 2) (June 1993): 255–76; and Liao Jenn-Wang 廖振旺, "'Wansuiye yisi shuo': Shi lun shijiu shiji lai Hua Xinjiao chuanjiaoshi dui *Shengyu guangxun* de chuban yu renshi"「萬歲爺意思說」：試論十九世紀來華新教傳教士對《聖諭廣訓》的出版與認識 ["The meaning of the emperor": On Protestant missionaries' publishing and understanding of the Sacred Edict in nineteenth-century China], *Chinese Studies* 漢學研究 26 (3) (September 2008): 225–62. For Gützlaff's study of *Shengyu guangxun*, see Philosinensis [Karl Gützlaff], "Ta Tsing Hwang Te Shing Heun, or Sacred Instructions of the Emperors of the Ta Tsing Dynasty," *Chinese Repository* 10 (11) (November 1841): 593–605.
32. The English translations of *Shengyu guangxun* are modified from William Milne, trans., *The Sacred Edict, Containing Sixteen Maxims of the Emperor Kang-He* (London: Black, Kingsbury, Parbury, and Allen,

bujing 西洋教，宗天主，亦屬不經). Henceforth, Gützlaff was well aware of the official stance and popular sentiments toward Christianity while putting forth his arguments on religious orthodoxy.

Instead of engaging in theological discussion or highlighting the hostility toward Christianity, *Right and Wrong* foregrounds the cultural aspects of Christianity and the ways in which Christianity forms an integral part of the daily lives of the British people. The novel mentions that the British people only worship God the Holy Trinity, the Lord of all creation (p. 25), while the Bible, "the Book of books" (*geshu zhi kui* 各書之魁), has been revered as the religious classic that contains divine revelations and teachings to be followed not only by the British but also by all peoples in the world, including the Chinese (pp. 33–34). *Great Britain* stresses that each and every nation will enjoy peace and tranquility so long as the illustrious truths of the Bible are preached to the end of the world (ch. 5, p. 22). The legitimacy of the British crown resting on Christianity, the monarch will hold the Bible while taking an oath at the coronation, pray and seek for the blessings of God, the Lord of Heaven, and restrain himself from the willful abuse of power (ch. 1, pp. 5–6).

Convinced by the protagonist's eloquent discourse of the multifaceted Christian culture, the non-Christian friend in *Right and Wrong* shows his admiration of the British faith of Christianity by exclaiming that "[t]he people are upholding orthodoxy (*chishou zhengjiao* 持守正教), and Great Britain's adherence to the True Way, on top of its prosperity and superiority, displays the true mark of great prestige and glory" (p. 27). This carefully constructed compliment conveys an implication that a country with advanced technology, a mighty army, and thriving trade may not be sufficient to fully qualify as a great nation. It is the true religion that constitutes the secret of success of the "supreme nation." Proclaimed as the orthodox religion, Christianity has been portrayed to have formed an indispensable part of British culture, providing important guidelines of life, solidarity of the British people, the foundation of the authority of the crown, and most importantly the key to its national supremacy.

Factors behind Gützlaff's constructed British image

With a view to consolidating the British image as the "supreme nation," Gützlaff attempts to arouse the Chinese reader's admiration by depicting Britain's technological superiority, cultural achievement, and religious orthodoxy. However, it is worth investigating the underlying factors for Gützlaff, a Prussian missionary, to sing the praises of such a foreign nation as Britain. In fact, Gützlaff's intricate connections with Britain may offer some important clues to his construction of an embellished image of Britain.

1817), 126–55; and F. W. Baller, trans., *The Sacred Edict: With a Translation of the Colloquial Rendering* (2nd ed.) (Shanghai: American Presbyterian Mission Press, 1907), 72–87.

Right from the beginning, Gützlaff was closely associated with the British missionaries to China. Upon arrival in Indonesia in 1827, Gützlaff, sent by the Netherlands Missionary Society, stayed with Walter Henry Medhurst (Chinese name 麥都思, 1796–1857), of the London Missionary Society (LMS) and studied Chinese under his instruction.[33] Gaining interest in the Chinese missions, Gützlaff resigned from the Netherland Missionary Society and became an independent missionary. He set off for Malacca in 1828 and for some time participated in the missionary work of the LMS. In fact, some of his works, for instance *Right and Wrong*, were published by the Anglo-Chinese College, founded by the LMS in Malacca.[34] Furthermore, the London-based Religious Tract Society (RTS) sponsored a great proportion of Gützlaff's publications.[35] The RTS annual report of 1834 quoted from Robert Morrison that Gützlaff was supplied with Bibles and tracts from the Anglo-Chinese College for performing an extensive distribution on the Eastern coast of China.[36] The RTS also reported in 1835 that "[t]he committee have remitted, through the late Dr. Morrison, a grant to Mr. Gutzlaff of One Hundred and Twenty-five Pounds. A former grant of One Hundred Pounds has been also paid during the year. Mr. Gutzlaff has not only received direct assistance from the society, but has obtained considerable supplies of tracts from the missionaries at Malacca and Batavia."[37] Therefore, it is apparent that Gützlaff's close links with the British missionaries of the LMS and the London-based RTS greatly facilitated his acquisition of funding for publishing his works by the Anglo-Chinese College. On top of his personal knowledge and experience, Gützlaff's

---

33. Su Ching 蘇精, *Shangdi de renma: Shijiu shiji zai Hua chuanjiaoshi de zuowei* 上帝的人馬：十九世紀在華傳教士的作為 [Under God's command: Papers on early Protestant missionaries in China] (Hong Kong: Christian Study Centre on Chinese Religion and Culture, 2006), 36.
34. For the history and publications of Anglo-Chinese College, see Brian Harrison, *Waiting for China: The Anglo-Chinese College at Malacca, 1818–1843, and Early Nineteenth-Century Missions* (Hong Kong: Hong Kong University Press, 1979); Su Ching, *Zhongguo, kai men! Malixun ji xiangguan renwu yanjiu* 中國，開門！馬禮遜及相關人物研究 [Open up, China! Studies on Robert Morrison and his circle] (Hong Kong: Christian Study Centre on Chinese Religion and Culture, 2005), 56, 156–57; and Su Ching, "Malixun yu Yinghua shuyuan de jingfei" 馬禮遜與英華書院的經費 [Robert Morrison and the budget of the Anglo-Chinese College], in Lee Kam Keung, Peter Ng Tsz Ming, and Ying Fuk Tsang, eds., *Zi Xi cu Dong: Jidujiao lai Hua erbai nian lunji* 自西徂東：基督教來華二百年論集 [East meets West: Essays celebrating the bicentennial of Protestant Christianity in China] (Hong Kong: Chinese Christian Literature Council, 2009), 31–51.
35. Founded in London in 1799, the Religious Tract Society was an interdenominational missionary society that aimed at publishing evangelical books and tracts. RTS sponsored the publication of translated works in more than 34 languages and dialects in 1824, and up to 226 languages in 1898. For the history and publications of RTS, see David Bogue, *An Address to Christians, Recommending the Distribution of Cheap Religious Tracts* (London: Religious Tract Society, 1799), 10–13; "Address of the Committee," *The Fifty-first Annual Report of the Religious Tract Society* (1850), ix–xi; and *Centenary of the Religious Tract Society* (London: Religious Tract Society, 1898), 2–6. John T. P. Lai, *Negotiating Religious Gaps: The Enterprise of Translating Christian Tracts by Protestant Missionaries in Nineteenth-Century China* (Sankt Augustin: Institut Monumenta Serica, 2012), 59–90.
36. *The Thirty-Fifth Report of the Committee of the Religious Tract Society* (1834), 1.
37. *The Thirty-Sixth Report of the Committee of the Religious Tract Society* (1835), 5.

close collaboration with other British missionaries and societies was in all likelihood a major source of his information for his detailed description on the culture and religion of Britain as portrayed in *Right and Wrong* and *Great Britain*.

In addition to the British missionaries and societies, Gützlaff had frequent contacts with some British merchants. Before leaving China in 1832, Charles Majoribanks (Chinese name 馬治平, 1794–1833), of the East India Company, sent Hugh Hamilton Lindsay (1802–81) to visit the seaports north of Canton, particularly in Fujian and Zhejiang Provinces. On February 27, 1832, Lindsay commenced his sea voyage on the *Lord Amherst* and employed Gützlaff as his interpreter.[38] Other than textile and other manufactured products, *Lord Amherst* was loaded with many Chinese tracts for political and religious propaganda, including Robert Morrison's *Dayingguo renshi lüeshuo* (大英國人事略說 A brief account of the English character),[39] whose illustration of, and attitudes toward, Britain form an important basis for Gützlaff's composition of *Right and Wrong*.[40]

Gützlaff also had a close connection with William Jardine (1785–1843) and James Matheson (1796–1878), founders of British company Jardine, Matheson & Co. It is worth pointing out that the publication of both *Great Britain* and *Dongxiyang kao meiyue tongji zhuan* (東西洋考每月統記傳 Eastern Western monthly magazine, 1833–37), the first Chinese monthly magazine published on Chinese soil, were actually sponsored by William Jardine.[41] Jardine, the patron of *Great Britain*, was known as an opium trader in China. Gützlaff had also traveled along the coastal regions of China on board the *Sylph*, an opium ship owned by Jardine, Matheson & Co. in 1832. Gützlaff's connection with these British merchants might be the subtle, if not

---

38. See "Advertisement," in *Report of Proceedings on a Voyage to the Northern Ports of China, in the Ship Lord Amherst* (2nd ed.) (London: B. Fellowes, 1834).
39. *Dayingguo renshi lüeshuo* is the Chinese translation of *A Brief Account of the English Character*, written by Charles Majoribanks (1794–1833) of the British East India Company in 1831. Majoribanks invited Robert Morrison, an employee of the company, to translate the work into Chinese. The work introduces the characteristics of the British people, society, and their trading activities in China. See Su Ching, *Malixun yu Zhongwen yinshua chuban* 馬禮遜與中文印刷出版 [Robert Morrison and the Chinese printing and publishing] (Taipei: Taiwan xuesheng shuju, 2000), 51, 113–29; Li Hsiu-chin 李秀琴, "Yishixingtai yu fanyi: Yi Malixun *Dayingguo renshi lüeshuo* Zhongyiben wei li" 意識形態與翻譯：以馬禮遜《大英國人事略說》中譯本為例 [Ideology and translation: Robert Morrison's Chinese translation of *A Brief Account of English Character*], *Newsletter of the Institute of Chinese Literature and Philosophy, Academia Sinica* 中國文哲研究通訊 22 (2) (June 2012): 73–74.
40. For example, Gützlaff's expression of his sympathy in *Right and Wrong* toward the dire situation of the Chinese merchants who were oftentimes falsely prosecuted as traitors, being punished, tortured, or even killed in prison (只可惜匪類誣告，篤實忠厚商賈與遠客公道貿易，妄稱之漢奸，令之或受罰，或拷打，或冤獄斃命) (p. 15) is slightly modified from *Dayingguo renshi lüeshuo* (又且民商因被誣告，以與英國人勾結為漢奸，則致罰銀，或拷打，或冤獄斃命). See Robert Morrison tran., *Dayingguo renshi lüeshuo* 大英國人事略說 (Malacca: Anglo-Chinese College, 1832), 2.
41. David K. Y. Chng, "Dujin niaolong li de nahan: Guoshili zhengzhi xiaoshuo *Shifei luelun* xi lun," 265. For the relationship between Gützlaff and Jardine, Matheson & Co., see Alain Le Pichon, ed., *China Trade and Empire: Jardine, Matheson & Co. and the Origins of British Rule in Hong Kong, 1827–1843* (Oxford and New York: Oxford University Press, 2006), 144–45, 196–98, 205–6, 216–18, 426.

significant, factors of consideration in the process of his construction of the British image in the two novels. Most tellingly, not a single line about opium is found in *Right and Wrong* and *Great Britain*, against the background that opium importation to China grew substantially in the early nineteenth century, from 4,570 chests in 1800 to 23,570 chests in 1832.[42] Gützlaff should be well aware of the adverse consequences of the discussion of opium trade, strictly speaking opium smuggling, which might not only intensify the Chinese discontent and hostility toward Britain but also spoil all the efforts made in his two novels for the advocacy of equal trade.

Given his intricate connections with various British groups, it is highly likely for Gützlaff to take into account the complicated missionary/religious background, commercial interest, and political consideration behind the text, including the will of British missionaries and the entrenched interest and benefits of the British merchants in China. Gützlaff's collaboration with the British merchants can be seen to be mutually beneficial for both parties. While Gützlaff succeeded in securing a wider space for his missionary endeavors, his patron relied heavily on Gützlaff's rare linguistic and literary skills for constructing a positive British image that would benefit the British commercial enterprise in China.

Conclusion

Karl Gützlaff makes conscientious efforts in *Right and Wrong* and *Great Britain* to deconstruct the negative imagination toward Westerners before reconstructing a positive image of Britain among the Chinese people of the early nineteenth century. He attempts to challenge imperial China's Sinocentric mentality, the Qing court's protectionist policy, and the widespread Chinese biases toward Western people, trade, and religion, specifically, regarding the Westerners/British as "barbarians," trading between the West and China as "tribute paying," and Christianity as the "heresy of Western barbarians." The removal of these misconceptions serves the function of paving the way for the subsequent depiction of Britain as the "supreme nation." On top of the construction of an image of a technologically advanced and military powerful Britain, Gützlaff offers his explanation that Britain's source of the strength and wealth lies in Christianity, which is embedded in the foundation of British civilization. The establishment of a free trade and equal diplomatic relationship might not be the ultimate objective for Gützlaff's textual depiction of Britain as the "supreme nation" and the upholder of religious orthodoxy. It is reasonable to suggest that Gützlaff, as a Protestant missionary, was more concerned with evangelization work in China. The positive portrayal of British culture in general and Christianity in particular aims to remove the prejudice of the majority of Chinese toward Christianity. While these novels

---

42. Jonathan D. Spence, *The Search for Modern China*, 130.

were sponsored by British merchants with an intended purpose of commercial and political propaganda, Gützlaff took full advantage of this hard-to-come-by opportunity to clear some obstacles for the opening of China and for the promotion of missionary causes.

5
"Sacred Heart" and the Appropriation of Catholic Faith in Nineteenth-Century China

Ji Li[1]

On June 18, 1863, the feast of the Sacred Heart, a ceremony was held in Guangzhou. Attended by the viceroy of Liangguang, government officials, as well as missionaries and priests, the ceremony was to bless the cornerstone of a Catholic church. Two foundation stones were blessed and laid. The Latin words "Jerusalem 1863" were engraved on the east one and the words "Roma 1863" on the west one.[2] This grand project, which took the next twenty-five years to complete, was designed by French architects and financially supported by the French Emperor Napoleon III (1801–73) and donations from French Catholics. The church was later named the Cathedral of the Sacred Heart of Jesus, "one of the most beautiful religious monuments of the Far East."[3]

This is neither the first nor the last cathedral of Sacred Heart of Jesus in China built by the French. In October 1863, four months after the ceremony mentioned above, the construction of the Dazhangzhuang Sacred Heart Cathedral started in Zhangzhuang, Xian County of Hebei Province. With donations from French Catholics, this church was built and supervised by Bishop Adrien Languillat (1808–78), a French Jesuit and vicar apostolic of Southeastern Zhili (1856–64) and Jiangnan (1864–78). This cathedral was later praised as *Huabei diyi tang* (華北第一堂 the most magnificent Catholic Church in north China).[4] In fact, in the second half of the nineteenth century, more than twenty Sacred Heart cathedrals were built all over China. If, as Raymond Jonas argues, "the Sacred Heart defined 'Frenchness' for French Catholicism" within France

---

1. This chapter is supported by the General Research Fund from the Research Grants Council of Hong Kong Special Administrative Region, China (Project no. HKU17405414: "Making Religion, Making Local Society: The Social History of a Catholic Village in Northeast China").
2. Zhao Maogao 招茂皋, "Mantan shishi Tianzhu tang" 漫談石室天主堂 [On the Catholic Church of Shishi], in *Guangzhou jiuhua* 廣州舊話 [Histories of Guangzhou], ed. Chen Zehong 陳澤泓 and Chen Jinhong 陳錦鴻 (Guangzhou: Guangzhou chubanshe, 2002), Vol. 1, 210–11.
3. Valentine Montanar, "Kwang-tung," *The Catholic Encyclopedia* (New York: Robert Appleton Company, 1910), Vol. 8. Available at http://www.newadvent.org/cathen/08712b.htm. Accessed on November 20, 2014.
4. Qi Yongquan 祁永泉, "Zhangjiazhuang zongtang shihua" 張家莊總堂史話 [History of Zhangjiazhuang Catholic Church], in *Xianxian wenshi ziliao* 獻縣文史資料 [Cultural and historical data of Xian County] (Xianxian: The Committee of Cultural and Historical Data of Xianxian, 1987), 88.

for the nineteenth century and much of the twentieth century,[5] the considerable number of the Sacred Heart Cathedrals built by the French in China may showcase a similar story in the Far East: the Sacred Heart also signified France's "ecclesiastical colony" in nineteenth-century China.[6]

The enormous popularity of the devotion to the Sacred Heart of Jesus after the French Revolution (1789–99) demonstrates Catholic resistance in republican France. It was also one of the most popular devotions promoted by French missionaries in late imperial China. This chapter examines the devotion to and the appropriation of the Sacred Heart of Jesus in the nineteenth century from a comparative perspective. Catholic missionaries introduced the devotion to the Sacred Heart of Jesus to China. But the devotion within this cross-cultural context has been reinterpreted and appropriated by ordinary Chinese Catholics. I highlight such a boundary-crossing adaptation by looking into a set of letters written by Chinese Catholic women to their French priest in 1871, in which they attempted to fuse religious devotion with the articulation of personal emotions. By means of writing, these ordinary Chinese Catholics played with the ambiguity between Catholic doctrines and everyday discourses. The remarkable in-betweenness character provides us with a different angle to further explore the grassroots-level encounters between Christianity and Chinese people. I argue that the nineteenth-century political context facilitated the secularized appropriation of religious devotions in both France and China, which consequently changed the spiritual exercise such as the devotion to the Sacred Heart.

Origin and transformation in France

Devotion to the Sacred Heart of Jesus is one of the most widely practiced devotions in the Catholic Church. It denotes a religious devotion to Jesus' physical heart. Pictured with his bleeding heart, the Sacred Heart of Jesus represents his divine love for humankind and stresses the central Christian concept of loving and adoring the Son of God. The devotion to the Sacred Heart of Jesus can trace its tradition to the time of St. John and St. Paul, when devotion to the love of God was emphasized by the Church. In the eleventh and twelfth centuries, "the first unmistakable indications of devotion to the Sacred Heart" have been found in the Benedictine or Cistercian monasteries where "the wounded Heart was gradually reached, and the wound in the Heart symbolized the wound of love."[7]

---

5. Raymond Jonas, *France and the Cult of the Sacred Heart: An Epic Tale for Modern Times* (Berkeley: University of California Press, 2000), 7.
6. "Ecclesiastical colony" is a term borrowed from Ernest P. Young's book, *Ecclesiastical Colony: China's Catholic Church and the French Religious Protectorate* (New York: Oxford University Press, 2013).
7. Jean Bainvel, "Devotion to the Sacred Heart of Jesus," *The Catholic Encyclopedia*, Vol. 7. Available at http://www.newadvent.org/cathen/07163a.htm. Accessed on December 1, 2014.

The modern form of this devotion originates with a seventeenth-century French Catholic nun, Marguerite-Marie Alacoque (1647–90), who allegedly learned the devotion directly from Jesus in visions from 1673 to 1675. Alacoque was a young humble gentlewoman who entered the Order of the Visitation in the monastery at Paray-le-Monial at the age of twenty. In the convent, she became renowned for her practice of poverty, chastity, and obedience. In 1673, Alacoque recorded her first revelation. "He made me rest for a long time on His divine breast where He discovered to me the wonders of His love and the inexplicable secrets of His Sacred Heart."[8] The visions of Alacoque were, however, not unique in the history of spirituality in medieval Europe. It was in fact part of a long tradition of mystical celebration of Jesus' wound, which in many ways was similar to those appearing to thirteenth-century nuns such as St. Lutgarde d'Aywières (1182–1246), Béatrice de Nazareth (1200–1268), and St. Gertrude de Great (1256–ca. 1302).

Alacoque's visions brought new attention to this particular devotion in the seventeenth century, when France was in a critical period of the Counter-Reformation: the Jesuits were battling their rivals, the Jansenists.[9] Pope Innocent X (1574–1655) first condemned the Jansenist doctrines, including their discouragement of the use of the sacraments, notably the Holy Eucharist, as heresy in 1653. The importance of associating the Holy Eucharist with devotion to the Sacred Heart was later elaborated by Pope Pius XI (1857–1939) in his *Encyclical on Reparation to the Sacred Heart* (1928): "so in the most turbulent times of a more recent age, when the Jansenist heresy, the most crafty of them all, hostile to love and piety toward God, was creeping in and preaching that God was not to be loved as a father but rather to be feared as an implacable judge; then the most benign Jesus showed his own most Sacred Heart to the nations."[10] In contrast to Jansenism, the Jesuit order, defender of the Catholic doctrines, promoted the image of the Sacred Heart of Jesus as a symbol of divine love for humanity since the late seventeenth century. The popularity of the Sacred Heart of Jesus, according to some scholars, was part of the long humanistic tradition in the Catholic Church, especially due to the promotion of seventeenth-century missionary humanists such as de Sales, Eudes, and de la Colombière.[11] Promoted by the Jesuits in the eighteenth century, devotion to the Sacred Heart of Jesus became a popular theme targeted at lay Catholics and responding to religious reforms. After the eighteenth century, the

---

8. Saint Margaret Mary, *Gems of Thought from Saint Margaret Mary* (New York: Benziger Brothers, 1931), xiii–xiv.
9. On the battle between the Jesuits and the Jansenists, see Dale Van Kley, *The Religious Origins of the French Revolution: From Calvin to the Civil Constitution, 1560–1791* (New Haven: Yale University Press, 1996), 115–18.
10. Pope Pius XI, *Miserentissimus redemptor* (May 8, 1928). Available at http://w2.vatican.va/content/pius-xi/en/encyclicals/documents/hf_p-xi_enc_08051928_miserentissimus-redemptor.html. Accessed on December 15, 2014.
11. Alice B. Kehoe, "The Sacred Heart: A Case for Stimulus Diffusion," *American Ethnologist* 6 (4) (1979): 763–71.

Jansenists began to dismiss it as a sentimental and embarrassingly anti-intellectual devotion. The devotion of the Sacred Heart of Jesus, seen as a symbol for the defense of "God and King" during the French Revolution, was then associated with the devout and ignorant peasants. And the Sacred Heart as an object of Catholic devotion became a dominant symbol of royalty and an emblem of counterrevolution.[12]

In 1800, the Congregation of the Sacred Hearts of Jesus and Mary was established by Pierre-Marie-Joseph Coudrin (1768–1837). In the following decades, the emphasis on sentimental devotions slowly ushered the later burst of a new piety movement. Between 1840 and 1880, the emphasis on the devotion to the Sacred Heart of Jesus, the Immaculate Heart of Mary and the Holy Family "expressed the growing populist orientation of the revivalist Catholic Church against the anticlerical religious reform of the liberal-minded bourgeoisie."[13] To promote religious revival, the Sacred Heart became a central icon not only in France but also worldwide, until the Second Vatican Council (1962–65).

Introduction and adaption in China

In the nineteenth century, a new wave of overseas missionary enthusiasm welled up in France. With the issuing of Napoleon's Concordat of 1801 and the following restoration of three major missionary organizations—the Lazarists, the seminary of the Saint-Esprit, and the Missions Étrangères de Paris (MEP)—in 1804, the Catholic missionary movement began to revitalize and gradually became overwhelmingly French.[14] The revival of Marguerite-Marie Alacoque's case for canonization fits well with other restoration initiatives. The revived missionary movement witnessed the most extensive spread of Catholicism to other parts of the world, accompanied by France's worldwide agenda of colonialization.[15] In China, after the eighteenth-century prohibition of Christian missions, the expansion of French control over the Catholic faith in China was gradually confirmed between 1844 and 1865 by a number of treaties between the Qing court and the French government.[16]

---

12. This argument is well illustrated by Raymond Jonas' study in *France and the Cult of the Sacred Heart*.
13. Patrick Taveirne, *Han–Mongol Encounters and Missionary Endeavors: A History of Scheut in Ordos (Hetao), 1874–1911* (Leuven: Leuven University Press, 2004), 293.
14. J. P. Daughton, *An Empire Divided: Religion, Republicanism, and the Making of French Colonialism, 1880–1914* (New York: Oxford University Press, 2006), 33–38.
15. The MEP, for example, finally got the opportunity to expand into the southwest, southeast, and northeast borderlands of the empire. Within a single decade, the MEP had founded five new missions in China: Mongolia-Manchuria (1830), Tibet (1846), and Guangdong, Guangxi, and Hainan (all in 1848). In all, between 1822 and 1921, the MEP sent 2,932 missionaries to East Asia, in comparison to only 287 in the period from 1658 to 1822. Missions Étrangères de Paris, *Les Missions Étrangères de Paris: Inde, Indochine, Chine, Thibet, Corée, et Japon* (Paris: Séminaire des Missions Étrangères, 1921), 9.
16. These treaties included the Treaty of Whampoa (1844), the Treaty of Tianjin (1858), the Convention of Beijing (1860), and the Berthemy Convention (1865).

With the French "ecclesiastical colony" established in China in the nineteenth century, devotion to the Sacred Heart of Jesus also became popular in many China missions under the protectorate of the French government.[17] The devotion was not new to China as a modern form of spiritual exercise. As early as the seventeenth century, when the French Jesuits arrived in China, they brought with them a new impetus to the practice of the spiritual exercises. This type of retreat that the French Jesuits introduced to China was "often given to illiterate people, evolved in the direction of popular missions with catechesis, preaching, singing, commentaries on painted images, etc."[18] In the eighteenth century, inspired by the French spiritual tendencies of the previous century, French Jesuits such as Joseph Anne-Marie de Moyriac de Mailla (1669–1748), Antoine Gaubil (1689–1759), Alexandre de La Charme (1695–1767), and Francois Xavier Dentrecolles (1664–1741) began to promote the meditations for daily life and produced many writings for spiritual exercises. De Mailla, according to Nicolas Standaert, "certainly was affected by the devotion to the Sacred Heart as strongly propagated by Jean Croiset (1656–1738). The *abrégé de la devotion au Sacré Coeur* as mentioned in the *Lettres édifiantes et curieusΩes* refers to a translation of one of the editions of Croiset's *La devotion au Sacré Coeur de Notre-Seigneur Jésus-Christ* (first edition Dijon: Claude Michard, 1680), entitled *Shengxin guitiao* 聖心規條 (or *Shengxin guicheng* 聖心規程) (ca. 1740–45)."[19] The text includes a brief introduction that explains the essence of the devotion revealed to Marguerite-Marie Alacoque and the manner of praying the rosary in honor of the Sacred Heart of Jesus and the Sacred Heart of Mary. It is followed by the practice of the devotion, partly adapted to the local situations, and the rules for receiving the attached indulgence, or a remission before God of the temporal punishment due to sins. The central part consists of the prayers and the litanies of the Sacred Heart of Jesus and the Sacred Heart of Mary.

Given the spiritual exercise promoted by their predecessors, the nineteenth-century missionaries followed the domestic revival of Catholicism to spread popular devotions in China. They sought to substitute local popular religious traditions for popular Catholic devotions. They hoped to root the Catholic faith in the hearts of local Chinese converts. Therefore, they introduced the cordial devotions such as the Scared Heart of Jesus and Immaculate Heart of Mary, the Holy Family, the Guardian Angels and Saints, which had been nurtured in the sodalities of their rural towns and minor seminaries in Europe.

The nineteenth-century popular devotion to the Sacred Heart of Jesus and Mary with their colorful icons and statues appealed to the Chinese Catholics, who wore crucifixes, scapulars, and rosaries. The faithful also displayed their icons and liturgical

---

17. See Taverine, *Han-Mongol Encounters and Missionary Endeavors*, 434.
18. Nicolas Standaert, "The Spiritual Exercises of Ignatius of Loyola in the China Mission of the 17th and 18th Centuries," *Archivum Historicum Societatis Iesu LXXXI* (2012): 104–5.
19. Standaert, "The Spiritual Exercises of Ignatius of Loyola," 119.

calendars at home. Popular prayers in literary Chinese include "Stop! The Sacred Heart of Jesus is here together with me" (亟止步！耶穌聖心與吾偕焉). The missionaries have described Chinese converts' preservation of Catholic icons in nineteenth-century Mongolia: "the blue and red icons of the Sacred Hearts of Mary and Jesus respectively, a yellow cross on red paper and the Catholic devotional calendar substituted for the 'idols.'"[20]

The Church that had a statue of the Sacred Heart of Jesus became particularly appealing. In 1875, the Sacred Heart of Jesus Diocesan Cathedral of Shenyang, the largest Catholic Church in northeast China, began to be built. In the following decades, more Sacred Heart of Jesus cathedrals were built in other places of northeast China, including Harbin, Jilin, and Changchun. The Church promoted the icon and statue of the Sacred Heart of Jesus to compete with popular religiosity in local communities. Similar to the French domestic situation, in which the spread of the popular devotion was linked to Catholic education in rural areas, the instruction of the new devotion in China also owed much to the widespread Catholic schools or catechismal classrooms.[21] Catholic education promoted literacy in rural society, especially among female converts, hence facilitating local converts' appropriation of the popular Catholic devotion into their personal articulation of religiosity.

Also noticeable is that, in the second half of the nineteenth century, China was involved in a series of domestic crises and foreign threats. The "unequal treaties" signed between the Qing court and the Western powers paved the way for the missionaries to enter inland rural areas of China. Working with rural Chinese converts, who were mostly illiterate, the missionaries felt the urgent need to instruct Catholic faith and doctrines to these ordinary converts by introducing and promoting popular modes of devotion. Different from their predecessors, most nineteenth-century French missionaries worked in the countryside under the supervision of religious orders and the protection of the French government. This particular political context facilitated the secularized appropriation of religious devotion to the Sacred Heart in late Qing China.

Appropriation in the Du letters

The Du letters were written in 1871 by three Chinese Catholic women from a small village in today's Liaozhong County of northeast China. In the letters, the Du women emotionally requested the return of "Father Lin," or Dominique Maurice Pourquié (1812–71), a French missionary of the MEP who had worked in northeast China for

---

20. Taveirne, *Han–Mongol Encounters and Missionary Endeavors*, 471.
21. For the discussion on Catholic education in nineteenth-century Manchuria, see Ji Li, "Dissemination of Catholicism in Nineteenth-Century Northeast China: A Study of MEP Archives on Missions Mandchourie," in *Manuscripts, Memories, Localization, and Explanations: New Perspectives on Christianity in Northeast China and Sino-Western Cultural Exchange*, ed. Zhao Yifeng (Shanghai: Shanghai People's Publishing House, 2013), 107–27.

more than twenty years before he returned to Paris in 1870, due to illness.²² The letters came from three of Pourquié's Chinese Catholic women: Colette Du or Du Xiao'erniu (杜小二妞 the second daughter of the Du family), Marie Du or Du Xiaoshiyi (杜小十一 the eleventh of the Du family), and Philomene Du or Du Xiaodazi (杜小大子 the eldest of the Du family).

The Du women are unknown to history even though at the end of the letters they write their Chinese surnames, followed immediately by their baptismal Christian names. None of them, however, has a formal Chinese given name. Colette, Marie, and Philomene all carry Chinese names that merely reflect their birth order in the family. The namelessness of the Du women is common in rural Chinese society, but the Du women are uncommon among nameless rural Chinese women, for they all have their own Christian names. Marie, Colette, and Philomene are three common Christian names in the register of MEP's Manchuria Mission. According to Jean Baptiste Franclet's (1822–1907) 1854 register of Catholic families in thirteen Catholic villages in the mountainous region of western Manchuria, Marie is the most popular Christian name for local Catholic women.²³

Besides their Chinese and Christian names, the Dus calling themselves "God's little daughters" in the letters is another important appellation for deciphering their identity. "God's little daughter" is the literal translation of *xiao shennü* (小神女). *Xiao* means "little"; *shen* means "god," "spiritual," or "divine"; and *nü* means "daughter" or "girl." The term *shennü*, which to my knowledge does not appear in any other official Chinese Christian documents, seems to be unique to northeast China. It may refer to Catholic nuns or lay women affiliated with Catholic communities of virgins, such as the Du women. In some Chinese documents, they are often called *shouzhennü* (守貞女), or "girls who keep their virginity," who usually took the vow of chastity and continued to stay with their families without marrying out.²⁴

The Du letters arrived in Paris in 1871, unfortunately a few months after Father Pourquié's death. The priest passed away, but the letters were preserved in the church archives. These letters present, perhaps for the first time, the private sentiments of rural Chinese Catholic women. One of the Du women wrote, "Merciful father, if you are recovered, God's daughter begs you to come back!" "When God's daughter realizes that [she] cannot listen to your instruction any more, God's daughter misses you and

---

22. Du Letters, AMEP 0564: 569a–572a.
23. Covering 18 Catholic villages in today's western Liaoning, missionary Jean Baptiste Franclet's 1854 register of Catholic families recorded altogether 804 Chinese Catholics who belonged to 170 individual households which shared only 84 surnames. Of them, Marie is the most popular Christian name for females: Out of 385 Catholic women in Franclet's register, 102 are named Marie. Jean Baptiste Franclet, "Relevé: Géographique, Statistique, Enumératif, Historique & Magnifique du District des Monts Amba," AMEP 0563: 629–44.
24. For the study of Chinese Christian Virgins in northeast China, see Ji Li, "Chinese Christian Virgins and Catholic Communities of Women in Northeast China," *The Chinese Historical Review* 20 (1) (May 2013): 16–33.

cries."²⁵ Candid expressions, awkward handwriting, and numerous writing mistakes in the letters are, however, mixed up with their skillful use of religious vocabularies.

In her letter, Philomene Du vividly describes her desperation by using the passionate language of devotion.

> Father, please beg God to forgive God's daughter's big sin that [I] fail to live up to God's kindness. Jesus and Holy Ghost, please bring my father back! My father, you know all my big sins, big pride, weakness, and indifference. If you cannot come back to pray for God's daughter and minister daily mass, please [remember to] pray for God's daughter whenever you pray to God. My father, you said that you wanted God's daughter to enter the Sacred Heart of Jesus. Father, please ask Jesus to teach me how to enter the Sacred Heart and stay in there forever. Sometimes when [I] realize that [I] do not know on which day [I] can see my father again, God's daughter's heart suffers more. God's daughter [wants to] enter the Sacred Heart of Jesus to meet my father. Then Jesus can help me remember my father's instruction. My father, since you have gone, there is no other priest like you who knows my heart. The words that you told God's daughter come to my mind now. Other priests do not understand what I am saying and I cannot understand what they say. God's daughter's heart is so bitter.²⁶

The most frequent and distinctive devotion used in the above passage is the "Sacred Heart of Jesus" (*Yesu Shengxin* 耶穌聖心). The other two letters by Colette and Marie Du were written in a similar pattern. Apparently, the vision of Alacoque deeply affected the three Chinese women. But different from the popular Catholic devotions in Europe, the "Sacred Heart of Jesus" in the Du letter is intentionally appropriated by these female converts to articulate personal feelings and emotional requests on the absence of a foreign priest. Philomene, Colette, and Marie all use the "Sacred Heart" in their letters to describe their emotional attachment to the priest. In contrast to the vision of Alacoque, the Du women envision the Sacred Heart in relation to their beloved father. Philomene enters the heart of Jesus by herself to meet her father: "God's daughter enters the Sacred Heart of Jesus to meet merciful father. Then Jesus helps me remember merciful father's instruction." In Philomene's mind, she can see Pourquié again only if she enters the Sacred Heart. Colette has a similar expectation: "I hope to enter the Sacred Heart of Jesus just as you (my merciful father) do." "My merciful father, if I want your teaching, I will read it in the Sacred Heart of Jesus." Marie knows the most religious terms: "My merciful father [and] my Jesus please teach me to love Jesus wholeheartedly, to enter the Sacred Heart of Jesus, to become like Jesus, and to understand how to love God the Holy Trinity." As the Du women understand, entering the Sacred Heart of Jesus is the best means to meet their father and to define their religiosity. Unlike Alacoque, who is taken and led by Jesus to enter his heart, the Du

---

25. Marie Du Letter, AMEP 0564: 569a, lines 2–3. The letters are written in Chinese without any punctuation marks. I have translated the letters literally as far as possible to preserve the original clumsy writing style.
26. Philomene Du Letter (May 1, 1871), AMEP 0564: 572a, lines 12–19.

women all envision entering the Sacred Heart by themselves. For the Dus, the purpose of entering the Sacred Heart is intertwined with both spiritual pursuit and personal desire to meet their father and recall his teachings.

The Du women appropriate devotion as a personal appeal. Theologically in the devotion, there are two elements: a sensible element as the Heart of flesh and a spiritual element that the Heart of flesh recalls and represents. From the Catholic Church's point of view, "the word *heart* awakens, first of all, the idea of a material heart . . . which we vaguely realize as intimately connected not only with our own physical, but with our emotional and moral life"[27] The devotion is based entirely upon the symbolism of the heart. Hence, there is a close theological and philosophical association between the material, the metaphorical, and the symbolic sense of the word "heart." This symbolic association is an important foundation for the later popularization of the devotion in different cultural contexts. To the Du women, the Sacred Heart signifies only the Heart of flesh. The love of Jesus and the moral life of Jesus that is metaphorically signified and symbolized by the word "heart" are missing. The vividly described meetings with Pourquié in the Sacred Heart easily transcend time and space, allowing the illusion that both "God's little daughters" and their "merciful father" participate in the same present moment. They also easily bridge the gap of divinity between the priest and his converts. The women's repetitive use of the Sacred Heart to request Pourquié's return becomes a focal point of two intersecting devotional experiences: to God and to their priest. Their exclamations to Jesus are always juxtaposed with the exclamation of "father, my merciful father." Although the modern devotion to the Sacred Heart focuses on lay Catholics' attention to Jesus, in exploiting the forms and techniques of devotion, the Du women's ritual fascination with the Sacred Heart cultivates and articulates their own personal and emotional attachment to the priest. This displacement of sacred devotion and private emotion demonstrates the Du women's appropriation of what they learned from the Christian religion. The women display a gift for employing forms drawn from the religious context to demonstrate their own personal concerns.

As shown by the Du letters in the late nineteenth century, the devotion to the Sacred Heart of Jesus was not unfamiliar to rural Chinese Catholic women. They appropriated the devotion not only to articulate their personal feelings but also to express their preference for a "traditional" lifestyle of meditation. The later part of the Dus' letters explains the reason why they wrote the letters to request the priest's return. Philomene stated "now, there is no priest in residence in Santaizi. Father Bao has established a convent, but God's daughter does not want to join them. I cannot accept their rules. Whenever I think of staying in their convent, I feel upset. Whenever I recall your ideas and the convent you wanted to establish, I feel calm." Marie Du also wrote, "I cannot obey other regulations. I feel sad. I do not want to join them. I want

---

27. Bainvel, "Devotion to the Sacred Heart of Jesus." Accessed on December 1, 2014.

to join the Carmelite Order."[28] The Carmelite Order is also called the Order of Our Lady of Mt. Carmel in English, or Ordo fratrum Beatae Mariae de monte Carmelo in Latin. It was established by an Italian named Bertold on Mount Carmel in about the mid-twelfth century. The Carmelite Order entered China in 1869 and mainly worked in Shanghai, Chongqing, Hong Kong, and Kunming.[29] In 1874, the order established a convent in Shanghai. The Carmelite Order had no convents in Manchuria in the 1870s. The Du women might have heard about this order from Pourquié or from other priests. Unlike the nuns of other convents such as the Sacred Heart of Mary, who were trained to do active mission work, the nuns of the Carmelite Order were devoted to a life of prayer and contemplation. It seems that the contemplative life is what Pourquié introduced to the Du women. Philomene mentioned in her letter that Pourquié had wanted to establish a convent before he left Manchuria. Although the women did not mention the name of this convent, their letters suggest that the convent proposed by Pourquié would have been similar to those of the Carmelites and would have been devoted to contemplative religious life.

Most likely the Du women at Santaizi were aware of the different styles of religious communities and had their own preference on religious practice. A letter written at about the same time by another MEP missionary, Philibert Simon (1842–74), verified the story.

> M. Pourquié, June 2, 1871
>
> Mister and Revered Provicar,
>
> Here are the letters of your girls. I want to give you a translation of the Chinese characters, but I have absolutely no time. So I send you the rest of their letters sincerely. They always do the same things. Now the poor girls are bitterly struggling in a small storm. They do not want to enter the convent of M. Boyer because it applies only to active religious life. As they trust in me, I will make sure I can resolve this fight for the good of their souls. They have to go to the convent of the Sacred Heart of St. Mary. If in a year the block in their hearts is cleared, they will become saints. If the same disorder persists, they can simply leave. I advise them never to enter an institute, for it is of real repugnance. It is difficult for perfection to exist in the obstruction—All I fear is that they have wilted for the trifles and never get worked up—Pray for them. I think they are material to become saints—I second M. Boyer by all my efforts to lead this small foundation to a good end.[30]

---

28. Marie Du Letter, AMEP 0564: 569a, line 21.
29. Tiedemann, *Reference Guide to Christian Missionary Societies in China: From the Sixteenth to the Twentieth Century* (Armonk, NY: M.E. Sharpe, 2009), 54.
30. Philibert Simon Letter (June 2, 1871). AMEP 0564: 557–60.

Simon's letter summarizes the conflict between the Du women and Joseph Boyer (1824–87) and tells Pourquié that the Du women refused to enter the newly established convent by Joseph Boyer, called Father Bao by his Chinese converts.[30] The Carmelite Order mentioned by Marie Du promoted virtue through austerity and poverty, as well as meditation. These rules were different from Boyer's convent, which encouraged active participation in mission work. The resistance of the Du women demonstrated a tension between the Catholic Church's effort in institutionalization and the "traditional" Catholic lifestyle chosen by Chinese Catholic women, especially Chinese Christian virgins like the Dus.[31]

Therefore, the Du women wrote to Father Pourquié to request help. But they also wrote to articulate their religiosity. Their writing style, different from most other formal letters from Chinese Catholics, turns out to be very private and emotional. Religious discourses, such as the devotion to the Sacred Heart of Jesus, become the major expression template for them to imitate and to articulate their personal feelings. The popularity of Catholic devotion in nineteenth-century northeast China contextualizes the religious discourses presented in the Du letters. Patrick Taveirne describes a similar process of introducing the devotion of the Sacred Heart in Mongolia as a substitute for "local religious traditions (superstitions) for popular Roman Catholic devotion."[32] The Scheut missionaries chose the cordial devotion to the Sacred Heart of Jesus for their evangelization, for the popular devotion had appealed to rural lay Catholics back in their home country. This transcultural appropriation provided space for a set of new religious discourses to rural Chinese Catholics, especially to women, who could use it to articulate religiosity in their own terms.

The Sacred Heart of Mary

Similar to the devotion to the Sacred Heart of Jesus, the devotion to the Sacred Heart of Mary is one of the popular forms of meditation and spiritual exercise in northern China and appealed to many Chinese Catholics in the rural areas. The Sacred Heart of Mary or the Immaculate Heart of Mary is a devotional name used to refer to the interior life of the Blessed Virgin Mary. It is the expressive symbol of Mary's "joys and sorrows, her virtues and hidden perfections, and, above all, her virginal love for God, her maternal love for her Divine son, and her motherly and compassionate love for her sinful and miserable children."[33] The history of the devotion to the Sacred Heart of Mary is connected to the devotion to the Sacred Heart of Jesus. According to church

---

30. Ibid.
31. For discussion about the conflict and its historical background, see Ji Li, "Chinese Christian Virgins and Catholic Communities of Women in Northeast China," 16–33.
32. Taveirne, *Han–Mongol Encounters and Missionary Endeavors*, 305.
33. Bainvel, "Devotion to the Immaculate Heart of Mary." http://www.newadvent.org/cathen/07168a.htm. Accessed on December 1, 2014.

historians, "there is a close parallel" between the two devotions, for both the Sacred Heart of Jesus and the Immaculate of Heart of Mary are symbols of the sacred physical heart and divine love. The love of Mary symbolized by the heart is twofold: the divine love by which God has made a choice of her and in which he has enfolded her.[34]

The devotion to the Sacred Heart of Mary, although associated with the devotion to the Sacred Heart of Jesus, has its own history of development. From the end of the eleventh century to the twelfth century, slight indications of a regular devotion were perceived in a sermon by St. Bernard (1090–1153), from which an extract has been taken by the Church and used in the Offices of the Compassion and the Seven Sorrows. In the second half of the sixteenth and the first half of the seventeenth centuries, ascetic authors dwelled upon this devotion at greater length. St. Jean Eudes (1601–80) propagated the devotion to make it public and to have a feast celebrated in honor of the Heart of Mary, first at Autun in 1648 and later in a number of French dioceses. He founded several religious societies interested in upholding and promoting the devotion and published his book on the *Coeur Admirable* (Admirable heart) in 1681. In 1725, Père de Gallifet combined the cause of the Heart of Mary with that of the Heart of Jesus in order to obtain Rome's approbation of the two devotions and the institution of the two feasts. In 1729 his project was defeated, and in 1765 the two causes were separated to assure the success of the principal one. In 1855, the Congregation of Rites finally approved the Office and Mass of the Most Pure Heart of Mary without, however, imposing them upon the Universal Church.[35]

As the devotion to the Sacred Heart of Jesus and to the Sacred Heart of Mary became popular within France in the nineteenth century, due to the expansion of Catholic missions in Asia, the devotion and the institutions bearing the same name also became popular in China. The Sisters of the Sacred Heart of Mary was the first indigenous community of Catholic women in northeast China. Before it was officially approved by the Holy See in 1932, it had had a presence in the region for more than eight decades. Bishop Emmanuel-Jean-François Verrolles (1805–78), the first Vicar Apostolic of the Manchuria Mission, first established a community of the Virgins of the Sacred Heart of Mary in Xiaobajiazi in 1858, and he later founded a second house in Hulan.[36] This was the first form of communal religious life introduced to Catholic women in northeast China. In 1898, the Manchuria Mission was divided into the northern and the southern missions, and by the early twentieth century, the Virgins in the northern mission finally outnumbered those in the south. In 1938, the Apostolic Vicariate of Jilin had "188 professed Virgins, six novices, and thirteen postulants: eighty-three professed Virgins residing in twenty-four parishes and the rest in their convents. Their work consisted of catechetics and of service in schools,

---

34. Kevin McNamara, "Devotion to the Immaculate Heart of Mary," *The Furrow*, 36 (1) (1985): 599–604.
35. Bainvel, "Devotion to the Immaculate Heart of Mary." Accessed on December 1, 2014.
36. Tiedemann, *Reference Guide to Christian Missionary Societies in China*, 96.

orphanages, dispensaries, hospitals, etc."[37] In the southern mission, the Virgins joined the Sisters of the Providence of Portieux and helped them in orphanages and hospices. These Virgins later moved to Shenyang with the Sisters of Providence. In 1913, the MEP missionary Felice Choulet established a convent. During the chaos of the Second Sino-Japanese War and the Civil War in the 1930s and 1940s, the Sisters, led by Sister Hao Zhiying, first moved to Nanjing and later to Taiwan, and finally established their headquarters in Taizhong in the 1960s. About sixty sisters remained in Shenyang after 1949. Although not active, the convent survived various political movements in the following decades. In 1989, the convent began to recruit postulants, and it has more than ninety nuns today.

The legacy of the Sisters of the Sacred Heart of Mary in northeast China can be traced to the nineteenth century. As the Du women mentioned in their letters, the convent that Boyer wanted to establish in Santaizi was that of the Sacred Heart of Mary. The Du women refused to enter the convent because they could not accept its rules. Marie Du's letter makes clear that the women preferred a convent that emphasized contemplation, like the Carmelite Order, rather than one that encouraged an active religious life. The Sacred Heart of Mary was dedicated to active mission from the beginning. It required its Virgins to be trained before entering a period of probation, which lasted for at least six months. During the probation, the girls would receive instruction in basic theological knowledge and Catholic rituals. Then they would have the chance to enter a two-year period of novitiate. On satisfactory performance, the girls could then take vows of poverty, chastity, and obedience. These vows were temporary and were to be repeated annually for five to nine years until the Virgin took lifelong vows to be a Virgin of the Sacred Heart of Mary. The long process of training was very different from the practice of the Carmelite Order, which the Du women wanted to enter. When the Du women vividly described their encounters with Father Pourquié in the Sacred Heart of Jesus, they were describing their personal preference to this popular devotion. It is also possible that they were implicitly expressing their refusal to enter the institute of the Sacred Heart of Mary.

Devotion to the Sacred Heart of Jesus became highly political in France after the French Revolution and was associated with the Catholic Right in France. As the Sacred Heart defined "Frenchness" for French Catholicism, it was "an integral nationalism."[38] When this devotion, through systematic Catholic evangelical endeavors in nineteenth-century China, was introduced to ordinary Chinese Catholic converts, its original and political meanings were inevitably transformed in local and personal discourses. Many teachings and institutions bearing the names of Sacred Heart of Jesus or Sacred Heart of Mary appeared in China, instilling faith into these alien minds. At the same time, local believers through their limited religious education appropriated and

---

37. Ibid.
38. Jonas, *France and the Cult of the Sacred Heart*, 7.

reinterpreted this devotion in their own terms. Such boundary-crossing understanding not only signifies the transmission of a religious practice from one country to another, but also challenges the dichotomy between missionaries and converts: the religious discourse on the Sacred Heart in nineteenth-century China was not transmitted one way from Western evangelists to Chinese converts. Rather, it was mutually constructed by both parties, who found certain in-between space where they could negotiate with each other in reshaping the boundaries of the *self* and the *other*.

Conclusion

The Sacred Heart of Jesus is a key concept in Catholic theology, and the devotion to the Sacred Heart is part of the long tradition of Catholic spiritual exercise in Europe. There is a historical trajectory to view the transformation of the devotion to the Sacred Heart of Jesus from the medieval period to the early modern era. The modern form of the devotion, as revealed by the visions of Saint Marguerite-Marie Alacoque, is a product of the Catholic Counter-Reformation. This popular devotion in nineteenth-century France, manipulated by different political and religious players, finally became an emblem of counterrevolution. It reached its ultimate as a symbol of the royal in the construction of basilica of the Sacré-Coeur in Paris in March 1871, "a structure that celebrated the defeat of the people of Paris."[39]

In contrast to the symbolic meaning of royalty nurtured in French political culture, the Cathedrals of the Sacred Heart of Jesus constructed in nineteenth-century China may have displayed another set of meanings: a symbol of the success of the French religious protectorate in China and the celebration of France's "ecclesiastical colony" in East Asia. The devotion to the Sacred Heart of Jesus was introduced to Chinese Catholics as a key spiritual exercise that had been promoted since the seventeenth century. In the nineteenth century, this popular devotion was emphasized by Western missionaries with the main purpose to substitute indigenous religious practices. The local converts received the devotion as part of their catechismal education. However, the religious discourses associated with this popular devotion provided an opportunity for local converts to reinterpret the foreign discourse in their own terms and to organize their communal religious life in a new way.

Employment of the devotion of the Sacred Heart in the Du letters to demonstrate personal attachment makes it possible for religion more generally to serve as the cultural host for developing sentimental forms. The Du women's inner emotions are accented by the iconic object and vivid description. Later, in the early twentieth century, Chinese women writers would revel in exclamations of love and sexuality. But the Du women's articulation of personal sentiment simply borrows from the forms of religious devotion. In the second half of the nineteenth century, the lack of

---

39. Ibid., 2.

formal education for girls in rural China provided a nice opportunity for Western missionaries, whose religious education mingled spiritualties, sentiments, and passions. It empowered female converts to construct their individual contributions to the discourse of faith and religiosity.

The displacement of sacred devotion and private emotion demonstrates the Du women's gift to transform Western religious discourse to articulate their own individual and personal requests in a gendered Chinese context. They played upon ambiguities of religious languages across cultures, appropriating the spiritual forces of devotion to serve personal sentimental excesses. In turn, writing according to Catholic concepts and Chinese language becomes a means to construct a new in-between identity in the late Qing cross-cultural context.

6
Local Magistrates and Foreign Mendicants
Chinese Views of Shanxi's Franciscan Mission during the Late Qing

Anthony E. Clark

Introduction[1]

After the violence of the Boxer Uprising in 1900, a rash of missionary memoirs and hagiographies of Christian martyrs—European and Chinese—were published in Europe and North America, and as expected, in the wake of this era of Sino-Western tension, Western accounts portrayed China as "heathen," "backwards," and "ruthless." Among the most read and cited books from the post-Boxer era was Dr. Ebenezer Henry Edwards' memoir-cum-hagiography on the Protestant martyrs of Shanxi, entitled *Fire and Sword in Shansi*, which recounted in meticulous detail the anti-foreignism and anti-Christianism that spread through the province during the summer months of 1900.[2] In his opening sentence, Edwards wrote that:

> During the summer of 1900, while the eyes of the civilized world were turned towards Peking anxiously awaiting news of the beleaguered Legations, far away in the province of Shansi helpless men, women, and children—European and American—were being done to death.[3]

This is typical of Western sources on China in the early twentieth century; the "civilized world" watched China from afar while "uncivilized China" massacred Europeans and Americans. We might note, also, that foreign victims of Qing troop and Boxer violence were only a small portion of those who were killed in 1900; most victims were native Chinese.

---

1. I would like to acknowledge with special gratitude the kind support of the National Endowment for the Humanities/American Council of Learned Societies, the Chiang Ching-kuo Foundation, Minzu University of China, and the Bejing Center. I also thank, in particular, Dr. Wu Yinghui at Minzu University, Fr. Thierry Meynard, SJ, Fr. Roberto Ribeiro, SJ, and Fr. Jeremy Clarke, SJ, who have been most pleasant "office mates" at the Beijing Center. I also extend my gratitude to the archivists and staff at the archives and libraries consulted to complete this study.
2. See Ebenezer Henry Edwards, *Fire and Sword in Shansi: The Story of the Martyrdom of Foreigners and Chinese Christians* (London: Oliphant Anderson and Ferrier, 1903).
3. Edwards, *Fire and Sword in Shansi*, 20.

Since 1900, and perhaps even before, missionary representations of the "insidious" Chinese influenced Western depictions of China, and by the 1950s and 1960s there was a confluence between both missionary and secular portrayals. In 1907, the English Protestant missionary, W. E. Hipwell, recounted his impressions of a Chinese temple:

> I entered the temple for a few moments, but was compelled to withdraw quickly, on account of the horror by which I was overwhelmed as I watched those before the idol who with intense fervor besought the blessings which they desired... The place was reeking with sickening smoke, and horrible because of the almost manifest presence of the devil, glorying over these multitudes thus enslaved by him.[4]

Hipwell's description of China's indigenous religious culture is unflattering; followers of popular religions make offerings of "sickening smoke" to the devil, who has "enslaved" the people of China.

Only six years after Hipwell published this description in *The Church Missionary Gleaner*, an Anglican periodical, the English novelist Sax Rohmer (Arthur Henry Sarsfield Ward, 1883–1959) wrote a strikingly similar description of the lair of "the insidious Dr. Fu Manchu":

> From a plain brass bowl upon the corner of the huge table smoke writhed aloft... smoke faintly penciled through the air—from the burning perfume on the table— grew in volume, thickened, and wafted towards me in a cloud of grey horror.[5]

In other passages from Rohmer's novels, the reader is invited to "[i]magine a person, tall, lean and feline, high-shouldered, with a brow like Shakespeare and a face like Satan, a close-shaven skull, and long, magnetic eyes of the true cat-green."[6] Rohmer's representation of the "Satanic doctor" appears to have been inspired by Protestant descriptions of such Chinese temple worshippers, as one source describes them, "with their hideous, grotesque expressions, staring fixedly in front of them."[7]

To return to Shanxi: in his 1943 history of the Catholic martyrs of Shanxi, *La Testimonianza del Sangue*, Cipriani Silvestri, OFM, includes a line-drawn image of the Taiyuan governor Yuxian (毓賢 1842–1901), who orchestrated and conducted the massacre of thousands of Christians, which appears almost identical to conventional book cover and film representations of Rohmer's *Dr. Fu Manchu*.[8] In addition, later depictions of the mendicant friars and nuns of Shanxi who died under Yuxian's

---

4. W. E. Hipwell, "Union in Face of the Foe; or, Co-operation in Evangelistic Effort in China," *Church Missionary Gleaner* (December 1907), 185. I am indebted to Eric Reinders for alerting me to Hipwell's description quoted here.
5. Sax Rohmer, *The Insidious Dr. Fu Manchu* (Dover: New York, 1913/1998), 81–82.
6. Sax Rohmer, *The Return of Dr. Fu Manchu* (New York: A. L. Burt, 1916), 4.
7. "The Idol's Protection," *Homes* (January 1910), 4.
8. See Cipriani Silvestri, OFM, *La Testimonianza del Sangue: Biographie dei Beati Cinesi uccisi il 4, 7 e 9 luglio 1900* (Rome: S. Guisefpe al Trionfali, 1943), 43. Also see pp. 161 and 447 for other images mentioned in this study. This edition of Silvestri's book is held at the library of the Pontificia Università Antonianum in Rome.

command are characteristically hagiographical, theatrically presenting a tableau wherein the cultural lines between good (West) and evil (East) are unabashedly underscored; the victims of Yuxian's massacre are frequently seen below the impending figure of a Chinese executioner in the act of slaughtering a mendicant at prayer. During the first half-century following the Boxer Uprising, Western views of China were decidedly pejorative.[9] Western representations of China before the Boxer era, however, wavered between naïve adulation, such as the idyllic depictions of the Chinese "philosopher king" and caricatured Chinese beauties in European *chinoiserie* popularized in mid- to late seventeenth-century Europe, and the occasional imaginings of the "Yellow Peril," a phrase regrettably coined by Kaiser Wilhelm II (1859–1941) in 1895.[10]

I mention these Western views of China during the late imperial era only to highlight the mutual nature of cross-cultural misunderstanding and misrepresentation, and in this enterprise China had been an active participant. Perhaps the most extreme example of anti-Christian propaganda in China was the vitriolic text and illustrations of the *Bixie jishi* (辟邪紀實 A record of facts to ward off heterodoxy), published in 1861.[11] One of the more acerbic illustrations in this text, which encouraged severe forms of anti-foreignism, depicted an "Image of Feeding [Foreigners] Shit" (*Qi tuan guanfen tu* 齊團灌糞圖), while another depicted a Chinese person reclining on a bed while two European priests gouge out his eyes; the title of this caption reads: "Image of the pig grunt [homophone for Catholic] religionists cutting out eyes" (*Zhujiao wan yan tu* 豬叫〔主教〕剜眼圖).[12] Excrement was considered an apotropaic substance in imperial China; forcing Christians to eat feces was thought to hinder their practice of malicious magic. As this booklet was disseminated through Hunan and other provinces in northern China, its illustrations and anti-Christian descriptions are likely to have reached the common people and literati in Shanxi.

The first mendicant footsteps in Shanxi

The first Roman Catholic missionaries to enter Shanxi were not mendicant friars, but were rather Jesuits who had come to China in the footsteps of Matteo Ricci (Chinese name 利瑪竇, 1552–1610). The first Jesuit in Shanxi was Nicolas Trigault (Chinese name 金尼閣, 1577–1628), who opened a chapel in Jiangzhou (絳州) in 1624,

---

9. There are numerous post-1900 examples of pejorative Roman Catholic depictions of China. The widely disseminated works of Vincentian missionaries and their publications serve to illustrate how Western Catholic views of China had grown more negative after the Boxer Uprising. See J. M. Planchet, *Documents sur les martyrs de Pékin pendant la persécution des Boxeurs* (Beijing: Imprimerie des Lazaristes, 1920), and several letters reprinted in the *Annales de la Congregation de la Mission* dating after 1900.

10. For an example of late nineteenth-century uses of the term "Yellow Peril," see G. G. Rupert, *The Yellow Peril* (Britton, OK: Union Publishing, 1911), 9.

11. The *Bixie jishi* 辟邪紀實 [A record of facts to ward off heterodoxy] was authored under the nom de plume of Tianxia diyi shangxin ren 天下第一傷心人 or "the world's most heartbroken man" (Hunan 1861).

12. For these illustrations, see *Bixiejishi*.

and his nephew Michel Trigault (Chinese name 金彌格, 1602–67) was the first to bring Christianity to Taiyuan.¹³ Another Jesuit, Alphonse Vagnone (Chinese name 高一志／王豐肅, 1568–1640), later entered Shanxi, where he established pious associations and successfully earned the respect of the provincial authorities due to his ability to amalgamate Christianity with the hallowed virtues of Confucianism.¹⁴ The earliest official Chinese document that discusses the Catholic mission in Shanxi mentions Vagnone in complimentary terms. In an edict by the prefect of Jiangzhou published in 1635, the magistrate censured the emergence of "heterodox doctrines" that had spread throughout the county. After criticizing Buddhism and Daoism for "causing men's minds to become befuddled and disordered" (*Huoluan renxin* 惑亂人心), the Jesuit missionary is applauded.¹⁵

The edict praises the teachings and behavior of Father Vagnone, however, and after critical remarks about other religions the decree notes that:

> We are fortunate to have Mr. Gao, a Western Confucian, who cultivates virtue, serves Heaven, and loves others as himself. Because he imparts loyalty and filial piety as his principal teaching, he is given honor from our sagely Son of Heaven (emperor) and worthy ministers. Even the learned, officials, and all gentlemen revere him as their teacher and love him as a brother. The common people who follow his teachings are all transformed into virtuous persons.¹⁶

There are no complaints in this early document regarding Western foreigners or their religious teachings though I disagree somewhat with the way in which Fortunato Margiotti (1913–90), OFM, represents this edict in his study of Catholicism in Shanxi. Margiotti commends this decree as a proclamation "In Favor of the Catholic Religion" (In Favore della Religione Cattolica), but the magistrate nowhere mentions Christianity or Catholicism in his pronouncement. In fact, it is Vagnone's apparent Confucian tenets that are favored, and the Jesuit is referred to as a *Xiru* (西儒, or "Western Confucian"). It is clear that Vagnone had become, at least ostensibly, "Chinese"; his cultivated patina of a Chinese *literatus* underscored his "in-betweenness," being neither entirely Western nor entirely Chinese. Franciscan friars were assigned to the Shanxi mission in 1716, which was then combined with Shaanxi, and there are scant sources regarding Chinese impressions of the mendicants there until Sino-missionary tensions materialized following the calamitous events of the Opium War (1839–42). After the Sino-Western treaties of 1842, all of which favored and facilitated Western imperialist incursions into China, the Franciscan mission in Shanxi became increasingly powerful and visible. After 1860, Shanxi's cities and

---

13. Liu Anrong 劉安榮, *Shanxi Tianzhujiao shi yanjiu* 山西天主教史研究 [Research on the Roman Catholic history of Shanxi] (Taiyuan: Beiyue wenyi chubanshe, 2011), 34.
14. See Lazzaro Cattaneo, SJ, AL, Vice Province 1630, Hangzhou, September 12, 1631, BAJA 49-V-8:716v.
15. Fortunado Margiotti, OFM, *Il cottolicismo nello Shansi dale origini al 1738* (Rome: Edizioni "Sinica Franciscana," 1959), 594–96.
16. See Margiotti, 594. I have modified Margiotti's Italian translation of this edict.

countryside were progressively marked by large Franciscan churches with towering steeples. The Church of the Immaculate Conception, for example, was built by the Italian bishop Aloysius (Luigi) Moccagatta (Chinese name 江類思, 1809–91) in the provincial capital Taiyuan, near the city's north gate. The church's tall steeple, or clock tower (*zhonglou* 鐘樓) as it is called in Shanxi, appeared to challenge the two 52-meter-tall pagodas at Taiyuan's prominent Twin Pagoda Temple (Shuangta si 雙塔寺).[17] Suddenly a foreign building vied with the city's venerated religious monuments; it likely appeared to the Buddhists of Twin Pagoda Temple that a religious contest had begun. Local Chinese reflections—complaints, commendations, or otherwise—began to appear in earnest after the emergence of Boxer violence in northern China, especially after Yuxian's arrival at Taiyuan on April 19, 1900;[18] he had been transferred to Shanxi from Shandong, where he had already demonstrated his support for Boxer anti-Christianism.

Chinese views of the Franciscans during the Boxer era

Several themes emerge from within Chinese documents produced in Shanxi during the Boxer era, some of which appeared in the writings of local literati, often included in gazetteers (*difangzhi* 地方誌) and other texts that were posted publicly by local officials. These themes include: (1) contrived rumors of clandestine plots to overthrow the empire; (2) a superstitious fear of Christian black magic; (3) a belief that the emperor and the imperial court were cooperatively anti-Christian and anti-foreign; (4) an assertion that Christian missionaries were invaders who precipitated anarchy in Shanxi; (5) a critical view of Christianity as a heterodox doctrine, and official decrees calling for apostasy under threat of punishment; and (6) a post-Boxer violence *volte-face* by the imperial court and local officials, wherein efforts were made to redefine Christianity as orthodox and victimized, as well as an attempted rapprochement with Shanxi's Franciscan mission.

Other than a smattering of official documents exchanged between the governor's *yamen* in Taiyuan and the *Zongli yamen* (總理衙門) in Beijing, which deal little with their views of the Christian missionaries in Shanxi, the most important local Chinese materials are the reflections by the Confucian *literatus*, Liu Dapeng (劉大鵬 1857–1943), the agitated decrees of Governor Yuxian, and the post-Boxer decrees of Governor Cen Chunxuan (岑春煊 1861–1933), who was assigned to

---

17. For a brief history of the 1870 Church of the Immaculate Conception in Taiyuan, see Qin Geping 秦格平, *Taiyuan jiaoqu jianshi* 太原教區簡史 [A concise history of the diocese of Taiyuan] (Taiyuan: Catholic Diocese of Taiyuan, 2008), 97; and Li Yuzhang 李毓章 and Li Yuming 李毓明, *Shanxisheng Taiyuanshi Tianzhujiao baizhounian tekan* 山西省太原市天主教百週年特刊 [One hundred years of Shanxi Province Taiyuan Catholicism commemorative issue] (Taiyuan: Church of Taiyuan Bishop, 2006), 21–36.
18. Edwards, *Fire and Sword in Shansi*, 56.

replace Yuxian in 1901. All three of these men received a characteristically classical education, immersed in the Confucian textual tradition requisite for advancement in the late imperial exam system, though surprisingly the writings of Liu and Yuxian participate in the typical superstitious sensibilities and rumor mongering that were more common to less educated Chinese in Shanxi. Liu Dapeng and Yuxian's impressions of the Franciscan mission in Shanxi appear to have been based largely on, and informed by, the invented mythology that the friars and their native followers were surreptitiously plotting a widespread rebellion against the Qing empire. In Liu Dapeng's *Qianyuan suoji* (潛園瑣記 Trivial records while ensconced in the garden), Liu wrote at length about the Boxers and the role of local Christians in the Sino-missionary tensions of 1900.

Rebellion and black magic

After describing the abrupt emergence of Boxers in Shanxi, Liu recounts that "[t]he court ordered a military expedition, anxious that foreigners would gather their Christian forces in collaboration," and that the court decreed that "all of the foreigner barbarians from the hinterlands must be securely constrained."[19] The imperial pronouncement, Liu continues, declares that "anyone [Christians] who seizes the opportunity to rebel or collaborate in forming plots should be executed on the spot."[20] Yuxian, the Boxer-friendly governor in Shanxi, was so pleased when he heard the court's edict to suppress foreigners and Christians that reportedly, "he was moved to tears of gratitude."[21]

Liu Dapeng elaborates in detail how the foreign missionaries of Shanxi by that time "had already entered into deliberations with the Christians regarding how to initiate a rebellion in the province and take its cities and towns by force, and have summoned the militaries of their respective countries to march into Shanxi."[22] There is no evidence whatever in Franciscan correspondences, diocesan records, or in any available Western archival materials, that the friars and nuns in Shanxi had conceived any intentions of rebellion. It appears that these rumors of a collaborative missionary–native Christian insurgence were contrived to support Yuxian's aspiration to eradicate foreigners and Christianity in Shanxi.

In addition to allegations of sedition, the Franciscan mendicants were accused of sorcery, and Shanxi's Boxers disseminated leaflets throughout the province, especially

---

19. Liu Dapeng 劉大鵬, *Qianyuan suoji* 潛園瑣記 [Trivial records while ensconced in the garden], in *Yihetuan zai Shanxi diqu shiliao* 義和團在山西地區史料 [Historical sources on boxers in Shanxi], ed. Qiao Zhiqiang 喬志強 (Taiyuan: Shanxi renmin chubanshe, 1980), 31.
20. Liu, *Qianyuan suoji*, 31.
21. Ibid.
22. Ibid.

around Taiyuan, that the foreign missionaries along with their native Christian followers were casting fatal curses on non-Christians. Inventive tales of Christian magic had become so prevalent by 1900 that one Boxer notice advertised a protective formula to use as protection against their curses. This formula, reported to have descended from Confucius (551–479 BCE) and the Daoist patriarch Zhang Daoling (張道陵 AD 34–156), recommended gathering several ingredients, such as red orpiment, lime, and black beans, and placing them into a red pouch, which was to be "worn with your undergarments, suspended behind their doors, and placed on five branches of a willow tree."²³ Liu Dapeng, who one might expect would have maintained an educated distance from popular superstition, was in fact an enthusiastic sponsor of such mythologies.

In a lengthy reflection on the "Christian practice of black magic," Liu outlines a litany of imaginative practices. Other than performing rites involving the sprinkling of blood, steaming food in poisonous vapors, and enchanting streets and alleys with a mysterious "kill, kill sound,"²⁴ perhaps the most outrageous claim Liu Dapeng makes in his local record involved the animation of paper cutouts. He notes that the foreign missionaries and their Christian followers in Shanxi:

> Cut out paper men with yellow paper and past them in alleys and lanes in the night, desiring that these paper figures will kill a million Chinese people. The Boxers, however, broadcasted instructions to every household, informing them to set out water basins in their door thresholds and windowsills in order to destroy the paper men [as they fall into the water].²⁵

The heroic champions against Christian conjuring, Liu reported, were the Boxers who preemptively warned the common people and provided instructions regarding how to safeguard against these enchantments. As Liu recounted, these common rumors about Franciscan missionary magic precipitated an outbreak of terror through Shanxi: "In the daytime the common people were bewildered and at night they had nightmares of ghosts," and "the myriad people prayed to the gods asking for protection."²⁶ On July 12, 1900, Governor Yuxian announced in an official proclamation that "[t]he religious teachings of the foreigners employ black magic to confound the people, and poison and harm the land of China"; Boxers, literati, and mandarins alike promoted such rumors.²⁷

---

23. Taiyuan Diocese Archive 太原教區檔案館, Notice 6. Also in Qiao Zhiqiang, *Yihetuan zai Shanxi diqu shiliao*, 3.
24. Liu, *Qianyuan suoji*, 34.
25. Ibid., 35.
26. Ibid.
27. ACGOFM, Proclamation by Governor Yuxian on July 12, 1900; reprinted in Giovanni Ricci, OFM, *Barbarie e trionfi ossia le vittime illustri del San-Si in Cina nella persecuzione del 1900* (Parma: Tip. Egidio Ferrari, 1908), 630. This edition is held at the Zikawei (Xujiahui) Library, Shanghai.

An anti-Christian, anti-foreign court

One of the recurring themes in local Shanxi texts during the Boxer disturbances was that the imperial court, which was viewed as anti-Christian and anti-foreign, was powerless to punish missionary "offenses." After announcing the intention of foreigners to "delude the minds of China's people and turn China into a foreign country," Liu lamented that foreign power was such that "the court cannot rectify their crimes, and local officials are incapable of investigating their guilt."[28] Governor Yuxian presumed the court's unanimous anti-missionary position when he posted his decree, announcing that "[w]ar has been declared in the coastal regions, and the great military of China has won a victory. The officials and people must be of one mind, remain bound by a common thread of hatred for the enemy, eliminate the seed of Christianity, and eradicate foreigners at their root."[29] The operating assumption of Shanxi's literati and mandarins was that the court was decidedly on the side of the Boxers though this was far from unanimously true.

Perhaps one of the best sources we have regarding the court's actual position on Christians and foreigners during the Boxer Uprising is Li Xisheng's (李希聖 1864–1905) narrative account of debates conducted during the summer months of 1900 in the palace between the conservative faction of Empress Dowager Cixi (慈禧太后 1835–1908) and the reformist party of the emperor, Guangxu (光緒 1871–1908). During these deliberations Xu Jingcheng (徐景澄 1845–1900) remarked that "China has had relations with the foreigners for several decades, and there has not been a single year during this period free of animosity between the people and Christians."[30]

Xu's statement was followed by a response from Yuan Chang (袁昶 1864–1900), who "passionately" recommended that "[w]e cannot allow conflict to occur with foreigners. Toleration of the rebels [Boxers] will bring disasters of a magnitude which will make them impossible to handle," and he continued to predict that if the Boxers are allowed to attack foreigners and Christians, "civil wars and foreign invasions will follow."[31] After representatives of the Empress Dowager's faction countered that the Boxers must be supported due to threats of foreign invasion, the emperor himself argued that conflict with foreigners would be reckless: "How could there be any hope of success when we use riotous mobs [Boxers] to do our fighting?"[32] Contrary to

---

28. Liu, *Qianyuan suoji*, 32.
29. ACGOFM, Proclamation by Governor Yuxian in June or July 1900; reprinted in Cipriano Silvestri, OFM, *La Testimonianza del Sangue: Biographie dei Beati Cinesi uccisi il 4, 7 e 9 luglio 1900* (Rome: S. Giuseppe al Trionfale, 1943), 37.
30. Li Xisheng 李希聖, *Gengzi Guobian ji* 庚子國變記 [A record of the condition of the nation in 1900] (Beijing, 1902). I am using the translation in Scott Dearborn Colby, "The Boxer Crisis as Seen through the Eyes of Five Chinese Officials" (PhD dissertation, Columbia University, 1976), 328.
31. Colby, "The Boxer Crisis as Seen through the Eyes of Five Chinese Officials," 329.
32. Ibid., 332.

what literati and official impressions were in Shanxi—that the emperor and his court were unanimously in support of collaboration with Boxers to rid China of foreigners and Christians—the emperor was in fact adamantly opposed to any support of the "riotous" and superstitious Boxers who threatened China's long-term security. In the end, however, the Empress Dowager and her conservative court allies won the debates, and war was affirmed.

Franciscan invasion and anarchy

After a series of unequal treaties were pressed upon the Qing Court in the wake of Britain's attack of China's shores during the Opium War, agreements permitted unconditional missionary freedom throughout the empire, and in keeping with European ecclesial custom, churches and mission structures were constructed in a fashion that illustrated the ascendency of God over humanity and human institutions. Suddenly, the plains, cities, and villages of Shanxi were punctuated with grand Franciscan edifices, many of which soared above the other structures—Buddhist, Daoist, popular religionist, and civic. Thus, Liu Dapeng reflected on what he saw as he passed through of the Franciscan village of Dongergou, which was where Taiyuan's bishops housed and trained Shanxi's seminarians. He writes:

> The villagers all follow the foreign religion. The village lies at the foot of the hills, with the church standing on the slope of the hill, surrounded by a wall. There are many buildings within the wall. The site is impressive and the buildings are all in the foreign style.[33]

From his point of view, Shanxi was not only being overrun by foreign Christians, but Franciscan buildings built in non-Chinese styles appeared to claim the province.

In addition to the construction of new and looming churches, which Shanxi's literati viewed as itself a distortion of social hierarchies, the Italian Franciscans were accused of confusing proper human relations. As Yuxian asserted in his decree of July 5, 1900: "Foreign missionaries wreak havoc, despising the [Chinese] deities and abusing the [Chinese] people."[34] And just three days after he had executed all of the Franciscans and Protestant missionaries in his *yamen* courtyard on July 9, 1900, Yuxian posted another decree justifying his actions: "They completely destroy the five human relations and

---

33. Liu Dapeng, *Tuixiangzhai riji* 退想齋日記 [Diary from the study for retreat and contemplation], in *Jindaishi ziliao Yihetuan shiliao* 近代史資料義和團史料 [Materials for modern history: Materials on the Boxers] (Beijing: Zhongguo shehui kexue chubanshe, 1982), 819. Translated in Henrietta Harrison, "Village Politics and National Politics: The Boxer Movement in Central Shanxi," in *The Boxers, China, and the World*, ed. Robert Bickers and R. G. Tiedemann (Lanham, MD: Rowman & Littlefield, 2007), 3.

34. ACGOFM; reprinted in Giovanni Ricci, OFM, *Barbarie e trionfi ossia le vittime illustri del San-Si in Cina nella persecuzione del 1900*, 379. The date of this proclamation, which is not indicated in the original text, has been handwritten on the document as July 5, 1900.

have dared to plot rebellion, so I myself have seized them."[35] Liu Dapeng's estimation of Shanxi's Christian missionaries was similar to Yuxian's: "Foreign Christians are said to encourage people to behave well, but in truth they annoy our government, rebel against our institutions, destroy our customs, and delude our people," and he lamented that Shanxi's missionaries could not be eliminated because they "rely on the support of foreign powers, which is vast and imposing."[36] The Franciscan mission was, according to Yuxian and Liu Dapeng, intrusive and divisive, and despite local protests it was sheltered under the defensive arms of its foreign protectors, which were in any case far away in Beijing and Tianjin and were actually too far away from Shanxi to pose a serious threat.[37]

Christianity as a heretical doctrine and the call for apostasy

Other than the complaints of Chinese Catholics themselves, who mentioned several unsavory practices by the missionaries, perhaps the most common grievances expressed in local documents against foreign presence in Shanxi, of which the Franciscan mission occupied the greatest portion, was that Christianity was a heterodox doctrine that must be abnegated for the province to remain authentically Chinese.[38] This notion was mainly promoted in Shanxi by Governor Yuxian; in fact, the Franciscans were already well aware of Yuxian's opinion that Christianity was a precarious and heterodox religion long before he was assigned to Taiyuan. In an apprehensive letter written in May 1900, the mendicant friar Andrew Bauer (Chinese name 安振德, 1866–1900) wrote: "He has come to Taiyuanfu, the notorious persecutor of Christians in Shandong.

---

35. ACGOFM; reprinted in Giovanni Ricci, OFM, *Barbarie e trionfi ossia le vittime illustri del San-Si in Cina nella persecuzione del 1900*, 630. Yuxian's involvement in the massacre of Christians at Taiyuan on July 9, 1900 has been questioned by Roger R. Thompson, who states his suspicion of the sources he had as he conducted his research. See Roger R. Thompson, "Reporting the Taiyuan Massacre: Culture and Politics in the China War of 1900," in *The Boxers, China, and the World*, ed. Robert Bickers and R. G. Tiedemann. Evidence—both Chinese and Western—that establishes Yuxian's personal involvement in the July 9 massacre of Christians in 1900 is overwhelming. A partial list of sources that note Yuxian's orchestration and participation in the event include Li Di (李杕, 1840–1911), *Quanhuo ji* 拳禍記 [A record of the Boxer catastrophe] (Shanghai: Tushanwan yinshuguan, 1909), 340; the collected witness testimonies held at the Archivio Segreto Vaticano, such as the ASV, Congr. Riti., especially Processus 4628; and Liu Dapeng, *Qianyuan suoji*, in *Yihetuan zai Shanxi diqu shiliao*, ed. Qiao Zhiqiang, 32, where Liu directly states, "Yuxian donned his military regalia . . . Everyone was arranged outside the West Gate of his yamen, and one after another was slain." For another contemporary account involving Yuxian, see the University of Oregon Special Collections, Dr. Charles F. Johnson Papers (Ax 268), Box I, Folio p. 66.
36. Liu, *Qianyuan suoji*, 32.
37. For an exhaustive discussion of the French protectorate over the Roman Catholic missions in China, see Ernest P. Young, *Ecclesiastical Colony: China's Catholic Church and the French Religious Protectorate* (Oxford: Oxford University Press, 2013).
38. For examples of abuses and discrimination against Chinese by missionaries in Shanxi, see Henrietta Harrison, *The Missionary's Curse and Other Tales from a Chinese Catholic Village* (Berkeley: University of California Press, 2013).

What can we expect of him at any time now except persecutions?"[39] Bauer's concerns proved prophetic, for soon after Yuxian arrived in Shanxi he invited the native Chinese population to his *yamen* to present their accusations against the Franciscan mission and other foreigners. Indeed, Yuxian wasted no time amassing "confirmation" that Shanxi's Christians were dissenting mischief makers.

Yuxian's decrees after his arrival in Shanxi included a call for Chinese Christians to apostatize. In his July 5, 1900 decree, Yuxian posted a severe and foreboding ultimatum for Shanxi's Christians to consider:

> The righteous people will burn and kill, and calamities will come down.
> I exhort you who are Christians to reform before it is too late.
> Correct your evil and return to what is proper and all shall be benevolent.
> If you maintain this distinction [between Christian and non-Christian], you will become a respectable person.
> Officials accept this command to protect yourselves.
> For those who do not know to change, they will have regrets for no reason.
> To this end explicit directions are given, and all should revere [this decree] with trepidation.[40]

Yuxian's view of Christian heterodoxy as a cause of social disorder was so extreme that he warned Christians that "righteous people," that is non-Christians, would soon "burn" the property and "kill" persons who refused to "correct your evil and return to what is proper." In other words, apostatize or die.

In his July 12, 1900 decree, Yuxian repeated his exhortation though by then he had already demonstrated that his threats were far from idle. In this announcement he stated, "I have executed these criminals according to their names [list] in order to extinguish calamities and all Christians at their root. It is urgent to make a new beginning; Christians apostatize and it shall pacify the people."[41] In yet another decree Yuxian reasserted his call for Christians to depart from their "heterodox" teaching, albeit in a somewhat softened tone: "The court has recommended magnanimity, granting [Christians] a chance to reform."[42] In this pronouncement the court is also mentioned, which as Shanxi's new governor reports, agreed with Yuxian's urgent summons for Christians to abandon "deviant" beliefs.

Yet another official announcement was posted on July 14, 1900, demanding that "all male Catholics who refused to apostatize must report to Beimen Street,

---

39. ACGOFM, Letter from Andrew Bauer, OFM, written in Taiyuan, May 6, 1900. Quoted in Georges Goyau, *Missionaries and Martyrs: Mother Mary of the Passion and the Franciscan Missionaries of Mary*, translated by the Very Reverend George Telford (Anand: Anand Press, 1944), 32.
40. ACGOFM, Yuxian Decree, July 5, 1900.
41. Ibid., July 12, 1900.
42. Ibid., June or July 1900.

Dongtoudao Alley [Taiyuan]."[43] His decree was clear; those who neglected to arrive would be pursued and executed, and those who obeyed the summons would be presented another opportunity for apostasy. Taiyuan's Christians, however, were determined to become martyrs, and the more than one hundred Catholics who arrived at the designated courtyard knelt in remonstration against Yuxian's decree. As Qin Geping recounts, the magistrate's order was received with intense resistance; the Catholics arrived three hours early, and as they knelt they wrapped their long queues around their foreheads, exposed their necks, and defiantly awaited the executioner's sword. Once the mandarin's runners had arrived to the gathering of audacious Christian protesters, he "shouted the order to 'kill,' and the executioner began arbitrarily beheading men; in a split second streams of blood flooded the ground."[44] Thirty-nine Chinese Catholics were killed before the executioner grew too exhausted to continue; conflicts between the governor and the Chinese attached to the Franciscan mission grew even more severe in subsequent weeks.

Local views of the Franciscan mission and native Chinese Christians in Shanxi vacillated from serene to strained; the Jiangzhou edict of 1635, which praised the Catholic mission for its apparent compatibility with Confucian tenets, was entirely reversed after the international tensions between China and the West in the wake of the Opium War. Shanxi's governor, Yuxian, and the famous *literatus* Liu Dapeng provide sharp examples of the late Qing transition from a predominantly tolerant attitude toward the Catholic mission to one of suspicion and superstition. By 1898 the Franciscan mission in Shanxi, directed by Italian Friars Minor, was rumored to be rebellious, involved with black magic, collectively abhorred by the emperor and his court, and determined to overcome the empire and disturb China's cultural cohesion with its heterodox teaching. The only recourse local officials had, they argued, was to execute the Franciscan mendicants and call all native Christians to apostatize. By late August 1900, eight foreign militaries, for better and worse, marched into China's imperial capital and began a bifurcated campaign of relief and revenge. In early 1901, the court issued an edict ordering the capture of Yuxian, who had fled to Lanzhou, and on February 22, 1901, he was publicly beheaded.[45] The Empress Dowager's once trusted governor of Shanxi was summarily executed in an imperial *volte-face*; local Chinese views of the Franciscan mission, and of Christians in general, were radically revised and restated.

---

43. Qin Geping, *Taiyuan jiaoqu jianshi*, 320.
44. Ibid.
45. Ibid., 323.

Shanxi's official *volte-face*: Christianity redefined as orthodox and victimized

When Yuxian had left Shanxi on October 12, 1900 he was seen off with great fanfare; the people and gentry of Taiyuan reverently bid him farewell, and the local merchant guilds erected a memorial tablet in the governor's honor at the city's south gate.[46] Once Cen Chunxuan, Yuxian's replacement, had settled in Taiyuan, he invited missionaries to return to the province and then exacted swift punishment on the Boxers who were enlisted and supported by Yuxian only a few months previously. In the official *volte-face*, buoyed by the central court in Beijing, the violence of the Boxer Uprising was turned upon the Boxers themselves. As Zhang De and Jia Lili recount: "After Cen Chunxuan had replaced Yuxian as the new governor of Shanxi, every day there were Boxers who were executed, and above the gates of Taiyuan and every city in the province were hung their heads, dripping with blood."[47] Having executed the Boxers, Cen labored to repair relationships with the Franciscan mission in Shanxi, which returned to discover that its churches, hospitals, and orphanages had all been razed; what remained was a diminished and beleaguered Catholic community.

Suppressing Boxers was one thing; recasting social stereotypes of foreign missionaries and their religion was another matter. Cen Chunxuan's about face followed a deliberate pattern, which carefully reversed the assertions made about missionaries and Christians since the mid-nineteenth century. In 1901, Governor Cen posted a rather long decree at the south gate of Taiyuan (replacing the earlier monument in the same location praising Yuxian), celebrating the erection of a commemorative stele for the Franciscan and Baptist foreign missionaries and the large number of native Christians who were killed under the order of Cen's predecessor. The extent to which foreign pressure influenced post-1900 edicts of reconciliation cannot be underestimated though the rash of official proclamations exonerating martyred foreigners and Christians had an undeniably salutary effect on general impressions of foreigners and Christianity.

Rather than perpetuate rumors that the Franciscans were partisan to machinations to rebel against the empire, which he knew to be contrived, or preserve superstitious fears of Christian black magic, which were manufactured by Boxers and Red Lanterns, Governor Cen Chunxuan issued a series of decrees to exonerate the Franciscan mission and extol the virtue—rather than the heterodoxy—of their religion. In his commemorative decree, Cen begins by asserting the emperor's consternation regarding what had besought the missionaries in Shanxi.

> The Son of Heaven commemorates the missionaries of Shanxi who were cruelly and unexpectedly slaughtered, and it has been ordered that the official in charge of

---

46. Edwards, *Fire and Sword in Shansi*, 117.
47. Zhang De 張德 and Jia Lili 賈莉莉, *Taiyuan shihua* 太原史話 [A history of Taiyuan] (Taiyuan: Shanxi renmin chubanshe, 2000), 163.

the area where they were killed record the names of the missionaries for posterity. Now I have been appointed the magistrate of Shanxi and solemnly honor the will of the Court.[48]

In no uncertain terms Shanxi's new governor avowed the emperor's support of and remorse for the missionaries, and whether or not his remarks were politically motivated, the sea change in official attitude was clearly articulated.

Cen continues: "Looking into the rebellion of 1900, the Protestant and Roman Catholic missionaries encountered difficulties and were willing to die for their benevolent way, and in all 150 people died."[49] And before enumerating the names of the missionaries killed in Yuxian's *yamen* courtyard, which begins with the Franciscan bishops, Cen notes his intention to "exonerate [these Catholics] in order that they never be forgotten"; official proclamations beginning in 1901 systematically reversed those published during the height of the Boxer conflicts. In another decree, issued also in conjunction with a commemorative stele erected to commemorate the missionaries who died in Shanxi, acclaims the missionaries' merits in very explicit terms, stating, "I commend the sincere virtues of those missionaries and grieve over the cruelties they encountered."[50] In addition to his edicts of support and commemoration, the new governor provided funds and land for a Franciscan cemetery, where the martyrs' bodies could be interred and memorialized, as well as assisted in the reconstruction of the Catholic orphanages, schools, hospitals, and churches that had been destroyed.

Both Catholics and Protestants hailed Cen Chunxuan as a friend of foreigners and Christianity though to what level his actions were ordered by the central court, or to what level they were motivated by political rapprochement, may never be known. From the historian's point of view, Shanxi serves as an excellent example of how local Chinese views and representations of foreign missionaries, in this case Franciscan mendicants, were transformed after the Boxer era from pejorative to positive and from accusing foreign missionaries of insurrection and black magic to acknowledging them as victims of "cunning" officials. Sadly, while local Chinese views of foreigners and foreign missions improved after the turbulence of the Boxer era, Western views of China began a several-decade period of negative depictions of China, depictions that were admittedly encouraged by what had happened in China in 1900.

Perhaps the most interesting turn of events in Shanxi after the Boxer era had concluded was that local Chinese depictions of the Franciscan mission began to be produced almost entirely by Chinese Catholics attached to that mission; as the number of converts increased after 1900, so too did Chinese attempts to *re*-present

---

48. AFMM, Proclamation by Cen Chunxuan of Taiyuan, Shanxi, in 1901.
49. Ibid.
50. TDA, Proclamation by Cen Chunxuan of Taiyuan, Shanxi, in 1901. "Taiyuan guanfu jinian ting shibei," 太原官府紀念亭石碑 [Taiyuan official commemorative pavilion stele]. A transcription of this stele exists in Qin Geping, *Taiyuan jiaoqu jianshi*.

the mendicants who served the population of Shanxi. Mandarins then shared literary space with Chinese Christians who added their own voices to the Franciscan history of late imperial Shanxi. As one Chinese Catholic wrote, those who suffered during the Boxer violence of 1900, "were prepared to give their lives when in danger, and spend their lives selflessly," which is precisely the message taught by the Franciscan mendicants who first entered Shanxi in the early eighteenth century.[51] Chinese views of Shanxi's Franciscan mission during the late Qing were transformed after the Boxer incidents of 1900; they shifted from mythological to objective, from a rhetoric of enemy to friend, and from a mode of representing the Franciscan *other*, to a predominant representation, as the number of Chinese friars grew to outnumber the foreign missionaries, of the Chinese and mendicant *self*.

Abbreviations

ACGOFM	Archivio Curia Generalizia Ordo Fratrum Minorum (Rome)
AL	Annual Letter, Society of Jesus
ASV	Archivio Segreto Vaticano (Vatican City)
AFMM	Archive of the Franciscan Missionaries of Mary (Rome)
TDA	Taiyuan Diocese Archive 太原教區檔案館 (Taiyuan)

---

51. TDA, monument inscription by an anonymous Chinese Catholic in 1901. A transcription of this stele exists in Qin Geping, *Taiyuan jiaoqu jianshi*.

7
A Religious Rhetoric of Competing Modernities
Christian Print Culture in Late Qing China

Melissa Wei-Tsing Inouye

Introduction

The imbalance of power in the encounter between China and the West during the late Qing dynasty makes it easy to describe the encounter between Western Protestant missionaries and Chinese Protestant converts in terms of a flow of ideas, beliefs, and resources from Westerners to Chinese. This flow has been viewed negatively, as in the nationalistic narrative about how Western imperialists devalued Chinese religious practices and imposed their own beliefs and values on Chinese citizens. It has been viewed positively, as in narratives about how Chinese Christians' access to Western-style education enabled them to play a disproportionately influential role in the modernizing projects of the late Qing and early Republican era.[1]

And yet while the momentous nature of the influx—for good or ill—of people, products, ideas, and institutions from the West to China in the late Qing cannot be denied, the flow of exchange was not always unidirectional. Nor did it traverse a cultural gap as wide or as clearly defined as the historical actors presumed.

In this volume, the concept of "in-betweenness" is raised to capture this sense of bidirectionality and mutual exchange in Christian encounters bridging China and the West. Indeed, Chinese Christian publications and Western missionary records reveal that Western-Chinese exchange in the late nineteenth and early twentieth centuries was more than a transfer—negative or positive—of ideas, technologies, and influence from the West to China. It was a jostling two-way exchange transacted in the rapidly multiplying interstices of the modern world.

Miracle-oriented devotional discourse by both local and foreign Protestant Christians provides an example of this "in-betweenness" and how people experienced modernity in early twentieth-century China. Whole books have been written to argue over the defining characteristics of modernity; I will not attempt to solve this problem in the limited scope of this chapter. For the sake of this chapter's discussion, I define

---

1. Ryan Dunch, *Fuzhou Protestants and the Making of a Modern China* (New Haven: Yale University Press, 2001), 15.

"modernity" in China very broadly, as the experience of new ideas, culture, and technologies, often from abroad, which fed a discourse of the transformation and progress of Chinese society. "Rationalistic modernity," in which reliance on science is taken to be modernity's dominant ethos, was one of the dominant ideologies underneath the umbrella of modernity, but, as we will see, it was one of many others.

Chinese Protestant periodicals not only contributed to a burgeoning national print culture but also popularized reports of world news and the latest scientific breakthroughs. And yet their espousal of scientific modernity never extended to their own metaphysical faith in the saving power of Christ, the malicious power of Satan, and God's ability to intervene in people's lives. Miraculous popular Christian devotional narratives in early twentieth-century China were perpetuated by lay Christians and missionaries alike. Local Christians eagerly received news of Christian miracles because miracles provided validation in a religious culture that prized efficacious demonstrations. Foreign missionaries, despite their self-identification with modern scientific rationality, likewise yearned for manifestations of divine power that would break with everyday patterns and evoke the divine manifestations described in the Bible.

Without a doubt, Protestant denominational endeavors to establish hospitals, schools, universities, and civic organizations such as the YMCA are well documented and justifiably contribute to a strong historical association between Protestant Christianity and modernity. For example, Ryan Dunch's compelling research on Fuzhou Protestants has shown that, in Fuzhou around the early twentieth century, Christian adherence was often aligned with progressive civic values and a rationalistic modern outlook, especially as it was transmitted over the generations. Dunch writes:

> Literacy, education, and knowledge of the outside world tended to follow Protestant belief, particularly for second-generation and later Protestants in any given locale. As a result, Protestants became more educated and more inclined to claim a place in Chinese elite society, and the stress on supernatural experience gave way to an emphasis on the association of Christianity with science, rationalism, and progress.[2]

As an example, he contrasts the more supernatural worldview of Xu Bomei (許播美, 1827–?), an early Christian convert who, in the late nineteenth century, staged an Old Testament–style competition between the Christian God and the local deity in offering prayers for rain, with the more scientific approach of Xu Bomei's son, a Christian doctor who responded to requests for exorcism "not by prayer and fasting, as his father probably would have done, but by the more prosaic means of holding an ammonia-soaked cloth over the nose of the patient whenever the evil

---

2. Dunch, *Fuzhou Protestants and the Making of a Modern China*, 15. Dunch qualifies this observation, importantly, by saying, "[t]hat modern alignment was not an inevitable consequence of conversion, however, and we would be mistaken to equate conversion with detachment from Chinese society and entry into a westernized, missionary-dominated, or modernist cultural reality."

spirit manifested itself."³ Dunch's well-researched study convincingly captures one mode of Chinese Christianity, a rationalistic sort of Christianity that was influenced both by the programs of Western missionaries and the interests of a rising Chinese professional class.

When discussing an alignment of "Western missionaries" and "rationalistic modernity" it is important to point out that Western missionaries did not share a common approach to the question of faith and science. In the 1920s, a theological rift formed between "modernist" and "fundamentalist" Protestant factions in the United States and United Kingdom. As Daniel Bays has pointed out, the tensions between modernist and fundamentalist points of view carried over into the Protestant missionary presence in China.⁴ Bays writes that, at the turn of the twentieth century, these divisions were not merely philosophical but also marked by a stark gap in institutional resources:

> [T]he mainstream ("liberal" or "modernist") denominational mission establishment "remained firmly in control of the great majority of important institutions of the Sino-foreign Protestant community in China: the large urban church edifices; the schools and hospitals; the administrative positions interfacing with Chinese government and foreign consular authorities; and the influential monthly magazine, *The Chinese Recorder*.⁵

Hence those civic institutions that most closely overlapped with the Chinese modernizing project (as propounded in government policy and intellectual advocacy, for instance) tended to be supported by a certain strain of theologically modernist Protestants. For this reason, the rationalist tendencies of some Western missionaries are clearly visible in the historical record but not necessarily representative. The world of Chinese Protestant Christianity in the late Qing could be a self-consciously modern world, characterized by international awareness and access to recent technology. And yet local and foreign Christians alike left a significant gap in their discourse of scientific rationality in order to make space for the occurrence of miracles, because miracle stories bolstered the validity of their religious endeavor. Christians saw seeking miracles within a non-Christian context as "superstition," but within a Christian context a miracle was a sign of God's favor.

How did miraculous Christian modes shape Western and Chinese Christians' engagement with modernity and with each other? How did modern printing technologies multiply the contradictions between rationalist rhetoric and miraculous yearning?

---

3. Dunch, *Fuzhou Protestants and the Making of a Modern China*, 9–15.
4. See, for instance, Daniel Bays, "Christian Revival in China, 1900–1937," in *Modern Christian Revivals*, ed. Edith L. Blumhofer and Randall Balmer (Chicago: University of Illinois Press, 1993), 161–79; "Indigenous Protestant Churches in China, 1900–1937: A Pentecostal Case Study," in *Indigenous Responses to Western Christianity*, ed. Steven Kaplan (New York: New York University Press, 1995), 124–43.
5. Bays, "Christian Revival in China, 1900–1937," 161–79, 169.

In this chapter, I first show how Western missionaries' introduction of modern printing technology to China led to the propagation of not only national, mass-mechanized commercial publishing practices but also projects such as the promotion of charismatic practices in Chinese Christian publications. I next highlight in-betweenness in the Chinese Christian publications that simultaneously attacked efficacy-oriented popular religious practices and promoted efficacy-oriented Christian practices. Finally I highlight in-betweenness in the historical records in Western missionaries' letters, in which they excitedly related accounts of divine intervention. Both these Chinese Christian publications and Western missionary letters share a curious mix of competing assumptions and desires that reflected the dynamic cultural exchanges in Chinese society in the early twentieth century.

Chinese Christian print culture

Western printing technologies came to China in the nineteenth century via Christian missionary organizations and quickly took on a life of their own, developing along publishing avenues that diverged from the scientific ethos that had given rise to these technologies. The increasing prevalence of Christian miracle stories in nationally distributed Chinese-language publications such as the *Church News* (*Jiaohui xinbao* 教會新報, 1868–74) and the *Chinese Christian Intelligencer* (*Tongwenbao* 通問報, 1902–48) normalized "miraculous" practices such as healing, exorcism, and particularistic protection as part of the Christian experience across China.

The role of Western missionary organizations in expanding mass-mechanized modern print culture in China in the nineteenth century is well-known. It is important to point out that advanced printing technologies and well developed regional networks of publishing and book distribution had existed in China for centuries. Indeed, throughout the early modern period, China led the world in printing technology and print culture.[6] Christopher Reed has estimated that, prior to the nineteenth century, more books were likely written and published in Chinese than in any other single published language.[7] Despite the sophistication and scope of Chinese print culture in the early nineteenth century, however, certain features of the Chinese publishing environment up until the late Qing tended to prevent the development of modern, mass-audience print culture founded on industrialized printing technology.

---

6. Christopher A. Reed, "From Woodblocks to the Internet: Chinese Printing, Publishing, and Literary Fields in Transition, circa 1800 to 2008," in *From Woodblocks to the Internet: Chinese Publishing and Print Culture in Transition, circa 1800 to 2008*, ed. Cynthia Brokaw and Christopher A. Reed (Leiden and Boston: Brill, 2010), 1–38; see also Brokaw, "Commercial Woodblock Publishing in the Qing (1644–1911) and the Transition to Modern Print Technology," in *From Woodblocks to the Internet*, 44; Andrea Janku, "The Use of Genres in the Chinese Press from the Late Qing to the Early Republican Period," in *From Woodblocks to the Internet*, 130; Cynthia Brokaw and Kai-wing Chow, eds. *Printing and Book Culture in Late Imperial China* (Berkeley and Los Angeles: University of California Press, 2005).
7. Reed, "From Woodblocks to the Internet," 4.

Although wooden, clay, and metal movable type technologies were in use in China at this time, they were not widespread because a huge initial investment of time and money was required to create a set of type that covered tens of thousands of Chinese characters. Across China most printers continued to rely on xylography (woodblock printing). However, because one set of wooden blocks could only create about 25,000 copies, these networks were often only local or regional in scale.[8]

In the nineteenth century, Western missionaries introduced printing technologies such as lithography, then letterpress printing, and eventually photolithography. Missionaries turned to publishing in their need to address China's sheer size and their inability to travel freely. Robert Morrison (Chinese name 馬禮遜, 1782–1834), the first Protestant missionary in China, who arrived in 1807, devoted the majority of his efforts to biblical translation, a Chinese-English dictionary, and other publishing endeavors.[9] In 1815, Morrison and other early London Missionary Society (LMS) missionaries published the *Chinese Monthly Magazine* (*Cha shisu meiyue tongji zhuan* 察世俗每月統記傳) in Malacca on the Malay peninsula. It was distributed in Malacca and among overseas Chinese communities in the South Seas.[10] The first periodical to appear on the Chinese mainland, in 1833, was the *Eastern Western Monthly Magazine* (*Dongxiyang kao meiyue tongji zhuan* 東西洋考每月統記傳), a monthly published in Guangzhou by the Prussian Protestant missionary Karl Gützlaff (Chinese name 郭實獵, 1793–1851).[11]

The *Chinese Serial* (*Xia'er guanzhen* 遐邇貫珍), published monthly between 1853 and 1856 by the London Missionary Society Press in Hong Kong, was the first Chinese-language paper to use lead type (letterpress printing).[12] Although the *Chinese Serial* was only in existence for a few years, its printing equipment was used to launch the first Chinese-run daily newspaper in Hong Kong in 1874, the *Universal Circulating Herald* (*Xunhuan ribao* 循環日報).[13] In the meantime, the treaty port city of Shanghai was quickly emerging as a new publishing powerhouse, fueled first by missionary and subsequently commercial publishing ventures.

The *Church News*, published in Shanghai from 1868 to 1874 by the Methodist missionary Young J. Allen (Chinese name 林樂知, 1836–1907), later renamed *Review of*

---

8. Brokaw, "Commercial Woodblock Publishing in the Qing (1644–1911) and the Transition to Modern Print Technology," 44.
9. Su Ching 蘇精, "Jindai diyizhong Zhongwen zazhi: *Cha shisu meiyue tongji zhuan*" 近代第一種中文雜誌：察世俗每月統記傳, in *Ma Lixun yu Zhongwen yinshua chuban* 馬禮遜與中文印刷出版 (Taipei: Xuesheng shuju, 2000), 153.
10. Su, "Jindai diyizhong Zhongwen zazhi," 153–58.
11. Janku, "The Use of Genres in the Chinese Press from the Late Qing to the Early Republican Period," 132.
12. Ibid., 134.
13. Although Western missionary publications pioneered the use of the latest printing technologies, older technologies such as lithography and xylography were not abandoned entirely. For instance, Janku notes (132) that the American Baptist Mission used lithography to publish a Chinese-language newspaper in Ningbo between 1854 and 1861, the *Chinese and Foreign Gazette* (*Zhongwai xinbao* 中外新報).

the Times (*Wanguo gongbao* 萬國公報) and published from 1875 to 1907, was China's first magazine devoted to news reports and background essays and the first magazine concerned with social criticisms and suggestions for reform. The Catholic Imprimerie at Tushanwan (土山灣) in the Shanghai suburb of Zikawei (Xujiahui 徐家匯) in 1882 used state-of-the-art lead type to print *Yiwen lu* (益聞錄, Record of useful news). *Yiwen lu* was also the first Chinese periodical with a native Chinese editor, Jesuit priest Li Wenyu (李問漁, 1840–1911). In 1900, the Imprimerie pioneered the use of photo-engraving technology.[14]

These missionary publishing projects sowed the seeds of a publishing boom not only in technology but also in human capital. Hundreds of printers and apprentices were trained in the Protestant and Catholic missionary printing operations in Shanghai. They then went on to staff other missionary presses and commercial operations in the surrounding Jiangnan (江南) region and beyond.[15] Before long, missionary publications had to contend with increasingly stiff competition from commercial publications like the *Shanghai Journal* (*Shenbao* 申報, 1872–1949), the *Shanghai Daily* (*Xinwenbao* 新聞報, 1893–1960), and the *Eastern Times* (*Shibao* 時報, 1904–39).[16]

The number of copies printed and distributed by missionary institutions was certainly less than the circulation eventually attained by major national commercial publications in Shanghai. And yet as these Christian publications traveled from station to station, they established national networks of Christian printing, distribution, and consumption that paved the way for commercial operations that expanded as rapidly as technology and industrialization allowed.[17] Chinese Christian print culture also strengthened Christian identity by providing widely shared devotional resources. As ideological resources and points of shared identity also spread throughout China via commercial printing networks, modern realities such as awareness of current global issues and strong national identity became possible. Hence, Chinese Christian print culture was at the forefront of emerging modern consciousness in China in the nineteenth century.

---

14. Joachim Kurtz, "Messenger of the Sacred Heart: Li Wenyu (1840–1911) and the Jesuit Periodical Press in Late Qing Shanghai," in *From Woodblocks to the Internet*, 82–91, 96.
15. Kurtz, "Messenger of the Sacred Heart," 82.
16. Janku, "The Use of Genres in the Chinese Press from the Late Qing to the Early Republican Period," 112.
17. Missionary publication numbers were modest compared to commercial competitors, but not insignificant. For instance, Young J. Allen's the *Church News* reached 2,000 copies per week in 1874 (Adrian A. Bennett, *Missionary Journalist in China: Young J. Allen and His Magazines, 1860–1883* [Athens, GA: University of Georgia Press, 1983], 104). The *Chinese Serial* was published by James Legge in runs of 3,000 copies (Janku, 132); the *Messager du Sacre-Coeur* (*Shengxin bao* 聖心報), June 1887–May 1949, was a monthly periodical published by Jesuit priest Li Wenyu that reached a subscriber base of about 3,000 through the end of the imperial era (Kurtz, 105). In contrast to this, the *Shanghai Journal* claimed a circulation of 10,000 in an 1877 editorial although publisher Ernest Major cited a more modest figure of "only 5,000" in consular papers in 1876 (Janku, 134).

Spread of miracle stories by means of printing

At the same time that modern print culture was spreading awareness of science, however, it was also facilitating the spread of a range of miracle stories, including accounts of particularistic protection, healing, visions, cathartic worship, and exorcism. Proponents of this miraculous worldview found easy support for supernatural efficacy in the Bible. The Old Testament and New Testament both contain numerous depictions of prophets, apostles, and Jesus himself as healers and exorcists. A more conservative or literal interpretation of the significance of these miraculous accounts occurred with regularity among essays and reports published in Chinese Christian periodicals. These supernatural characterizations of Christianity embodied more than one expression of modernity: the technology and sophisticated communication networks on one hand, and on the other hand, the printed miracle stories that flaunted rational analysis.

This war of competing modernities escalated as both trends accelerated. Christian missionaries and organizations could dramatically expand their capacity to communicate with mass audiences through publications and to build ideological communities that stretched across provincial and national boundaries. At the same time, the supernatural mode of Christianity normalized in such publications encouraged imitation and shaped Chinese Christian popular culture.

Here I share several examples of this miraculous mode of Christianity from just two early Chinese Christian publications. The first was a weekly published in Shanghai by Young J. Allen, first as the *Church News* (1868–74) and later, with the aim of attracting non-Christian readers, *Review of the Times* (1875–1907). The second was printed in Shanghai by the Presbyterian Missions in China and was called the *Chinese Christian Intelligencer* (1902–48).[18] According to a 1907 book written to commemorate a century of Christian missionary work in China, the *Chinese Christian Intelligencer* had the highest circulation of any religious weekly in China (3,700).[19] By 1938, the *Chinese Christian Intelligencer* had a circulation of 5,000 and was classified among a minority of Protestant periodicals with circulations reaching this size.[20]

---

18. *Chinese Christian Intelligencer* (*Tongwenbao* 通問報) (Shanghai: The Presbyterian Missions in China), hereafter *CCI*. Accessed via microfilm in the Shanghai Library (catalog number 5030). Rudolph Löwenthal confirms that *Tongwenbao* was published by the Presbyterian Mission and not simply printed on its presses by another group. See Rudolph Löwenthal, *The Religious Periodical Press in China* (Peking: The Synodal Commission in China, 1940), 113–14.
19. Presbyterian missions claimed the highest number of baptized adherents in the country. Having 52,258 communicants, they far outnumbered those claimed by other major categories of Western missionary societies including Congregationalists, Episcopalians, Methodists, "interdenominational" groups such as Bible Societies and the China Christian Youth Association, "unclassified" societies, and independent missionaries. Donald MacGillivray, ed., *A Century of Protestant Missions in China (1807–1907): Being the Centenary Conference Historical Volume* (New York: American Tract Society; Shanghai: American Presbyterian Mission Press, 1907), 674. On the circulation of the *Chinese Christian Intelligencer*, see MacGillivray, 403.
20. Löwenthal, *The Religious Periodical Press in China*, 113–14.

Although *Review of the Times* targeted a secular as well as a Christian audience, the *Church News* and the *Chinese Christian Intelligencer* were directed at a Christian audience. The content of the two magazines included theological sermons, Bible illustrations, world and church news, and testimonies. These testimonies and reports frequently included miracle stories, such as accounts of healing, exorcism, and particularistic protection.[21]

For example, in 1874, the last year of the *Church News* before it became *Review of the Times*, two stories drove home the message of the superior efficacy of the Christian God compared to all other deities. The first article, written by a Li Zhuxiu (李竹修), gave an account of a village smitten with a deadly disease. Despite the villagers' energetic propitiations to local deities, the disease spread unchecked. According to the author, only after a local scholar gathered up and destroyed the ritual implements for the offerings, thus rejecting the local deities, were the sick in the village healed. The moral of the story according to the author was that local deities were little better than demons (*gui* 鬼) and that one could reject and destroy their power. "Is this not the great grace of God made manifest in this world?" the final line read.[22]

Another story printed in the *Church News* in 1874 told the tale of a catastrophe at sea in which one vessel transporting a foreign missionary back to China from a conference in New York collided with another ship in the night. The missionary, "Gu Yiweili" (谷以未利), and another pastor colleague told the panicked passengers to pray. According to the account, Pastor Gu spoke cheerfully, telling people not to be afraid, for deliverance was at hand: "I feel in my heart that in the morning there will be rescue." Just before dawn, another boat, *The Queen of England*, appeared on the scene. The shipwrecked passengers and the author took this as an example of miraculous deliverance. "How could it be an accident?" the article asked. "It is God's doing, and nothing else."[23]

In the *Chinese Christian Intelligencer*, printed in Shanghai but with a growing national and international circulation, the greater proportion of reader-submitted articles yields an even richer harvest of miracle stories.[24] My research in the *Chinese*

---

21. One interesting thing to note is that, although miracle stories do exist in both publications, they are much more frequent in the *Chinese Christian Intelligencer* than in the *Church News*. This is largely due to structural and editorial differences at the two periodicals. The regular sections of the *Church News* featured theology, foreign and domestic political news, and science, with an occasional section on church news (the arrivals and departures of missionaries, statistics of converts, etc.). Only occasionally were reader-submitted articles on Christian topics included. Content in the *Chinese Christian Intelligencer*, however, was much more eclectic. Lengthy articles on theology or missionary biography were accompanied by numerous shorter reports submitted by reader-writers from all over China. These shorter reports often gave accounts of faith-promoting and even miraculous happenings in a given locale.
22. The *Church News* (*Jiaohui xinwen* 教會新聞), Vol. 6 (1874), 2715.
23. Ibid., 3184.
24. Rudolf Loewenthal, *The Religious Periodical Press in China, with 7 maps and 16 charts* (Peking: The Synodal commission in China, 1940), Chart III.

Christian Intelligencer sampled issues from 1906 to 1948.[25] I found that accounts of miraculous beliefs and practices, from particularistic protection, healing, visions, and cathartic worship, appear regularly throughout the run of the *Chinese Christian Intelligencer* during this period. With every jump into a new interval, it usually took no more than a few pages or at most one or two weekly issues before I found miraculous material. For example, in one of the earliest issues of the *Chinese Christian Intelligencer* held by the Shanghai Library from January 1906, one can read a miracle story in which God's particularistic protection is given in response to a Christian's prayer. The Christian is an umbrella maker surnamed Chen (陳) in the southeastern city of Wenzhou (溫州). His shop was threatened by a terrible fire blowing mercilessly through the city on the back of great winds. According to the account, when faced with this approaching disaster, instead of rushing into his shop to save what goods he could, Chen simply prayed. "He calmly answered his neighbors, 'You do not need to be worried for me. I am praying to the High Lord, and the Lord will surely protect me. It is not needful to raise a finger. The One who hears my prayer will always answer.'"[26] Chen and his family members kept their nerve even as the fire approached, coming from the east and heading west. Upon reaching the shop, the account reads, the flames stopped, then suddenly turned south. After turning south and avoiding Chen's shop, they continued heading west. Chen's shop was surrounded on all sides by over one hundred scorched shops, and only his umbrella shop was spared.[27] This article concluded with a commendation of Chen's "unwavering faith" and a reference to the power promised in the Bible to believers.[28] While the modern solution to urban fires might be to improve funding for fire brigades, here the promoted course of action could have been taken straight out of the Old Testament.

Another miracle story advocating the power of particularistic prayer to the Christian deity appears in another story from the first lunar month of 1909. In this account, a mother surnamed Zhang (張), living in Fengtian (奉天), Xi'an County (西安縣), fretted over her 8-year-old son, who had been sickly since he was very young and who was most recently afflicted with a lung disease that two years of medicine had been unable to cure. A woman surnamed Xie (謝) visited Zhang and urged her to convert to Christianity, assuring her that "if ordinary people petition the Lord, the Lord will grant it," and to abandon her faith in other gods such as the Bodhisattva Guanyin, who

---

25. I accessed the source in the Shanghai Library. Although the library's holdings of the *Chinese Christian Intelligencer* for this period have a few gaps so as to prohibit the use of absolutely uniform sampling intervals, miraculous stories exist throughout.
26. *CCI*, December 26, 1905–January 24, 1906 (#183, 8 [Microfilm (hereafter MF) Juan 1, 0025]), available at the Shanghai Library Modern Documents Reading Room.
27. In the December 1940 issue (#165, 11) of the *Hankou Griffith Church Monthly*, a similar story appears. It is the published letter of a woman from Chongqing (重慶), telling how her brother's dormitory was knocked over in a severe storm and how nearly everyone was killed. Only he and one other student survived, because, the woman surmises, of the protective prayer of the elders in her family.
28. *CCI*, December 26, 1905–January 24, 1906 (#183, 8 [MF Juan 1, 0025]).

was "just a person long dead."²⁹ After Xie's departure, Zhang was apparently emotionally moved; she "shed tears like rain" and then commenced to pray to the Christian Lord.³⁰ That night, she had a dream in which she and her son were walking together along a narrow and meandering road. They came to a waterfall flanked by large rocks on each side, which blocked their progress forward. Suddenly there was a bright path of light that descended in the air from heaven, leading them on. Upon awakening, Zhang concluded that God had spoken to her in the dream and had directed her onto the great path of eternal life. She then began to pray. She also awakened her son and had him pray with her. Henceforth, her son's health was greatly improved and they attended church services faithfully.³¹

In addition to miraculous stories about particularistic protection, healings, and visions, numerous accounts of revivals or preaching meetings in the *Chinese Christian Intelligencer* describe ecstatic worship, characterizing intense expressions of emotion as an involuntary manifestation of the presence of the Holy Spirit. It is the involuntary, external nature of the experience of the Holy Spirit as described in these accounts that leads me to categorize cathartic worship as "miraculous"—without the divine presence of the Spirit, the stories suggest, these dramatic displays of emotion would not occur. One early 1906 account of a revival in Shandong reports that the audience engaged in hours-long sessions of kneeling prayer and confession of sins: "There were those who wept, those who prayed repeatedly . . . Men and women, young and old, no one thought to be tired . . . Truly, all felt the Holy Spirit pouring out, filling their hearts with comfort and liveliness."³² Another story from the same year and month described a revival in Fuzhou (福州), Fujian, in which "the hall was filled with weeping and prayers being repeated over and over again . . . One youth prayed, confessing his sins in a loud voice, fervently pleading for grace, praying unceasingly. Then there were two people who prayed together in sorrowful voices. In a few moments the sound of mournful pleading and weeping prayer filled the hall like the roar of thunder, like the splitting of mountains."³³ A 1909 report of a revival in Hangzhou (杭州) reported that, in the packed hall, nearly everyone expressed repentance for their sins, "some crying and confessing their sins, others weeping as they prayed, and still others quietly shedding tears in the dark. If it were not the Holy Spirit that had descended, how else could this have come to pass?"³⁴ A 1919 article reporting on a revival meeting of the China Inland Mission in Yuwu (余吾), Shanxi, also describes the descent of the

---

29. *CCI*, January 22, 1909–February 19, 1909 (#335, 4 [MF Juan 1]).
30. Another story involving a miraculous apparition (or in this case, audition) can be found in *True Light*. It was reported by the Haicang Christian Church (海滄基督教堂) in Xiamen (廈門), Fujian: The voice of Preacher Lin (林), a former church leader who had been dead for twenty years, was recognized and heard to be discoursing on Scripture during a meeting. *True Light*, August 15, 1924 (89–92).
31. *CCI*, January 22, 1909–February 19, 1901 (#335, 4 [MF Juan 1]).
32. *CCI*, January 25, 1906–February 22, 1906 (#186, 3 [MF Juan 1, 0049]).
33. *CCI*, January 25, 1906–February 22, 1906 (#187, 4 [MF Juan 1, 0059]).
34. *CCI*, January 22, 1909–February 19, 1909 (#336, 7 [MF Juan 1, 0763]).

Holy Spirit.³⁵ Another 1919 account of a three-day revival meeting jointly presided over by a pastor from the Church of Christ in China (中華基督教會) and a pastor from the Jinling Theological Seminary (金陵神學院) describes an emotional audience in which people wept for the Church and wept for their families, so that "the mournful sound filled the hall and shook the eardrums, in a great outpouring of the Holy Spirit."³⁶

The high frequency of charismatic stories in national Christian publications at the end of the Qing dynasty and beginning of the Republican era contributed to the normalization of charismatic modes within the culture of Protestant Christianity in China. In the countryside and in cities alike, to this day the charismatic mode of Christianity is the norm.

Efficacious expectations: Mixed messages

Another way in which we see the in-betweenness of the Chinese Christian response to modernity is the *Chinese Christian Intelligencer*'s strange admixture of stories that criticize non-Christians for petitioning local gods for miracles of particularistic protection but that praise Christians for doing the same thing.

In the early years of the twentieth century, the *Chinese Christian Intelligencer* even had a regular section called "World of Darkness" (*Hei'an de shijie* 黑暗的世界) dedicated to debunking traditional popular religious beliefs. For instance, one article from the spring of 1906, titled "Lord Zheng Fails to Protect His Own Temple from Hail," related the legend surrounding the god of a local village in Laizhou (萊州), Shandong (山東). The temple of this god, "Lord Zheng," was said to have the power to ward off hail. When a Christian preacher tried to evangelize in the village, the villagers cast him out. That very night, however, thunder boomed and hailstones "as big as black bowls" rained down, forming a thick layer on the ground. Everyone's roofs were destroyed, including the roof of Lord Zheng's temple. "Everyone was homeless," the article reported with grim satisfaction. "Everyone wept. Those who had thought that Lord Zheng was efficacious had a rude awakening." While the testimonials in the *Chinese Christian Intelligencer* lent positive support to the Chinese Christian project, trying to highlight the authenticity and validity of the divine presence within the Church, these anti-testimonials leveled negative criticism at its chief rival, traditional religious beliefs, intending to show the fruitless and ignorant nature of local worship.³⁷

Another story from the same issue discussed the destruction of the Lü (呂) clan's ancestral temple in Huixian (徽縣), Shandong, as a matter of administrative expedience. Bandits had been taking refuge in the Lü ancestral temple, and so the local

---

35. *CCI*, April 1919 (#845, 2 [MF Juan 2, 0319]).
36. *CCI*, July 1919 (#859, 6 [MF Juan 2, 0426]).
37. *CCI*, May 1906 (#200, 19 [MF Juan 1, 0162]).

official ordered the village head to organize a group to destroy it. "An old woman" said, "The gods are powerful and they will never stand to have their temple destroyed by petty people." To this, the official answered, "Clearly, idols are not efficacious at all," and went on till the temple was destroyed. "This is a sign of getting rid of the false and returning to truth," the *Chinese Christian Intelligencer* reported.[38]

In yet another "World of Darkness" report from early 1907, the *Chinese Christian Intelligencer* related the tragic tale of a family who got up early on the day for worshipping the God of Wealth so that they could perform all of their religious devotions properly. Unfortunately, while they were making paper offerings to the God of Wealth, the flames rose up, the roof caught on fire, and their house and scores of other houses were burned. "How pitiful!" said the commentary. "We truly hope that those who worship the God of Wealth will switch their reverence to the true God and be happy." The particular focus of the critique in this story was on the *methods* by which people worshipped the local Chinese deities: the physical burning of votive offerings. By wrongly ascribing spiritual value to crude materials and the physical process of burning, the *Intelligencer* article implied, the people had ironically destroyed the physical structures of their houses that "actually" had value. The only thing that was real about their religious devotions, the article seemed to be saying, was the physical reality of fire, its chemical processes. Hence, to switch one's allegiance to the invisible Christian God, abandoning votive offerings to human-made idols, was also to affirm the primacy of the immutable laws of the physical world.[39] This is another example of how the *Chinese Christian Intelligencer* presented Christianity as being superior to native popular religion because of the latter's misguided blurring of distinctions between the physical world and religious delusions.

And yet as is apparent in the preceding section on miracles, feats of physical efficacy were commonly accepted by Christians as validations of their faith. What is interesting with this category of "World of Darkness" reports is the juxtaposition of "false" faith in native religious physical efficacy and "true" faith in Christian physical efficacy, because it becomes apparent that, structurally, the narratives are very much the same. The only difference is the proper noun: Guandi or the Trinitarian God, Guanyin or Jesus. The *Chinese Christian Intelligencer* fully encouraged faith in regular divine intervention as long as the object of petitions was the Christian God.

For example, the story of a devastating flood in Hunan simply replaced the "heathen" gods with the Christian God. "It rained incessantly," the report read. People drowned. The young sprouts in the field were destroyed. Water poured in through the city gates and domestic animals drowned. Someone had heard that, about twenty years ago, there had been this kind of flood. The officials went to the local temple and pleaded with local deities, even organizing the elaborate *jiao* (醮) ritual, but to no avail. Having

---

38. *CCI*, May 1906 (#200, 19 [MF Juan 1, 0162]).
39. *CCI*, January 1907 (#237, 2, 55 [MF Juan 1, 0412]).

lost their faith in the local deities, on a Sunday people went and "sincerely prayed to the Trinitarian God, so that God would soon stop the rain." Interestingly, we are never informed of the result. The thrust of the story is not to decry the futility of praying for rain to stop, but to highlight the failure of local deities to respond to prayers, clearing the stage for prayers to the Christian deity.[40]

The proximity between scornful dismissals of the miraculous assumptions of traditional popular religion and fervent affirmation of the miraculous assumptions of Christianity creates another space for in-betweenness, the coexistence of scientific rationalism and charismatic expectation. Of course, such a coexistence of physical and metaphysical perspectives is a perennial feature of human experience. And yet, the conspicuous lack of self-reflectivity about nonrationalistic expectations and behavior in these narratives shows a curious sort of disconnect, a jumble of different and competing ideological paradigms.

Western missionaries and modernity

Another way in which we see the in-betweenness of the interaction between Westerners and Chinese in the late Qing is in missionaries' religiously inflected perception that Chinese popular religion was completely antithetical to the modern project with which they saw themselves as being wholly aligned. Missionaries saw Christianity as a potent antidote to the irrationality and backwardness that they perceived as endemic to traditional Chinese civilization. In an effort to attract more people to their message, Western Christian denominations had founded schools, colleges, hospitals, and orphanages that were important institutions at the forefront of social progressivism in China. In their letters home reporting on Chinese mission developments, missionaries reported on their work to replace Chinese popular religious beliefs with Christian faith as being one with the ultimately secular aims of modern political, civic, and educational reform.

For instance, in Peking (Beijing) in the fall of 1898, E. Curwen of the London Missionary Society reported, "Buddhist and Taoist temples in the eighteen provinces are to be turned into elementary schools ... In all these schools Western learning is to be taught, and it is to be hoped that the result of this educational movement will be really satisfactory."[41] Instead of seeing the commandeering of sacred spaces for secular education as an incursion against religious institutions that also threatened Christianity, Curwen viewed the decline of Buddhist and Daoist religious influence and the rise of "Western learning" as a victory in whose fruits he and the other Christian missionaries shared as campaigners for progress.

---

40. *CCI*, May 1906 (#203, 3 [MF Juan 1, 0175]).
41. Council for World Missions Archives, North China, MFC 266.0095/L846 CN (216), available at Hong Kong Baptist University Special Collections.

Similarly, in Tianjin around the same time, another London Missionary Society evangelist, Jonathan Lees (1862–1902), wrote: "The China of today is not the China of 20 years ago. It is changing with bewildering rapidity . . . The days of stolidity are gone forever, and the mind and heart of this great people are opening to a new life. The twentieth century will see the end of its idolatry, and I believe the very grandest triumph of the cross. You will be privileged to see and to help in the new birth of a nation."[42] Like Curwen, Lees posited that the birth of the modern Chinese nation would be partially achieved through the defeat of "idolatry," by which he meant Chinese popular religion. The missionary associated "the triumph of the cross" with the great ideological transformations of Chinese society in the twentieth century.

Because many missionaries were also doctors who staffed the missionary hospitals where Western medicine was practiced, it may not be surprising that many missionaries associated the spread of Christianity with the spread of modernity in China. What is interesting is that, in the eyes of the missionaries, the spread of rational enlightenment that they celebrated in reports of the decline of "heathenism" always stopped short of implicating the nonrational foundations of Christianity itself.

For instance, in January 1905, London Missionary Society preacher T. Howard Smith, writing from Peking, credited the ongoing spread of Christianity with a decline in traditional religiosity in Chinese society at large: "Another result of this gospel leaven is the growing tendency on the part of very many to give up idolatry. It is becoming quite a common experience to find that enquirers have given up heathen worship and customs long before they enter the enquiry room."[43]

In Smith's first sentence, he seems to be suggesting that the decline in traditional religious belief is a necessary result of China's rapid modernizing transformations, one of which is the spread of Christianity. And yet Smith then concludes that people who have given up Chinese popular religion then "enter the enquiry room" to explore conversion to Christianity. It becomes apparent that Smith never expected the decline in traditional religious belief to lead to wholesale secularization. He merely expected that Western-style education and other "modernizing" influences would lead the Chinese to replace traditional popular worship of local deities with Christianity even though Christianity was similarly founded on beliefs in a superhuman being whose existence could not be scientifically verified.

In fact, when drawing a contrast between Chinese popular religion and Christianity, Smith did not do by presenting Christianity on the desirable side of an "irrational versus rational" dichotomy. Instead, he portrayed Chinese popular religion as a static, stolid sort of religious experience in contrast to a dynamic, charismatic religious experience of Christianity, including the miraculous Pentecostal manifestations recorded in the Book of Acts. "[I]n God's own time and way," he wrote, "We may be privileged

---

42. Council for World Missions Archives, North China, MFC 266.0095/L846CN (217).
43. Council for World Missions Archives, North China, MFC 266.00951/L846CN (690).

to see the people of this great heathen city awakened out of their indifference and visited by Pentecostal showers of blessing."[44]

Hence, even though Western missionaries identified with the cause of modern, scientific reform in China, their interaction with modernity in fact took more forms than one. They supported Western-style education and scientific learning, but in another way, their religious world was fundamentally just as enchanted as the Chinese popular religion that they sought to evict in the name of modern progress. The missionaries' condemnation of Chinese popular religion as "superstitious" and "backward" was not the modern secular critique of religious beliefs without a rational basis. Rather than advocating strictly rational approaches to knowledge and morality, missionaries' denunciations of "idolatry" and "heathenism" simply defined their view of acceptable and unacceptable expressions of supernatural belief: belief in a single formless, invisible Christian God was acceptable, and multiple embodied, personalistic Chinese gods was not.

In this sense the struggle between some Western missionaries and Chinese popular religious beliefs was not a clearly defined clash between "modern" scientific rationality originating in the West and "antimodern" religious traditions originating in China. Although they may have seen themselves as heralds of Western science and rationality to a backward Chinese audience, their project originated from the same ground occupied by Chinese popular religion. In both Protestant Christians and Chinese popular religion, the defining experience took place in the liminal space between the borders of the supernatural realm and the dusty contours of everyday human existence. In missionaries' acknowledgment of—or expressed longing for—Christianity's supernatural manifestations, they all stood much closer to the traditional Chinese popular religious position than they may have cared to admit. Instead of encountering each other from opposite poles of a "modern" spectrum of rationality, both Protestant missionaries and native Chinese popular religionists occupied the in-between space somewhere between the critical standard of modern rationalism and the inherited assumptions of religious tradition.

Conclusion

The encounter between China and the West during the late Qing as embodied by foreign Protestant missionaries and their Chinese interlocutors was characterized by more than mere *transmission*, but also innovation, negotiation, and misrepresentation. Modern printing technologies and print culture from the West were quickly adapted for diverse purposes, including the normalization of miraculous Christian discourse in the Chinese environment, and Christian converts and Western missionaries alike

---

44. Council for World Missions Archives, North China, MFC 266.00951/L846CN (686).

viewed this Chinese environment, including their native religious rivals, through the lens of their own assumptions about modernity.

It is worth noting that using the terms "China" and "the West" as shorthand for the interactions and relationships between individual people in China during the late nineteenth and early twentieth centuries is an extreme simplification. Of course, it is only natural that in hundreds or thousands of individual encounters between people from England and Guangdong, France and Sichuan, Los Angeles and Beijing, or Hong Kong and Malacca, cultural exchange would manifest itself in diverse and often contradictory ways. Manifestations of in-betweenness are inevitable when the two historical entities coming together are such gross simplifications as "China" and "the West." This does not mean that such shorthand is not useful at all to discuss broad concepts. However, it does remind us that the historical writing that scholars do is also an expression of the in-between. Mediated by extant publications and documents, in the world of the past there are real people whose lives possessed a richness and depth that we as historians can only hope to glimpse.

The development of Chinese Christian print culture enabled by Western missionary organizations' importation of modern printing technology in the late Qing had significant long-term effects. First, it propelled the Christian community to the forefront of a modern publishing revolution in China decades before the commercial publishing sector became well established. Second, it had a long-term influence on the character of popular Christian beliefs and practices in China. Western-run publications such as the *Church News* and the *Chinese Christian Intelligencer* and subsequent Chinese-run publications contributed to the normalization of miraculous experience as a regular feature of the Christian experience in China. The resulting prevalence of practices relying on miraculous efficacy such as healing, exorcism, particularistic protection, and Pentecostal tongues not only during the Republican era but throughout the twentieth and twenty-first centuries in Chinese Christian churches has been well documented.[45]

Chinese converts' and Western missionaries' equation of Christianity with rationalistic modernity and their intriguing understanding of Chinese popular religion as being simultaneously antithetical to both also gives us the opportunity to reflect on the complexities involved in the notion of modernity. Not only Christians in China in the early twentieth century, but also we scholars who try to make sense of their experiences and the reality within which they lived, have sometimes failed to confront

---

45. Deng Zhaoming, "Indigenous Chinese Pentecostal Denominations," in *Asian and Pentecostal: The Charismatic Face of Christianity in Asia*, ed. Allan Anderson and Edmond Tang (Baguio City, Philippines: Regnum Books International, 2005), 437–66; Gotthard Oblau, "Pentecostal by Default? Contemporary Christianity in China," in *Asian and Pentecostal*, 411–12; Lian Xi, "A Messianic Deliverance for Post-Dynastic China: The Launch of the True Jesus Church in the Early Twentieth Century," *Modern China* 34 (4) (October 2008): 407–41; Lian, *Redeemed by Fire: The Rise of Popular Christianity in Modern China* (New Haven: Yale University Press, 2010).

hidden assumptions in the way in which we have understood and interpreted what is "modern."

The apparent paradox of the "modern" miracle stories of Chinese Christian print culture and in missionaries' "modern" campaign against certain forms of supernatural religion helps us to understand that modernity is more than simply the border between the rational/irrational, scientific/unscientific, secular/religious, or any other number of dichotomies. Modernity is expressed in forms of organization, ways of conceiving of ideas and the audience for those ideas, new networks of communication and exchange. The human experience of modernity is not unmade but rather defined by these complexities of contradiction, conflict, and the uncertainties of being in-between.

Contributors

Anthony E. Clark is an associate professor of Chinese history at Whitworth University. His recent research focuses on Catholic Christianity in late Qing China. He has published *Heaven in Conflict: Franciscans and the Boxer Uprising in Shanxi* (University of Washington Press, 2015), *China's Saints: Catholic Martyrdom during the Qing (1644–1911)* (Lehigh University Press, 2011), *Ban Gu's History of Early China* (Cambria, 2008), and two edited volumes, *A Voluntary Exile: Chinese Christianity and Cultural Confluence since 1652* (Lehigh University Press, 2014), and *Beating Devils and Burning Their Books: Views of China, Japan, and the West* (University of Michigan Press/Association for Asian Studies, 2010).

Melissa Wei-Tsing Inouye is a lecturer in Asian Studies at the University of Auckland, New Zealand. Her research interests include the history of religion and morality in China, charismatic religious experience, global Christianity, Mormon studies, and the history of women and religion. She is currently finishing a book manuscript on the history of the True Jesus Church and Chinese Christianity in the twentieth century.

John T. P. Lai is an associate professor in the Department of Cultural and Religious Studies at the Chinese University of Hong Kong. His research interest focuses on Chinese Christian literature. He has published *Negotiating Religious Gaps: The Enterprise of Translating Christian Tracts by Protestant Missionaries in Nineteenth-Century China* (Monumenta Serica, 2012), *The Afterlife of a Classic: A Critical Study of the Late-Qing Chinese Translations of the Pilgrim's Progress* (Christian Study Centre on Chinese Religion and Culture, 2012, in Chinese), *The Doctrine of Redemption: The Collected Christian Novels of Karl Friedrich August Gützlaff* (CCLM Publishing, 2013, in Chinese), and *The Chronicles of Christian Publishing Enterprise in China (1860–1911)* (Chinese Christian Literature Council, 2015, in Chinese).

Ji Li is an assistant professor in the School of Modern Languages and Cultures and the Hong Kong Institute for the Humanities and Social Sciences, the University of Hong Kong. Her research interests focus on the social, cultural, and religious history of late imperial and modern China, with a particular emphasis on Christianity in China and cross-cultural studies between China and France. She has published a book titled *God's Little Daughters: Catholic Women in Nineteenth-Century Manchuria* (Seattle: University of Washington Press, 2015).

Nikolay Samoylov is a professor in the Faculty of Oriental Studies, head of the Department of Theory of Asian and African Social Development, and director of the Center for Chinese Studies at St. Petersburg State University. He works mainly on the history of East Asian countries and the history of Sino-Russian relations, especially the Russian Ecclesiastical Mission in late imperial China. He has published more than 150 articles and books (mostly in Russian).

Song Gang is an associate professor in the School of Chinese, the University of Hong Kong. He has broad interests in the cultural exchanges between China and the West in history, and his research mainly focuses on Christianity in late imperial China. He has published a number of articles in this field. He also has two forthcoming books, one on late Ming Christian-Confucian dialogism and the other on Catholic Bible translations in Qing China.

David Francis Urrows is an associate professor of music at the Hong Kong Baptist University. His research and teaching focuses on music history, including the history of the pipe organ in China and nineteenth-century studies on German émigré musicians in the United States. He is the author of *Keys to the Kingdom: A History of the Pipe Organ in China* (Leuven Chinese Studies Series, Ferdinand Verbiest Institute, Leuven, Belgium, forthcoming), the co-author of *Randall Thompson: A Bio-Bibliography* (Greenwood, 1991), and the editor of a three-volume critical edition of the music of German-American composer Otto Dresel (A-R Editions, 2002–15).

Thijs Weststeijn is professor of art history of the early modern period at Utrecht University, where he chairs the research project *The Chinese Impact: Images and Ideas of China in the Dutch Golden Age* (2014–19). He has published widely on Dutch art of the seventeenth century, including *Art and Antiquity in the Netherlands and Britain: The Vernacular Arcadia of Franciscus Junius (1591–1677)* (Leiden and Boston: Brill, 2015).

Index

Académie Royale des Sciences, 33
Academy of Fine Arts (Russia), 45
Aesop, 16
Africa, 18, 67
Alacoque, Marguerite-Marie, 78–80, 83, 89
Albazin (in Beijing), 38
Aleni, Giulio, 27n92, 50
Alexander I, 44
Alexy (Vinogradov), Hieromonk, 44
Allen, Young J., 110
Amsterdam, 10, 11, 13, 14, 15, 17, 18, 19, 20, 22, 25, 26, 33n121
Anglo-Chinese College, 72
anti-Christian (anti-foreign), 91, 93, 95, 98
Antwerp, 11, 13, 14, 16, 17, 22
apostasy, 95, 100–102
Arundel, Countess of, 33n121
August the Strong, 33n121
Avvakum (Chestnoj), 46

Bahr, Florian, 54
Barthes, Roland, 52n8
Batavia, 19, 25, 72
Bauer, Andrew, 100–101
Bayle, Pierre, 31
Becanus, Willem, 22
beheading, 102
Beijing (北京), 11, 13, 14, 18, 25, 28, 37, 38, 39, 40, 42, 43, 44, 45, 46, 49, 50, 52, 56, 95, 100, 103, 118
Belinsky, Vissarion, 42
Benkendorff, Alexander von, 41
Bible, 30, 41, 71, 72, 107, 112, 113, 114
Bixie jishi (辟邪紀實), 70, 93

black magic, 93, 95, 96–97, 99, 102–4
Blaeu, Johannes, 13, 21
Bloemaert, Cornelis, 14n23
Bodleian Library, 26
Bouvet, Joachim, 24n80
Boxer Uprising, 91, 93, 96–99, 103
Boyer, Joseph, 85–86, 88
Boyle, Robert, 26
Brac, Albert, 27n94
Brinck, Ernst, 15
British East India Company, 73
Brune, Pierre de la, 25n82
Buddhism, 23, 38, 94, 95, 99
Buys, Jan, 14n22

calligraphy, 29
Canton Trade System, 64
Carmelite order, 85–86, 88
Cartesianism, 30
Catherine II (Yekaterina Alexeevna), 39
Cen Chunxuan (岑春煊), 95, 103–4
Central Asia, 10
Charme, Alexandre de la, 80
Charmoy, François Bernard, 40
Chibei outan (池北偶談), 51n6
China Inland Mission, 115
Chinese Christian Intelligencer (*Tongwenbao* 通問報), 109, 112
Chinese Christian Virgins, 82, 86–88. See *shouzhennü*
Chinese Monthly Magazine (*Cha shisu meiyue tongji zhuan* 察世俗每月統記傳), 110
Chinese Recorder, 108

Chinese Serial (*Xia'er guanzhen* 遐邇貫珍), 110
chinoiserie, 32, 93
Chmutov, Ivan, 46
Church News (*Jiaohui xinbao* 教會新報), 109, 112
Church of the Immaculate Conception, 95
Cixi (慈禧), Empress Dowager, 98–99, 102
Clerc, Jean le, 25
Cleyer, Andreas, 12n14, 26
Cnobbaert, Michiel, 13
Cohong System, 64
Collegio dei Cinesi, 34n126
Collegio Romano (College in Rome), 13
Comenius, Jan Amos, 18, 20
Confucianism, 3, 21, 94, 95–96, 102
    Confucian classics, 3, 20–26
    Confucius, 11, 13, 21, 22–25, 31, 97
    Confucius Sinarum philosophus, 3, 21–25, 32
Congregatio de Propaganda Fide, 14
Coudrin, Pierre-Marie-Joseph, 79
Counter-Reformation, 78–79, 89
Couplet, Philippe, 13, 20, 21, 22, 23, 24, 25, 26, 31, 32, 33
Coxinga, 13n19. *See* Zheng Chenggong
Croiset, Jean, 80
Cruyl, Lieven, 14n23
Cunha, Simon de. *See* Wu Li

Daoguang (道光) Emperor, 44
Daoism, 23, 94, 97, 99
Dayingguo renshi lüeshuo (大英國人事略說), 73
Dayingguo tongzhi (大英國統志), 59, 60, 62, 63, 65, 66, 67, 68, 69, 71, 73, 74
Decker, Coenraet, 14n23
Deleuze, Léopold, 56
Deng Tingzhen (鄧廷楨), 61
Dentrecolles, François Xavier, 80
devil. *See* Satan
Dominicus (Martino Martini's Chinese assistant), 17
Douai, 12, 14n26
Dresden, 33n121
Dunch, Ryan, 107

Dutch Republic, 11
    and *Confucius Sinarum philosophus*, 21–22
    and the Jesuits, 12–15
Dutch United East India Company (VOC), 10, 12, 13, 15
Du women and letters, 81–86
Dyakonov, Osip, 39

Eastern Western Monthly Magazine (*Dongxiyang kao meiyue tongji zhuan* 東西洋考每月統記傳), 73, 110
ecclesiastical colony, 77, 80, 89
ecstatic worship, 115
Edelheer, Jacob, 17
Edwards, Ebenezer Henry, 91
Egypt, 18, 24n80, 30, 32
Eight-Nation Alliance, 7
Erasmus, 16
Eurocentric, 6, 42
execution, 93, 96, 99, 101–2, 103

Fengtian (奉天), 114
Fo (佛), 38
Formosa. *See* Taiwan
Four Seas (*sihai* 四海), 5, 67
Frähn, Martin, 40
Franciscan friars, 94–96, 97, 99–105
Franclet, Jean Baptiste, 82
Free Society of Science and Arts, 43
Fu Manchu, 92
fundamentalist, 108
Fuzhou (福州), 13n19, 115

Gallifet, Père de, 87
Gaubil, Antoine, 80
gazetteer, 95
Ghent, 14n26
God of Wealth, 117
Golius, Jacob, 15, 17, 18
Gravius, Daniel, 19
Great Britain, 5–6, 60, 65, 66–74, 99
Grimaldi, Filippo, 27n94
Grotius, Hugo, 11, 18, 30
Guangxu (光緒) Emperor, 98
Guangzhou (Canton), 9, 10, 76, 110
guoshi (國師), 44

Index

Gützlaff, Karl Friedrich August, 5–6, 59, 60, 61, 65, 67, 68, 69, 70, 71, 72, 73, 74, 75, 110
Gu Yanwu (顧炎武), 63

hagiographies, 91, 93
Hallerstein, Augustin von, 53
Hamme, Petrus van, 12n14
Hangzhou (杭州), 115
Harderwijk, 18
harmoniums, 56
harpsichord, 49
Hartoghvelt, Ignatius, 13
Heathenism, 120
Hebrew, 17, 18, 24, 30, 31, 32
heterodox doctrine, 93–94, 95, 100–103
Heurnius, Justus, 19
Heurnius, Otto, 15
hieroglyphs, 18
Hipwell, W. E., 92
Holy Family, 79–80
Hooghe, Romeyn de, 14n23
Hoorn, Pieter van, 25, 33
Hornius, Georg, 18, 31
Horthemels, Daniel, 22
Huangdi (黃帝, the Yellow Emperor), 32
Hugo, Herman, 16, 18
Huixian (徽縣), 116
Hulan (呼蘭), 87
Hunan (湖南), 93, 117
Hyde, Thomas, 26

Iakinf (Bichurin), Archimandrite, 40–43
idolatry, 119–20
Igorev, Leo, 46
Immaculate Heart of Mary, 79, 80, 86–87
imperialism, 94
in-between(ness), 2–3, 5, 6, 7, 8, 43, 47, 48, 58, 77, 89, 90, 106, 109, 116, 118, 120, 121, 122
Intorcetta, Prospero, 21n64
Islam, 18

Jansenist, 78–79
Janssonius, Johannes, 22
Japan, 28
Jardine, Matheson & Co., 73

Jardine, William, 73
Java, 34n128
Jellachich, Franz, 44
Jiangzhou (絳州), 93–94, 102
Jinling Theological Seminary, 116
Judaism, 18

Kaiser Wilhelm II, 93
Kangxi (康熙) Emperor, 9, 27, 34, 38, 55, 70
Karamzin, Nikolay, 44
Karsavin, Kondratii, 46
Kim Ch'ang-ŏp (김창엽／金昌業), 52–53
Kircher, Athanasius, 13, 14, 18, 19, 22, 27
Kneller, Godfried, 26
Korea, visitors from, 52
Kouduo richao (口鐸日抄), 50n4
Kovalevskiy, Yegor, 46
Krylov, Ivan, 40

Laegh, Willem van der, 14n23
Laet, Johannes de, 15, 18
Lagot, Ignatius, 27n94
Lairesse, Gerard de, 14n23
Laizhou (萊州), 116
Lama (喇嘛), 38
Lees, Jonathan, 119
Legashov, Anton, 45
Leibniz, Gottfried Wilhelm, 19, 33
Leiden, 17, 30
Leont'ev, Aleksei, 39
Leontevsky, Zakhar, 44
letterpress printing, 110
Liang Di (梁迪), 51, 56, 57
Liaozhong (遼中), Liaoning (遼寧)
Liebstein, Leopold, 52
Li Jiubiao (李九標), 50
Lindsay, Hugh Hamilton, 73
Lipovtsov, Stepan, 43
Lipsius, Justus, 16
Li Shiyao (李侍堯), 64
Liu Dapeng (劉大鵬), 95–97, 99–100, 102
Li Wenyu (李問漁), 112
London Missionary Society, 44, 72, 110, 118, 119
Lord Zheng, 116
Louis XIV, 26, 34n126
Low Countries, 3, 10–15, 21, 25, 27, 32–34

Lu Kun (盧坤), 63
Luocha (羅剎), 38

Maastricht, 27n94
Macartney, Lord George, 56, 61
Macau, 9, 14, 48, 50–51
Madre de Deus, church of (Macau), 50, 51
magic lantern (magick-lanthern), 28
Mailla, Joseph Anne-Marie de Moyriac de, 80
Majoribanks, Charles, 73
Manchu, 15
    Manchu Fulahe, 39
    Manchu language, 20, 37, 29, 40, 43, 44
    Manchu people, 39, 45
    Manchu region (Manchuria), 82, 85, 87
    Manchuria Mission, 82, 87
Martini, Martino, 12, 13, 17, 21, 30
massacre, 91–93, 100n35
mass-mechanized printing, 109
Matham, Theodoor, 14n23
Matheson, James, 73
Mechlin, 13, 14n26
Medhurst, Walter Henry, 72
Mei Yingzuo (梅膺祚), 17n40
Mentzel, Christian, 26
Meurs, Jacob van, 13
miracles, 107
miracle stories, 113, 114, 115, 116, 117, 118
Missions étrangères de Paris (MEP), 79, 81–83, 85, 88
modernist, 108
modernity, 107, 118
Mongols, 32n117
Moretus, Balthasar, 17n43
Morrison, Robert, 72, 110
Moses, 24
movable type, 110
Müller, Andreas, 26
Munnichuysen, Jean van, 14n23

Namur, 13
Nanjing Incident, 49
Nantang (南堂, South Church, Beijing), 52, 53n10, 53–54
Naples, 34n126
Nazareth, Béatrice de, 78

Netherlands, 10–11, 12, 12n14, 12n15, 13–16, 26, 28, 30
Netherlands Missionary Society, 72
Nieuhof, Johan, 13, 28
Noël, François, 33
Northeast Passage, 9
Novaya Zemlya, 9

Odoevsky, Vladimir, 40, 42
Olenin, Alexey, 40
Opium War, 60, 66, 94, 99, 102
Ouluoba zhuzhici (歐羅巴竹枝詞), 53
Oxford, 26

Pak Chi Won (박지원／朴趾源), 53n10
Palladiy (Kafarov), Archimandrite, 40
Papenbroeck, Daniel, 14, 16n33
Paris, 22, 26, 82
Paris Asia Society, 41, 43
Passe, Crispijn van de, 14n23
Pauw, Cornelis de, 34n127
Pentecostal, 119–20, 121
Pereira, Tomás, 27n94, 52
Peter (Kamensky), Archimandrite, 40
Peter the Great, 37
Petlin, Ivan, 36
Philemon, Ierodiakon, 39
Philippines, pipe organs from, 56
pipe organ, 48–58
    as *fengqin* (風琴), 49
    as machine, 49
    as *xiqin* (西琴), 50
    Gray and Davison, 56
    Rieger-Kloss, 57
Polo, Marco, 18n46, 29
Pope Innocent X, 78
Pope Pius XI, 78
Pourquié, Dominique Maurice, 6, 81–86, 88
prisca philosophia, 24, 30
Pronk, Cornelis, 10n7
Pushkin, Alexander, 41, 42

Qianlong (乾隆) Emperor, 56, 61
Qianyuan suoji (潛園瑣記), 96
Qing Empire, 37, 39, 45, 47, 96, 99, 102, 105
Qu Dajun (屈大均), 10, 50

Index

ratio studiorum, 14
Ravary, François, 56
red-haired barbarians (*hongmao fan* 紅毛番), 3, 10, 10n8
red-haired devils (*hongmao gui* 紅毛鬼), 62
Red Lanterns, 103
Reland, Adriaan, 18
Religious Tract Society, 72
Rembrandt, 26
Renaissance, 11
Review of the Times (*Wanguo gongbao* 萬國公報), 111, 112
Ricci, Matteo, 12, 27, 28, 49, 53, 93
Rohmer, Sax, 92
Rossokhin, Illarion, 39, 44
Rougemont, François de, 13, 22
Royal Society of Northern Antiquities at Copenhagen, 43
Rudamina, Andrzej, 50
Russian Academy of Sciences, 41, 43, 44
Russian Ecclesiastical Mission in Beijing, 37–40
Russian Foreign Ministry, 40

Sacred Heart of Jesus, 76–90
    Cathedral of, 76–77, 81, 89
    devotion in China, 79–81
    devotion to, 77–81
Sacred Heart of Mary, 80, 85–88
Saint Petersburg, 4, 34n126, 40, 41, 42, 44, 45
Saint Petersburg University, 40, 44
Salmasius, Claudius, 30
Sanzijing (三字經), 41
Sas, Theodorus, 12n14
Satan, 92
Scaliger, Joseph, 15, 30
Schilling, Pavel, 42
Second Vatican Council, 79
Senkovsky, Osip, 40
Septuagint, 31n111, 32
Shandong Revival, 115
Shanghai (上海), 20, 56
Shanghai Journal (*Shenbao* 申報), 111
Shen Fuzong, Michael, 21, 25, 26
Shengxin guitiao (聖心規條), 80
Shengyu guangxun (聖諭廣訓), 70

Shen Que (沈㴶), 49
Shenyang (瀋陽), 81, 88
Shifei lüelun (是非畧論), 59, 60, 62, 63, 64, 65, 66, 67, 68, 69, 71, 72, 73, 74
shouzhennü (守貞女), 82. See Chinese Christian Virgins
Shuzui zhi dao zhuan (贖罪之道傳), 70
Sibyls, 24, 25n81
Simon, Philibert, 85
Sinkan language, 15, 19
Sino-barbarian dichotomy (*Hua-Yi zhi bian* 華夷之辨), 1, 5, 61
Sinocentric mentality, 1
Sinology, 3, 4, 14, 37, 40–41
Sinophile, 33, 34, 42
Sioertsma, Anthonie Heeres, 14n23
Siraya language, 19
Smidt, Frans de, 14n22
Smith, T. Howard, 119
Smotritsky, Meletij, 39
sociocultural interactions, 35–37
Sophronius (Gribovsky), Archimandrite, 44
sorcery. See black magic
Spinoza, 31
St. Bernard, 87
St. Gertrude de Great, 78
St. Louis, church of (Tianjin), 57
St. Lutgarde d'Aywières, 78
St. Paul, church of (Macau). See Madre de Deus
superstitious. See black magic

Taiwan (台灣), 9, 19, 88
Taiyuan (太原), 92, 94–95, 97, 99, 100, 102, 103
Talbot, Aletheia. See Arundel, Countess of
temple worship, 92
Thévenot, Melchisédech, 26
Thomas, Antoine, 13, 14n26, 20, 27
Tianjin (天津), 57, 119
Tournon, Charles-Thomas Maillard, 34
Treaty of Kyakhta, 37
tributary, 5, 61, 66, 67
Trigault, Michel, 94
Trigault, Nicolas, 12, 16, 17, 19, 28, 93
Trismegistus, 25n81
Tsar Nicolas I, 42

Tushanwan (土山灣), 111
Twin Pagoda Temple, 95

Universal Circulating Herald (*Xunhuan ribao* 循環日報), 110
Universal Flood, 30, 31n111

Vagnone, Alphonse, 94
Vasiliev, Vasiliy, 40
Veniamin (Morachevich), Archimandrite, 42, 45
Verbiest, Ferdinand, 12, 20, 27, 33, 34, 50
Verrolles, Emmanuel-Jean-François, 87
Vietnamese language, 18
Vlierden, Henrik van, 27n94
VOC. *See* Dutch United East India Company
Vondel, Joost van den, 11, 33
Vossius, Gerard, 15, 17
Vossius, Isaac, 29, 31, 33
Voyeikov, Luka, 39
Voytsehovsky, Osip, 45
Vulcanius, Bonaventura, 15

Wang Linheng (王臨亨), 48–49, 57, 58, 62
Wang Shizhen (王士禎), 51
Wanli (萬曆) Emperor, 49
Warwijck, Wybrand van, 15n31
Wei Yuan (魏源), 69
Wenzhou (溫州), 114
Weyerman, Jacob Campo, 33n125
Wilkins, John, 18
William IV, 6, 68
Witsen, Nicolaes, 10, 26, 33
Wu Changyuan (吳長元), 54n12
Wu Li (吳歷), 29n102
Wu Pu, 15

Xavier, Henri, 27n94
Xi'an (西安), 114
Xiaobajiazi (小八家子), 87

xiao shennü (小神女), 81
Xifang dawen (西方答問), 50
Xifang yaoji (西方要紀), 50
Xiru (西儒), 94
Xitang ji: Waiguo zhuzhici (西堂集：外國竹枝詞), 51
Xu Bomei (許播美), 107
Xu, Candida, 20
Xujiahui (徐家匯). *See* Zikawei
xylography, 110

yamen courtyard, 95, 99, 100n35, 101, 104
Yanpu zaji (簷曝雜記), 54n12
Yenjing Diary. *See Yŏnhaeng ilgi*
YMCA, 107
Yongzheng (雍正) Emperor, 38
Yŏnhaeng ilgi (燕行日記／연행일기), 53n10
You Tong (尤侗), 53, 54, 56
Yuan Chang (袁昶), 98
Yue jian bian (粵劍編), 48n1, 62n11
Yuwu (余吾), 115
Yuxian (毓賢), 92–93, 95–96, 97, 98–100, 101–2, 103–4

Zhang Daoling (張道陵), 97
Zhao Yi (趙翼), 53–54, 55, 56, 57
Zheng Chenggong (鄭成功), 9. *See* Coxinga
Zheng Xianchen (鄭獻琛), 62
Zheng xie bijiao (正邪比較), 70
Zhifang waiji (職方外紀), 50
Zhou Meiye (周美爺), 26
Zhu Xi (朱熹), 39
Zikawei, 56, 112. *See* Xujiahui
Zizhi Tongjian Gangmu (資治通鑑綱目), 39
Zoes, Gerard, 14n22
Zou Yigui (鄒一桂), 29n102
zuoshizhe (作史者), 44